Schooling Teachers

MEGAN BLUMENREICH
BETHANY L. ROGERS

Foreword by Michèle Foster

Schooling Teachers

TEACH FOR AMERICA
and the Future of
Teacher Education

TEACHERS COLLEGE PRESS

TEACHERS COLLEGE | COLUMBIA UNIVERSITY
NEW YORK AND LONDON

Published by Teachers College Press,® 1234 Amsterdam Avenue, New York, NY 10027

Library of Congress Cataloging-in-Publication Data

Names: Blumenreich, Megan, author. | Rogers, Bethany L., author.
Title: Schooling teachers : Teach For America and the future of teacher education / Megan Blumenreich, Bethany L. Rogers ; foreword by Michèle Foster
Description: New York, NY : Teachers College Press, 2021. | Includes bibliographical references and index.
Identifiers: LCCN 2020055791 (print) | LCCN 2020055792 (ebook) | ISBN 9780807764688 (paperback) | ISBN 9780807764695 (hardcover) | ISBN 9780807779231 (ebook)
Subjects: LCSH: Teach for America (Project) | Teachers—Training of—United States.
Classification: LCC LB1715 .B559 2021 (print) | LCC LB1715 (ebook) | DDC 370.71/10973—dc23
LC record available at https://lccn.loc.gov/2020055791
LC ebook record available at https://lccn.loc.gov/2020055792

ISBN 978-0-8077-6468-8 (paper)
ISBN 978-0-8077-6469-5 (hardcover)
ISBN 978-0-8077-7923-1 (ebook)

Printed on acid-free paper
Manufactured in the United States of America

For Jon, Hank, and Maggie
—Megan

For Rhys
—Bethany

Contents

Foreword

Mention the group Teach For America (TFA) and the responses may vary, but in general they will be visceral. People, particularly in education, have strong feelings—positive or negative—about the program. Policymakers disagree over its relative merits. Some hail the program, considering it a needed corrective to their view that the existing teacher force is to blame for underperforming schools. These leaders argue that the lowest-achieving students enter the teaching profession, are woefully underprepared by schools and colleges of education, and are responsible for below-par student outcomes. Under this logic, one solution is to get higher-achieving people to enter the teaching profession.

In 1989 Wendy Kopp, a Princeton undergraduate, proposed in her honor thesis the idea of creating a program to do this. Her idea morphed into Teach For America, a program that recruited undergraduates from elite institutions into teaching and sent them to underresourced rural and urban school districts. Rather than becoming bankers, bright, high-achieving, and motivated young people would offer a bromide for underperforming schools by becoming the teachers that schools needed. A domestic Peace Corps, these young enthusiastic people would fan out into cities like Baltimore, Chicago, New York, and New Orleans, as well as small towns in Texas and Mississippi.

Quickly funded by private donors, Teach For America was embraced by both urban and rural school districts that had teaching shortages as a solution to staff schools. In 2000, TFA raised more than 25 million dollars from private grants, foundations, and government grants. By 2016, TFA funding had increased almost tenfold according to *Forbes*, securing a spot among the top 100 nonprofit organizations.[1]

TFA alums play outsized roles in educational settings. A few founded charter school networks, such as the well-known KIPP or less well-known networks like Noble Street Charter School. Others, like Michelle Rhee and Kaya Henderson, have served as chancellors and superintendents of urban and smaller school districts. Several have become college or university professors, including one of the authors of this book. One, currently president of Fort Lewis College, was deputy director for U.S. programming in K–12 schools for the Bill and Melinda Gates Foundation and dean of a well-respected college of education. Other TFA alums have secured positions in politics and political life.

Critics of Teach For America have accused the organization of weakening the teaching profession, hastening the dismantling of public schools in favor of charter schools, imperiling the schooling of the most disenfranchised pupils, and destabilizing public schools by placing inexperienced teachers in underresourced classrooms and schools. Others have noted that TFA serves as an escalator for young people who can climb the educational hierarchy, thus avoiding the traditional routes to the top.

Worth mentioning is that Teach For America is not the first program to recruit and place teachers in underresourced urban and role public schools. A quarter-century before TFA, The National Teacher Corps, referred to as the Teacher Corps, which was part of President Johnson's Great Society, was established by the United States Congress in the Higher Education Act of 1965 to improve elementary and secondary teaching in predominantly low-income areas. Like TFA, the Teacher Corps solution for improving elementary and secondary teaching was to place teachers in underserved and low-income districts.

Although not as widely discussed in the research literature as TFA, there is a dissertation and some articles written about Teacher Corps. One of the articles traces legislation, how it shaped Teacher Corps initiative, the early efforts to recruit Teacher Corps members, and compares and contrasts Teacher Corps with Teach for America. Anyone seeking to understand Teacher Corps and its distant cousin, Teach for America should read these works. One article[2] compares Teacher Corps members against other teachers matched by years of experience, teacher and pupil ethnicity, pupil sex, types of school, and grade levels. The research found that although there was no difference in the achievement of students taught by Teacher Corps or regular teachers, students taught by Teacher Corps members brought about changes in students' self-concept that were significantly higher than other teachers. The article also notes that Teacher Corps graduates were more likely to develop culturally relevant curricula, use community resources in teaching, initiate contact with parents, and hold positive attitudes about reading development and causes of poverty in society.

Scouring through old government documents reveals several reports about Teacher Corps, including a *Report to the Congress, Assessment of the Teacher Corps Program at the University of Southern California and Participating Schools in Los Angeles and Riverside Counties;* a report of the National Teaching Corps Program in The Atlanta Public Schools the 1966–67 school year; a collection of abstracts entitled *Teacher Corps: A Collection of Abstracts, A Program to Improve Educational Personnel Development and to Strengthen Educational Opportunities in Low-Income Schools (1965–1982),* culled from ERIC documents and published in May 1982 by the

Department of Education.[3] The evidence about what happened to Teacher Corps members is sparse. However, I know of at least one Teacher Corps member who parlayed his experience into a career in education policy and still works in this arena. A 1971–72 Teacher Corps member in Salinas, CA, he later became a training specialist for the Peace Corps, assumed several positions in foundations and politics, and currently runs a consulting firm founded in 2013 (edgepartners.org) that is described as a "consulting boutique dedicated to educational excellence for all" and concentrates on "policy, strategy, implementation, and continuous improvement."

We don't know nearly enough about what happened to Teacher Corps members during their training, as well as after they left. Hopefully researchers will take up this topic and fill this gap. Fortunately, we do not have to wait to find out about the experiences of the first cohort of Teach For America. Megan Blumenreich and Bethany Rogers have written *Schooling Teachers: Teach For America and the Future of Teacher Education,* a powerful account that draws on the experiences of 30 members of the first cohort of TFA. Previous research on TFA has depended mainly on quantitative methods, those likely to get policymakers' attention. Although ideally quantitative and qualitative methods are joined to provide in-depth understanding of a particular phenomenon, the former are typically privileged in policy discussions. Every so often, however, research that uses qualitative methods opens up avenues for quantitative researchers to pursue that may have been previously overlooked. One area where this occurred is the study of the positive impact of Black teachers on Black student academic outcomes, where many years of qualitative research on the topic caught the interest of quantitative researchers who have taken up the topic. Their findings have been striking. Policymakers paid little attention to the topic until the numbers made the findings stick. One lesson to be drawn from this recent research is that qualitative research can uncover key ideas that aren't obvious for quantitative researchers to investigate and this volume offers quantitative researchers who want to pursue promising areas for future research. Using oral histories, Blumenreich and Rogers capture the lived experiences and all the complexity of those who, depending on one's point of view, were either pioneers or guinea pigs—or, in all likelihood, were both.

The book consists of seven well-crafted chapters. The first five chapters provide the history that gave rise to TFA; explore the motivations of those who joined; examine the summer training institute; tackle the conflicts that ensued; and discuss members' first year of teaching. The last two chapters explore teacher educators' responses to TFA and the mutual effects of each on the other, and the final chapter appraises the influence TFA has had on the educational landscape. The authors don't shy away from controversial subjects. They grapple with the way race comes up among TFA candidates from different backgrounds, particularly, who is best suited to teach urban students and how ideas about shared background and privilege factor into these discussions. No matter what your views are about Teach For America, you will gain insight not only into the program, but also learn what is entailed—the challenges and possibilities—in preparing high-quality teachers for America's schools.

—*Michèle Foster*

Acknowledgments

There is a whole universe of people to whom we are grateful, though we will name just a few here:

We are immensely thankful for and profoundly indebted to the 30 participants who shared their personal testimonies with us: Eric Bird, Constance Bond, Diane Brewer, Christina Brown, Furman Brown, Nichole Childs Wardlaw, Felicia Clark, Spencer Downing, Kathy Feeley, Leo Flanagan, Carlos Gomez, Jennifer Denino, Scott Joftus, Lori Lawson, Priscila Leon-Didion, R. Brent Lyles, Andrew McKenzie, Suzanne Murray, Bill Norbert, Marife Ramos, Lisa Robinson, Ellen Rosenstock, Caroline Sabin, Jane Schneider, Arthur Schuhart, Jeffrey Simes, Mark Stephen, Avis Terrell, Jan Trasen, and Heather Weller.

We appreciate the financial support provided by the CUNY Collaborative Incentive Research Grant and PSC-CUNY Grants, from which we benefited at just the right moments.

Our friends, family, and colleagues who read drafts and provided feedback, ideas, and inspiration—in particular, Gene Blumenreich, Kate Blumenreich, James Fraser, Ken Gold, Jon Zimmerman, and the many colleagues from conferences throughout the last decade, deserve our special thanks.

We would like to recognize Brian Ellerbeck, our editor, who helped us broaden the scope of the manuscript, and all those at Teachers College Press who aided in producing the book.

And we would especially like to acknowledge Carolyn Comiskey, Jonathan Greenberg, Judith Kafka, Heather Lewis, and Emily Straus for their substantive contributions and emotional support.

Introduction

For 30 years, coauthor Megan Blumenreich has held on to a Teach For America (TFA) recruitment poster from 1990, a keepsake that represents the life-defining 3 years she spent teaching 7th grade in Compton, California, as part of the inaugural TFA cohort. Not that she needs the reminder: She has been a professor of teacher education at The City College of New York for 19 years, set on that path largely because of her Teach For America experience. But when her mother sent her that poster in an orange cardboard mailer, suggesting that Megan frame and hang it in her office, Megan found herself feeling conflicted. Despite the intertwined histories of TFA and university-based teacher education, the gulf that has divided alternate routes from "traditional" teacher education factions seemed too vast to bridge. It felt disloyal, or embarrassing, to mount a TFA poster in a teacher educator's office. But it got Megan and her coauthor, Bethany Rogers, to thinking. The general story of TFA, which has often been told, is also a story about teacher education and the struggle to attract, prepare, and support effective teachers for all children, especially low-income students of color. At the same time, there is a more intimate story to be told, about the historical moment in which a group of young college graduates, hoping to "give something back" and figure themselves out, signed onto the untested TFA experiment in 1990; about their experiences and the impact of those experiences on their lives; and about how their experiences might inform what we know about the process of becoming a teacher. This book, grounded in the voices of 30 inaugural TFA participants and a rich body of scholarship about the making of teachers, aims to tell those stories.

* * *

Schooling Teachers tackles the persistent and pressing issue of how the United States will attract and prepare high-quality teachers for all students, particularly those in our most underserved classrooms. Drawing on participant voices from that first 1990 cohort of Teach For America (TFA), this book situates their experiences within the larger context of teacher education and reform of the last 3 decades. Through investigation of TFA, one of the more radical and (at the same time) politically popular departures from traditional, university-based teacher preparation, this book sharpens the dimensions of the "teacher problem" and also illustrates why solutions remain elusive and limited. *Schooling Teachers* makes three critical contributions to our current understanding of teacher education: It illuminates persistent issues associated with conventional practices of teacher recruitment and teacher education; it analyzes the assumptions and experiences associated with a key reform effort designed to challenge those traditional practices; and, perhaps most importantly, it highlights the ways in which neither the familiar university-based model of teacher education nor one of the most vaunted reform efforts of the period has satisfactorily solved the problem of preparing high-quality teachers for underserved classrooms.

BELOVED ALTERNATIVE: TEACH FOR AMERICA

From the moment of its 1990 launch, Teach For America was wildly successful in capturing the public imagination. Touted as a domestic Peace Corps for teaching, TFA called for bright, idealistic graduates from elite colleges and universities to spend 2 years teaching in the nation's most challenging classrooms, with minimal preparation. *Schooling Teachers* locates TFA's beginnings within the reformist zeal of the late 1980s and early 1990s that gave rise to alternate pathways to teaching. In alternate pathways, preparation occurs primarily on the job rather than in advance; TFA is easily the best-known representative of this genre.[1] TFA, which arrived at a moment when the public was eager to see improvements in schooling, symbolized an opportunity to think differently about how to attract and prepare teachers for underserved public schools. Harnessing the ascendant principles of the free market and entrepreneurialism, alongside the idealism sweeping elite college campuses, TFA promised an innovative solution to what had become the "teacher problem": simply put, TFA suggested that the "right" people—enthusiastic, well-educated, but untrained graduates of the nation's most selective institutions of higher education—could learn how to teach on the job and, further, that recruiting such people to become public school teachers could solve the broader difficulties of struggling schools and districts. Because of the reform context and social networks within which it was conceived and developed, and in which it expanded over the subsequent 30 years, TFA has had tremendous influence on a generation of entrepreneurial school reforms and leaders.

    Schooling Teachers grapples with this legacy, using in-depth research into the experiences of TFA alumni themselves to explore the issues and solutions that have characterized the battles over teacher preparation since the late 1980s. One might ask, why study an outlier such as TFA that supplies only a tiny fraction of the nation's teachers? Or why write a book about an initiative that has already garnered so much attention, particularly in attempts to determine the efficacy of these alternate route teachers?

TFA matters because it has powerfully affected the larger educational policy context, determining the field of battle for partisans on all sides. It has helped to shape debate about how best to educate underserved students; it has challenged many of the assumptions and practices that characterize conventional teacher recruitment and preparation in this country. It has inspired the design of other alternate route and market-driven programs in school districts across the country, and both the organization and its alumni have occupied a prime position within the broader wave of recent reforms (including charter schools, school choice movements, and vouchers) that have challenged existing ways of doing business.

TFA achieved this impact above all by assuming the rhetoric of a social movement for equity, claiming that access to a high-quality education, especially for children in underserved communities, was the "civil rights issue of our era." Whether one views this rhetoric as sincere, cynical, or some combination of both, it succeeded in igniting the passion of many well-educated young people. Thousands of such individuals have applied to the program each year since 1990; those selected have taught under the auspices of TFA for two years in underserved schools and have, in many cases, gone on to influence the dialogue and practice of education, from the highest decision-making levels to the most local and informal venues. TFA is a juggernaut worth understanding, not only on its own merits as an experience and intervention, but as commentary on the perceived problems of conventional teacher training and the reforms intended to address them.[2]

CONVENTIONAL VS. ALTERNATIVE TEACHER EDUCATION

Neither conventional teacher education nor alternatives such as TFA have managed to adequately resolve crucial difficulties associated with preparing and supporting high-quality teachers for all schools. However, in the process of trying to solve these difficulties, traditional teacher educators and their entrepreneurial counterparts have engaged debates that continue to roil the field. What constitutes a "highly qualified" teacher for the most vulnerable populations? How long should newly prepared teachers stay in teaching? What is the role of professional preparation? Of what should such preparation consist? When should it occur (at university vs. on the job)? Is there a distinctive body of professional knowledge associated with teaching? And what kind of work is teaching—a profession? A craft? A vocation? An altruistic or social justice mission? While it would be foolish to assume widespread agreement on the answers to such questions, the common challenges identified by both traditional teacher educators and alternate route proponents demand and deserve a thoughtful, informed response.

Over the past 30 years, entrepreneurial reforms of the 1990s have mushroomed to occupy a substantial part of the teacher education and schooling market. This expansion, and the conflicts provoked, suggests that the time is ripe to look back and attempt to understand how we got here. How did TFA galvanize a generation of educators and reformers? To what ends? With what successes and what challenges? And, perhaps most meaningfully, what can be learned from such efforts?

A STUDY OF 30 ALUMNI OF THE INAUGURAL COHORT OF TFA

To offer our retrospective analysis of these issues, we draw on 30 oral histories that we gathered from individuals who participated in the inaugural 1990 corps and focus on the experiences and professional trajectories they describe. Specifically, we look at how participants explained their choices to join TFA and teach in low-income, underserved schools. We take into account participants' backgrounds, their perceptions of their post-collegiate options, their ideas about teaching, and the historical context of the late 1980s and early 1990s. We also explore the ways that participants characterized their teaching experiences—in particular, how these experiences align with what we understand about beginning teachers, how they affected participants, and what they say about the particular moment of 1990s education in underserved communities. Finally, we turn to the broader field of university-based teacher education, examining the responses and changes that have come about since the advent of TFA, and reassess significant aspects of TFA's legacy on the participants' lives and the field of education.

Why the 1990 TFA Cohort?

While the TFA program has been hotly debated for decades now, actual participants' experiences, their understandings of those experiences, and their subsequent professional lives have gone largely undocumented. In choosing to study TFA participants, we introduce important untapped perspectives into the conversation about urban teaching and education reform. In selecting individuals from the initial 1990 cohort, we hoped both to maximize the number of years over which we could see individuals' paths play out and to tap memories that have become well integrated into a longer life story. Such perspectives, important in themselves, can also add to and alter what we know about TFA and its influence on urban teaching.

In fact, TFA participants occupy a unique place in this history. Existing studies show that TFA participants have represented a distinct subgroup within the teaching population (and even among alternate route candidates) by virtue of their elite undergraduate education as liberal arts majors, their conceptualization of teaching, their reasons for choosing to teach, and their high level of cultural and symbolic capital.[3] Moreover, because TFA participants tend to parlay their experiences into socially influential positions, the ways that TFA participants have made sense of, understood, and acted on their experiences constitute rich grounds for analysis, analysis that illuminates the context of urban teaching and trends that have defined urban education and teacher policy debates over the last 3 decades.[4]

Finally, our focus on TFA also arises from our own situations. We, the authors, both attended elite undergraduate institutions and belong to the generation of young people that first embraced TFA. Our friends, our classmates, and even one of us took part in TFA. As teacher educators, we came of age professionally with TFA; many of our understandings and practices in teacher preparation have emerged against the backdrop of TFA. In this regard, our interest in TFA participants' lived experiences and the ways in which participants have framed, shared, understood, and incorporated these experiences within their lives is both personal and professional.

Why Oral History?

Oral history is a transdisciplinary means of gathering information that elicits individuals' personal perceptions and firsthand accounts of the past. Such testimonies provide a valuable source of knowledge about the past, offer new interpretive perspectives, and illuminate the current moment as well.[5] This makes oral history an ideal methodology for unearthing new details about this particular group of urban teachers' experiences and lives, and new understandings of "the structural and material conditions" that surrounded participants' work.[6] At the same time, we are aware that the very questions we bring to the stories of our TFA participants reveal our own location in the educational milieu of today—its concerns, challenges, and assumptions.

For many years, social scientists and historians treated personal narratives, including oral histories, as anecdotal and "unreliable as a basis for generalization."[7] Increasingly, however, scholars recognize the integrity of oral histories in yielding a distinct type of knowledge, in which their subjective character can be considered a strength. For our purposes, the oral histories we gathered not only gave details about participants' lives and experiences, but also revealed how individuals have made meaning of their TFA teaching tenure. This project of more nuanced understanding depends upon being able to examine participants' recollections about TFA within the thicker narrative of their lives, which in turn helps to contextualize both the explicit and implicit reasons behind their choices related to TFA.

Although oral history analysis traffics in the individual and the personal, it also recognizes the narrators as "persons in context . . . whose stories reflect their lived experiences over time and in particular social and historical settings."[8] The personal stories of our TFA participants thus contain not merely documentation of their individual lives, but also memories about the conditions of urban schools in the early 1990s, the cultural expectations for graduates of elite colleges, the general status of teachers in America at the time, and the social gestalt that shaped notions of what was possible for this generation of relatively privileged young people.

TEACHING FOR AMERICA: OUR STUDY

By interviewing individuals from the initial 1990 cohort, we meant to maximize the number of years over which we could see participants' professional paths play out and to tap memories that had become well integrated into a longer life story. Unlike larger aggregate and quantitative studies, this close-in investigation of a select number of TFA participants' experiences breaks new ground by documenting their explanations for and understandings of the choices they made and placing these understandings within the larger context of knowledge about teacher preparation. As our work shows, the details of individual lives, as understood by those individuals, deepen our understandings of the challenges we face in preparing teachers to provide high-quality education in all classrooms.[9]

Schooling Teachers consists of seven chapters. In the first chapter, we set the context for the book. In the late 1980s and early 1990s, many factors converged to spur TFA to prominence and popularity. Among these were widespread dissatisfaction with the performance of schools and teachers, shifting governance roles, the incipient entrepreneurial spirit in education, backlash against the bureaucratic requirements of teacher preparation and credentialing, and, finally, the revival of an old tradition linking teaching with "service." Given the "greed is good" ethos of the Reagan-era 1980s, it may seem an inauspicious time to have initiated a teaching corps reliant on altruism. Yet as the 1980s came to a close, the decade's policy direction having exacerbated many social ills, the country embraced a resurgence of idealism (particularly on elite college campuses), such that TFA's appeal for young people to "make a difference" met with remarkable success. Fittingly, the schools where TFA recruits taught were situated in those very neighborhoods most neglected by 1980s conservatism, suffering from poverty, homelessness, segregation, AIDS, the crack epidemic, and high violent crime rates, which took a toll on schools and students. It was within these educational and social contexts that the inaugural TFA participants began their adventure and from them that the reforms that have shaped today's educational milieu emerged.

Chapter 2 limns the motivations and desires that brought our participants to TFA. The theory of action behind TFA promoted the idea that if only the "right" people—a definition that has shifted according to the historical moment—could be induced to teach, the "teacher problem" would be solved. Who were these "right" people and why did they respond to the call of TFA? To answer this question, we draw on aspects of *life course theory*, which highlights how individuals and their choices are related to their broader social context. Specifically, we consider how the first-year TFA participants' choices were shaped by the transitional developmental moment of leaving college and assuming adult roles in society, their upbringing and college experiences and, finally, the historical moment in which they found themselves, especially the surge of idealism among the young and the prevailing critique of schooling. Looking across participants' stories, we found distinctive narrative patterns and common themes, including their assumptions that teaching would be a manageable challenge.

The book devotes two chapters to participants' experience of the 1990 TFA Summer Institute. Where traditional teacher education is predicated on the belief that teaching calls for specialized knowledge and training, to be acquired before becoming a teacher of record, TFA banked on the idea that the right people could learn how to teach on the job. The 1990 corps accordingly commenced with a brief 8-week Summer Institute that, according to participants, did little to prepare them for the practical realities of teaching. Chapter 3, working from participants' narratives and secondary sources, outlines the Summer Institute's attempt to prepare corps members for teaching. It focuses on TFA alumni's grievances regarding this preparation, particularly their sense of what they did not get in the way of preparation, while also recognizing their frustrations as surprisingly similar to those of traditionally trained teachers. This confluence in criticism suggests real shortcomings in how the field has operationalized teacher training—so far, neither the mainstream university-based programs nor the alternate routes such as TFA seem to have figured out how to effectively prepare teachers to be ready for what they will face when they take up their own classroom.[10] But perhaps these persistent difficulties also indicate just how hard it is to prepare individuals to teach effectively, especially in underserved communities. Unfortunately, because

TFA placed its figurative bet on the quality of the recruits over preparation and development, the initiative missed an extraordinary opportunity to seriously rethink how to develop and support effective teachers.

Chapter 4 continues consideration of the Summer Institute, but with a focus on the question of who was fit to teach low-income students of color. By 1990, critics had suggested that university-based teacher education had been slow—and not necessarily very effective—in responding to the challenge of preparing teachers to work with diverse student populations.[11] TFA called for deploying its recruits in classrooms serving children from low-income families, who were racially and ethnically different from the TFA participants. Thus, multiculturalism became the watchword of the Institute. According to participants interviewed, the Institute defined and presented multiculturalism simplistically, divisively, and with little practical connection to the environments or classrooms in which the recruits would teach, undermining recruits' opportunity to grapple substantively with the issues of identity politics and cultural difference. The chapter situates these accounts of the Summer Institute within the larger context of multiculturalism as it played out in elite college academics and campus movements of the late 1980s and early 1990s, as well as within the debate among teacher educators about how to adequately prepare teachers to teach students who were culturally different from them.[12]

Chapter 5 follows our interviewees into the classroom, as they assumed their teaching placements in high-need schools across the country. The question of how new teachers get from the "survival" phase of beginning teaching to teaching that effectively promotes student learning lies at the heart of current teacher preparation debates.[13] This chapter focuses on obstacles the TFA participants encountered—the difficulties of classroom management, assuming authority, functioning within school cultures, and dealing with the larger social context that students bring to school—to illuminate general challenges inherent in first-year teaching, even among so-called traditionally trained teachers. Ultimately, the chapter raises questions about how teachers can be prepared, finding fault with both the postwar, university-based model of teacher preparation and more recent alternatives, few of which have managed to provide the kind of supports needed at the most crucial time of a teacher's development.

TFA represented a much broader set of reforms challenging the educational status quo that have reshaped the field over the last 35 years. Chapters 6 and 7 widen the lens to examine the ways in which the broader field of teacher education has been challenged by and responded to these upstart alternatives, and to address the legacy of TFA. Fundamentally, the emergence of TFA was made possible by the success of critics and reformers in tagging traditional teacher education with a persistent "narrative of failure."[14] New advocacy organizations publicized this theme of failure to promote alternatives (though some of the fiercest critiques came from within the field itself), buoyed by a zeitgeist that favored deregulation and market competition. As TFA and related reforms infringed on teacher educators' authority over the "market" of teacher preparation, university-based teacher educators were pressed to respond and adapt. Chapter 6 sets the more recent critiques into historical context, identifies significant contemporary factors that have shaped teacher education debates, and briefly explores some of the ways in which university-based teacher educators responded. Ultimately, Chapter 6 suggests that while teacher educators are hemmed in by distinct disadvantages and continue to struggle for legitimacy, the respective efforts of traditional providers and alternatives have also intersected in ways that have pushed the field forward in confronting the persistent difficulties of preparing high-quality teachers.

The book's last chapter examines the impact of TFA on the broader discussion about teachers and teaching in this country as well as on participants. TFA has highlighted estimable weaknesses in our existing system, yet it has also carried the banner for a reform movement fraught with problems of its own. Chapter 7 argues that it is essential to acknowledge the challenges and affordances of both models if we are to imagine the future of more effective teacher preparation. Closing with an investigation of TFA's influence upon the lives of our interviewees, the chapter suggests the power of changed perspectives and small-scale advocacy toward educational justice.

CHAPTER 1

TFA and the Paradox of the 1980s

At the onset of the 1990 school year, the *New York Times* offered a "bittersweet" pronouncement on the nation's efforts to improve teaching in K–12 education: "More and better qualified people" were choosing teaching, but not enough to mitigate the "acute shortage of academically talented teachers, minority teachers and math and science teachers." The article noted one bright spot, however, in "teaching programs modeled on the Peace Corps, like Teach For America," that brought "different and smarter teachers" into the field.[1] At the same time the article appeared, the first cohort of Teach For America (TFA) teachers had just begun teaching in the classrooms of low-income schools across the nation. As participants began what would be a formative chapter of their own personal and professional journeys, their foray into classrooms by way of TFA ignited a heated debate over the policies and practices that govern teacher recruitment, training, and retention. And though TFA may have captured the headlines, it was no anomaly. Rather, the program was at the leading edge of a much larger wave of change and disruption that has transformed American education since the 1980s.

This book offers an analysis of these transformations. To set the stage, this chapter examines the place of TFA within the broader political, social, and educational histories of the 1980s, illuminating the forces that collectively enabled TFA and propelled it to prominence. As the most visible of several alternate routes to classroom teaching that emerged in the late 1980s, TFA captured the zeitgeist, attracting the attention of corporations and philanthropic organizations, teacher educators, young college graduates, and the general public. Part of this fascination lay in the program's origins, and how dramatically Princeton undergraduate Wendy Kopp nurtured her idea for a domestic teacher corps (loosely modeled on the Peace Corps) from undergraduate thesis to fundraising proposal to reality in the space of a year.[2] Most compelling, however, was the way the program became a powerful manifestation of efforts begun in the 1980s to challenge and ultimately circumvent existing educational systems and institutions.

Many of the complaints that spurred the development of TFA and fed its enthusiastic reception—discontent with the quality of teachers and their training; frustration with the supposed shortcomings of K–12 education; a shortage of teachers, especially in urban areas; and the lack of diversity that characterized the teaching force—were longstanding. Nor were the solutions that TFA presented wholly new. And yet something about the moment when it emerged enabled TFA to catch fire as both a harbinger and nascent expression of powerful new forces and attitudes in education.

In her original vision, Kopp meant for her "Teaching Corps" to address both the "dilapidated state" of K–12 education and the existing shortage of certified, qualified teachers.[3] Interest in the job of teaching was at a low ebb in the early 1980s and, by the decade's end, urban districts had begun to experience the "harsh reality" of what was predicted to be a nationwide teacher shortage.[4] Many at the time suggested that the rapidly changing economy of the 1980s (from an industrial to an information-based society) demanded a more rigorous education for all students, which would in turn require teachers who were up to the task.[5] In popular opinion, most teachers were not up to it; they were disparaged as not smart enough, and poorly prepared to boot. A 1980 *Time* headline, "Help, Teacher Can't Teach," for example, and a 1990 special edition of *Newsweek*, in which a cover story purported to lay out "How to Teach Our Kids," provide apt bookends for the decade's persistent critique of teachers' perceived failures.[6]

This framing of problems, which emerged at a particular moment in time, may have generated Kopp's idea, but complaints about teachers and their preparation long predated the 1980s, as Chapter 6 details. Though teachers have enjoyed lip service as the honored purveyors of a special service, they have also been roundly blamed for school failure and pilloried for their supposed shortcomings.[7] These attacks have most recently emphasized teachers' purported low academic standing, but historical criticism has also taken aim at teachers' gender, race, ethnicity, character, and moral standing as limitations that have precluded their ability to educate, suggesting the ways in which they and their occupation have been victimized by larger social circumstances.[8] As for their preparation, numerous reports and histories since the mid–20th century have engaged in the blood sport of bashing teacher education. Persistent critiques have taken issue with low standards, "Mickey Mouse" coursework, and the misplaced emphasis on theory over practice said to characterize university-based teacher education.[9] The decade of the 1980s, however, marked an abrupt departure, in which critics not only criticized but also attempted to circumvent or replace the traditional university-based route to the classroom, to the point of spawning a cottage industry of alternative routes to the classroom. Even though such initiatives represented only a tiny share of the larger market that produced teachers, they had the effect of undermining fundamental assumptions about who was qualified to teach and on what basis that had guided the field for at least 3 decades.

Why, in the 1980s, did these challenges jump from criticism and reform of university programs to, in some cases, outright competition with university-based teacher education? The historical exigencies of teacher education certainly played a role, but we argue that American politics and culture in the 1980s exerted new pressures on existing systems and encouraged new, entrepreneurial approaches to problem solving. Indeed, the social and political attitudes of the 1980s had a far-ranging impact on educational policy and practice, as the primary emphasis on equity and access that prevailed in the 1960s and 1970s transformed to an overarching quest for "excellence" and an increasing contestation over control of schooling. Perhaps most potently, the era effectively revised the public narrative about education. Redefining what counted as problems of schooling and teacher preparation enabled a confluence of powerful stakeholders to circumscribe the potential solutions to those problems.

1980s WRIT LARGE

In historian Doug Rossinow's formulation, the 1980s represented "an era of crucial choices for Americans—a time of political transformation and alterations in social values and ways of life."[10] The 1980 election of Ronald Reagan ushered in a decisive rightward turn to the nation's politics. Many voters hoped for a new direction in economic policy (tax relief and an end to runaway inflation), and many—business and religious conservatives, as well as a populist "New Right"—cast their votes in protest against the liberal movements of the 1970s (including feminism, gay rights, and civil rights) to push Reagan into office.[11] The result was a decade shaped by the ideals of unfettered capitalism, individualism, entrepreneurialism, anti-government sentiment, and so-called traditional values. Or, as Democrats such as Bill Clinton would put it at the end of the decade, a "gilded age of greed, selfishness, irresponsibility, excess and neglect."[12]

Reagan's denunciation of government and advocacy of deregulation framed the market as an antidote to government control, which, according to its critics, "hardened bureaucracy, stifled incentive, and discouraged fiscal discipline."[13] In this way, Reaganism made a target of the liberal welfare state itself. By the decade's close, the end of the Cold War and collapse of communist regimes seemed to vindicate free-market ideology.[14] This creed seeped into realms long guided by motives other than profit, reshaping the incentives and operations of fields such as health care and education. Capitalizing on a distrust of bureaucratic institutions dating back to Watergate and shared by the right and the left, the desire to dismantle "big government" found its analogue across a variety of domains, where nimble, entrepreneurial entities sprang up to compete against hidebound companies and public systems that seemed ineffective and unresponsive. This set the template for an upstart such as TFA to emerge against the backdrop of the heavily criticized, bureaucratic system of teacher preparation and credentialing.

But if anti-government sentiment and consumerism flourished, the "go-go" 1980s also had a dark side, laced with fears of economic decline, international enemies, and a threat of crime and disorder explicitly linked to urban spaces.[15] Such fears were not entirely misplaced. Americans worried about the nuclear arms race with the Soviet Union and fretted that Japan was outpacing them economically. But it was low-income communities—where TFA recruits would teach—that most tangibly bore the brunt of this dark vision. Globalization and job migration hollowed out cities, exacerbating the "immiseration, criminalization, and isolation of the worst urban neighborhoods."[16] Reagan's government downsizing took cruel aim at those programs (AFDC, Medicaid) serving the neediest, gutting crucial supports for marginalized communities. In the interstices, devastating social ills—poverty, AIDS, homelessness, crime, and crack cocaine—multiplied.[17] The crack epidemic in particular served as a pretext for the militarization of the police and the punitive crime and drug control programs unleashed in cities, even though, as historian Elizabeth Hinton has observed, crack abuse was primarily a manifestation of the "devastating impact of unemployment and urban divestment."[18]

Yet even amid this anti-government and rightward trajectory, liberalism remained a potent opposing force.[19] So-called front porch politics on behalf of social justice persisted through the decade, if not quite as successfully as in the 1960s and 1970s.[20] And by the late 1980s, various financial scandals—including the savings and loan debacle, insider trading, and the global market crash of 1987—muddied the case for unchecked capitalism. Indeed, if sharp new lines of division had emerged by the end of the decade, so had a new spirit, especially among young Americans, in which "the call to redeem those excluded from the era's wealth would be a source of . . . mobilization."[21] It would be a call that TFA would exploit.

"THE SKY IS FALLING": EDUCATION IN THE 1980S

The civil rights movement that swept the country in the 1960s and 1970s had found apt expression in education; its successes in pressing for school equity and access on behalf of low-income and Black and Brown students, as well as for girls and women and students with disabilities, were codified in a host of legislative protections. But these efforts also provoked a backlash. Racism surely accounted for some of the hostility, though the pushback was also stoked by zero-sum thinking, fears that integration and greater access for all would siphon off valuable resources and compromise the quality of education enjoyed by more privileged Americans.[22] Many also objected to the federal government's intrusion into the local workings of schools. Broadly, educational clashes at the time echoed the country's larger political conflict, which pitted those who believed in the power of the state to "organize social and economic life in the name of the public welfare and the social good" against others who subscribed to limited government, the power of individual or local control, and efficiency of markets.[23]

The ideological battles of national politics at the time played out in education through a messy assortment of beliefs about what ailed education and how to fix it. The period witnessed "serious divides in the world of school reform" that set social efficiency reformers against social justice activists, access advocates against the privileged, and free market thinkers against those who favored involvement of the state.[24] Such disparate views were visible across the era's major trends and initiatives: School finance cases seeking greater educational equity were filed while, at the same time, many state legislatures enacted sharp limits on tax revenues for education, such as those set by Proposition 2½ in Massachusetts or Proposition 13 in California. A burgeoning home-schooling movement, seeking relief from federal and state educational mandates, emerged alongside the dramatic expansion of special education requirements. And continued pressure to desegregate schools, as in Connecticut's *Sheff v. O'Neill*'s argument for a plan of racial integration, competed with the resegregation that occurred as districts across the country were released from court-ordered desegregation plans.[25] Acrimonious politics among education associations, increasing teacher militancy, the growth and balkanization of single-interest groups battling for their special program or need, and an economic recession further meant that, as one education policy scholar put it, "combative groups were fighting over a smaller and smaller pie."[26] One thing on which reformers did seem to agree, however, was that schools were in desperate need of change.

Making the Case for a Crisis

A flood of commissions and reports documented this "evident national soul-searching" about public schooling in America.[27] Philanthropic foundations, business groups, academic researchers, government commissions, education and teacher education associations, and political organizations issued dozens of reports bemoaning the state of education in the United States.[28] As many as 275 state and local task forces released reports critical of American schools.[29] High-profile educators, such as Theodore Sizer, John Goodlad, and Ernest Boyer, urged reform of American education.[30] Perhaps the best known among the reports is the federal government's 1983 *A Nation at Risk*, which set a prevailing tone with its dramatic prose: "If an unfriendly power had attempted to impose on America the mediocre educational performance that exists today we might well have viewed it as an act of war."[31]

Though the myriad reports and commissions of the 1980s may have diverged in substance, they shared a sensibility. They warned of a crisis in American education that threatened the very state of the nation and, across their differences, found common cause in the need for reform. Media coverage magnified this narrative of schools in crisis, pushing education to the top of the national agenda.[32]

Riding this crisis narrative, the *Nation at Risk* report broke open public debate about the quality of education and laid out a rationale for change. Unlike the educational criticisms of the 1970s, which took issue with the "lack of relevance and humaneness" in schools, the prevalent critique of the 1980s concerned the declining *quality* of schooling.[33] The report argued that coursework in the nation's schools had strayed from important basics, educational achievement had dipped precipitously, and schools suffered from a shortage of good teachers, especially in low-income communities and communities of color.[34] Responding to such complaints, the reforms unleashed by *A Nation at Risk* focused on excellence and higher standards. Twenty-five years earlier, in response to the 1957 launch of Sputnik, America had oriented educational efforts toward excellence, but the 1980s version of excellence exhibited several crucial distinctions. The 1980s reforms were more about nurturing talent to compete in a global economy than shoring up national defense, and "excellence" in the 1980s encompassed a broader constituency than did reforms of the Sputnik era. Specifically, the notion that "equity and excellence are connected," as Ernest Boyer observed in his 1983 report on secondary education, made room for both conservative and liberal education reformers under the banner of "excellence."[35] Indeed, *A Nation at Risk* advanced the idea that improving educational outcomes, while central to developing top-notch academic talent and prevailing in international competition, was also "essential for preventing the less privileged from becoming further disenfranchised" from society. Both the left and the right—that is, social justice advocates and proponents of economic competitiveness and elite achievement—had reason to come together around higher standards under the banner of "excellence for all."[36]

The report argued that the country's economic development relied upon improved education. Given that America was grappling at the time with an increasingly competitive globalized economy, the notion that "America could not prosper unless its schools were successful" hit home.[37] Educational success thus became tightly linked to national security and economic competitiveness. Meanwhile, owing to a confluence of policy trends, educational "success" was increasingly determined by standardized tests, which were used to monitor student progress and, over time, to hold schools accountable.[38] *A Nation at Risk* marshaled these metrics to make the case for educational failure and framed the 1970s downward trend in major indices of student performance, including NAEP scores and SAT results, as evidence of deteriorated school quality. These declines in test scores could have well been interpreted as the reasonable result of a larger number of diverse students taking these tests. But the dominant narrative of the era seized on the test scores as proof, instead, of the eroding quality of education. The report helped energize efforts to make achievement and accountability primary goals of state and federal education policy. In turn, the emphasis on test-based accountability measures suggested a larger shift in the criteria for educational quality, from inputs to outputs: "No longer would we view school quality through the prism of inputs and resources alone—degrees earned by teachers, the size of classrooms, the number of books in the library. Instead, we would look at outcomes."[39]

"Excellence" provided a common objective for reforms launched at the time, though the means of reaching that outcome remained contested. If, as Charles Payne argued, "The late 1980s and entire 1990s were a period of unprecedented experimentation with ways to improve schools . . . [especially those] serving low income children," those experiments tended to polarize along the lines of either increased regulation and requirements or decentralized, entrepreneurial initiatives.[40] Education scholars Thomas Timar and David Kirp identify, on the one hand, "hyperrationalists who believe that schools are infinitely manipulable," and, on the other hand, "romantic decentralists who believe that schools will flourish if only they are left alone." According to the authors, "Hyperrationalists' strategy for fixing schools is to create new policies and programs [such as teacher and student testing, increased graduation requirements, or longer schools days]," whereas "[t]he romantic decentralists . . . believe that relief from stultifying mediocrity lies in deregulation and local control of schools."[41] In his examination of Teach For America, education historian David Labaree came to a similar framing of the standards movement, the effort to impose standards and high-stakes tests, against the choice movement, described as a way of bypassing the "stifling bureaucracy of public schooling" through the accountability of the marketplace.[42] Over the next several decades, both approaches flourished. As states generated more rules and regulations about all aspects of education in this period, market-based reforms such as vouchers, school choice, and charter schools also emerged, all with the intention of raising education up from the "stultifying mediocrity" of the existing system.

In the mid- to late 1980s, the "hyperrationalists" began their work toward a standards-based, systemic reform policy strategy. The idea was to ensure an alignment of reforms, all working together toward higher student achievement, that included the development of challenging academic standards (to drive curriculum and instruction) tied to accountability measures, including testing and teacher certification.[43] Pushed forward substantially by federal efforts, including George H. W. Bush's gathering of governors in Charlottesville, VA, in 1989, and Clinton's "Goals 2000" state grants program, the standards and accountability movement culminated in the passage of the No Child Left Behind bill in 2001, which required every state to develop and implement a standards-based accountability system in line with the law.[44] No school or district across the nation was left untouched; the standards and accountability movement, especially as it was yoked to high-stakes assessments, indelibly shaped the work of schools and teachers over the last 20 years, in ways both intended and not.

Free Market Thinking

On the other hand, as indicated earlier, belief in the power of markets to solve social problems and increase efficiency gained traction with the larger political movement represented by Reaganism. The administration embraced new principles for governing education that emphasized deregulation, decentralization, and even disestablishment (of the U.S. Department of Education), reduction of education as a federal priority, and cutbacks in federal education dollars.[45] While *A Nation at Risk* compelled national attention to education, the federal government avoided launching any major initiatives, choosing instead to define its role as a bully pulpit and devolving to states and localities the responsibility (and costs) for actually enacting reforms recommended by the report. Reducing the role of government, along with the growing entrepreneurial ethos of the time, created a vacuum for new players to exploit.[46]

Because the rationale of increased economic competitiveness fueled much of the reform energy of the 1980s, it should come as no surprise that business became a dominant actor in defining the shape and tenor of educational reform at the time. Education historian Dorothy Shipps has written incisively of the "privileged status of business critiques and management solutions" in urban school reform during this period.[47] Her work helps to frame the growing role of business—in terms of strategies, monies, and human capital—in setting the agenda for education in the 1980s and early 1990s. She points out that reports commissioned by business organizations such as the National Business Roundtable, the National Alliance for Business, and the Conference Board tended to draw parallels between good business practices and good schools. Many such reports, along with statements by business leaders and CEOs, articulated the need for market incentives, to be created through choice, charter schools, or vouchers. Generally despairing of educators' ability to undertake meaningful improvement on their own, these leaders declared, "Business will have to set the reform agenda."[48] Over time, they would insist on fulfilling that agenda as well.

But efforts to elide the system or build alternatives also had roots in the civil rights movement and community control battles of the 1960s and 1970s. Communities of color found the system largely unresponsive to their efforts to secure high-quality education in their public schools.[49] At the mercy of a predominantly white teaching force that generally held low expectations of the Black and brown children they taught, families sought to control their educational destiny in the 1960s and 1970s by taking over district schools, as in community control, or creating alternative educative spaces, such as Freedom Schools or private community-based neighborhood academies.[50] By the 1980s and 1990s, on the other hand, choice, charter schools, and vouchers had become primary means for families of color to pursue their goal of good education when their local district school could not deliver.[51]

Indeed, the laboratory of the 1980s offered up a variety of alternatives, now familiar elements in the educational firmament, to challenge or go around the educational establishment. Public vouchers, first approved in Wisconsin in 1990, could be used by low-income families to attend non-public (private) schools. By 1991, Minnesota had initiated the first charter school legislation, which essentially provided for independently operated public schools, and was quickly followed by other states. Early on, charters enjoyed broad support among liberals and conservatives, as the charter model satisfied interests in both expanding opportunity and bypassing the entrenched bureaucracy of the public school system. Many of these efforts built upon and broaden the practice of public school choice. Pioneered in places such as Harlem's District 4, choice was popularized as a way for families—even poor families—to exercise the freedom to choose where and how their children were educated. Choice beautifully reflected the ethos of the 1980s. As one supporter put it, "Given a choice system, schools will compete with each other for students and will therefore improve academically in order to attract their maximum market share."[52] It also located agency in the hands of the "customer," aiming to make schools accountable to parents and students rather than to the larger bureaucratic system.

This turn away from the state, along with the widespread experimentation of the era, created a rich climate of opportunity for new sources of authority, including policymakers, states, and "outsiders," such as philanthropy and business, to significantly shape new approaches to education. Teach For America grew out of this heady moment, uniting the entrepreneurial spirit of the time and the language of equity to revolutionize the path to the classroom.

Focus on the Quality of Teachers and Teaching

A *Nation at Risk* explicitly attached teachers to the larger narrative of failure, connecting supposed educational decline to "disturbing inadequacies in the way the educational process itself is often conducted." Teaching was one aspect of the educational process that the report identified as particularly problematic.[53] In this, A *Nation at Risk* had good company, as reports of the 1980s generally agreed that teacher quality was central to the crisis in education. The findings from A *Nation at Risk* regarding teachers were ruthless: There weren't enough qualified teachers to go around, especially in the fields of math, science, and foreign languages; qualified specialists in special education, gifted and talented education, and bilingual education were wanting. Worse, many existing teachers lacked the necessary skills for their jobs, due to a dearth of "academically able" students and because typical teacher education failed to prepare them well. A *Nation at Risk* chided teacher preparation programs for emphasizing educational methods courses at the expense of subject matter courses, echoing a deeply rooted criticism of university-based teacher education.[54] Critics also pointed to the conditions of teaching—low salaries and lack of decisionmaking authority, for example, as well as the cumbersome process of preparation and certification—as driving away good candidates.[55] And, as Wendy Kopp astutely noted, interest in teaching had reached an all-time low in the 1980s, a result both of the poor conditions associated with teaching and increased opportunities elsewhere, especially for women and people of color.[56]

Reforming Teaching

Reforms around teaching mimicked the contradictory reform landscape of education in general, which seesawed between tighter regulation and deregulation. On the one hand, states enacted more than 700 statutes affecting the teaching profession between 1984 and 1986 alone, many of which called for stiffer requirements.[57] Many teacher educators also advocated their preference for new rules and regulations to strengthen existing licensure and preparation systems. In two major 1986 reports, the Carnegie Forum on Education and the Economy's *A Nation Prepared: Teachers for the Twenty-first Century* and *Tomorrow's Teachers: A Report of the Holmes Group*, teacher educators and their allies argued that the key to improving teaching was "to change drastically the practice of teaching so that it [would] be a true profession, not . . . [an] over-burdened and under-rewarded occupation."[58] Only by ratcheting up the quality of individuals recruited into the profession, increasing their academic preparation, and creating ladders within the profession to offer career advancement with "salary increases attached" could teaching attain the status of a profession and attract and retain excellent teachers.[59]

But the countervailing reform trend and the era's advancement of free market ideals gave rise to a contrary strategy, in which the existing licensure apparatus would be stripped down, so that able aspiring teachers could circumvent traditional preparation programs. This, according to proponents, would have the result of attracting better people into the field and also diminishing the influence of existing stakeholders, including teacher educators, who had, from the perspective of the deregulation advocates, presided over educational failure. Such beliefs, along with the shortage of teachers for urban schools, a fear of teachers' declining skills, and dissatisfaction with existing university-based teacher preparation encouraged the proliferation of alternative routes to teaching.

Alternatives such as TFA also benefited from specific complaints against university-based programs of teacher education, including the expense of such programs, their lack of diversity, and the growing belief that the field needed not just a one-size-fits-all model, but many types of preparation programs.[60] These complaints spanned the ideological spectrum: as education historian James Fraser observed, by the end of the 1960s and 1970s, conservative proselytizers of deregulation, liberals, and communities of color all agreed that "the university monopoly was a problem" and that, "by the 1980s . . . easing entry into the classroom for higher quality, better qualified candidates—whether that be defined by academic success or cultural competency—was ultimately a positive goal."[61] Their shared sentiments linked liberals and conservatives in a call for change, abetted by the on-the-ground frustrations of school district leaders, who were tired of dealing with teacher shortages and relying on emergency-credentialed individuals to teach. This agreement meant that wide adoption of alternate routes was politically viable, garnering philanthropic dollars and even federal funds to move forward "in a domino-like fashion."[62]

A "KINDER, GENTLER NATION":
STUDENT IDEALISM IN THE 1980S

On its surface, the materialistic era of the late 1980s seems an inauspicious moment to initiate a teaching corps aimed at redressing educational inequities and reliant on idealism. Yet TFA's savvy appeal for young people to buck the cultural ethos and "give back" to America met with remarkable success. In its first year of recruitment, TFA attracted 2,500 applicants for only 500 teaching positions, tapping a latent idealism on the part of young college graduates. In this seeming paradox, Teach For America feeds into an important counter-narrative of the 1980s, in which the same era that "glorified the triumph of capitalism around the globe and . . . made greed a virtue also generated its opposite, a concern with how to repair the torn fabric of community," notably through volunteerism rather than policy.[63]

Nowhere did these countervailing trends play out as dramatically as on elite college campuses. Research stereotyped college students of the 1980s as self-concerned, "looking out for number one," career-focused, and eager to acquire material rewards.[64] In the early 1980s, involvement in campus organizations declined, along with participation in altruistic and service activities.[65] Yet even while such attitudes persisted, researchers noted a "subtle change" that suggested the beginnings of a period of "social engagement" among young people.[66] Indeed, media accounts at the time observed a general "rebirth" of idealism among college-aged young people, which translated into the desire to "become involved in the life of the community, especially to help such current issues as homelessness, hunger, illiteracy, and . . . the crisis of AIDS."[67] These writers saw students' idealism as the wellspring for increased participation in civic life and community service, greater social awareness, and even more activism, as measured by protests and political engagement. Greater optimism about the social collective, the proliferation of service opportunities and organizations on campuses, and local, state, and national incentives all seemed to point toward greater social engagement among college students.

Other scholars, however, cautioned that growing involvement in voluntary or community service projects could not serve as a reliable indication of renewed idealism or social activism among young people, and suggest that students' motives and interests might be more complicated. Students often saw service as an opportunity to do good for others while also doing well for themselves; they looked to their community service participation to provide skill development and experience; and they perhaps favored what sociologist Robert Serow called "a norm of personal assistance," in which students engaged with problems as local, individual phenomena, rather than seeing them as part of a larger social or political structure. Idealism, then, coexisted with a variety of interests, and the kind of pragmatic idealism exhibited on elite college campuses seems often to have been anchored by social privilege.[68]

In fact, the idealism and the orientation toward serving society that emerged among college students in the 1980s balanced seemingly opposing drives. In one study that discovered greater optimism among college students in the late 1980s, the authors acknowledged this optimism "was not well described by words like naïve, innocent or pollyannish," but rather, that there was "a hard edge to it," which they found surprising among young people.[69] If young people both responded to the conservative self-interest of the time and also wished to make a difference through actions aimed at real, intractable social issues, perhaps that kind of hard-edged idealism is not so surprising, particularly in an era defined by George H. W. Bush's idea of "prosperity with a purpose."[70] As it was, campuses were held in thrall by corporate recruiters just as they were gripped by debates over multiculturalism, apartheid, and political correctness and characterized by a growing student interest in serving to improve society.[71]

Wendy Kopp formulated her idea for a teacher corps as an antidote to the "sorry state" of education in the late 1980s and a way of meeting the demand for academically able teachers. But if she framed the problem in terms of schools and teaching, she couched the solution in the terms of a social movement, which effectively tapped that growing idealism of college students at the time. Kopp's strategy involved attracting a different kind of candidate—academically strong, idealistic "leaders"—into the field, exploiting the idea that the "right" people could solve the "teacher problem."[72] Accordingly, she trained her sights on graduating seniors at elite colleges and universities, most of whom had not previously considered teaching as an option. Kopp's intended recruitment pool initially provoked disbelief. Even if people agreed that the idea of a teacher corps made sense, they didn't necessarily believe that outstanding college graduates in 1990 would want to teach in public schools in low-income neighborhoods. One inner-city district personnel director actually "laughed out loud" when he saw the colleges where TFA intended to recruit: "'You'll never get people from these colleges to teach here.'"[73]

Undaunted, Kopp argued that "today's students are as willing as ever to 'give something back' to America." She employed selectivity as part of the nascent corps' appeal, to "counteract teaching's image as a 'soft' and downwardly mobile career," and cannily likened TFA to the Peace Corps. Marketing and recruitment materials framed TFA less in terms of the work of teaching than as an exclusive, altruistic adventure and a "movement."[74] An early flyer personalized this appeal, reaching out to people of color, for instance, by suggesting that achievement of full equality lay in education, and to liberal arts majors by drawing their attention to low literacy rates in the country and by reminding them of the "great privilege" they had been given in their own education.[75]

Indeed, from the very beginning, Kopp insisted on the significance of what she called the "idea power" associated with a teacher corps.[76] Her corps would not only supplement the teacher workforce; the young people involved would "at the same time focus a new spirit on the educational system and the profession of teaching."[77] She argued that publicity and support from government and business leaders would be essential to the fledgling effort. Drawing on the lessons of major volunteer programs such as the Peace Corps and VISTA, Kopp recognized the crucial role that idealistic students would play in making TFA work, confident that TFA could attract "a great many highly qualified individuals even if salaries are low simply by capitalizing on a spirit of hardship and adventure."[78] As historians of the 1960s era have shown, the spirit of adventure, the search for authenticity, and the need to prove oneself were keys to youth movements as well as to programs such as the Peace Corps, VISTA, and (a precursor of sorts to TFA) the National Teacher Corps, in that era.[79]

Though cloaked in the appeal of a social movement, however, the roots of Teach For America were quite otherwise. As Kopp recalled, her first task following the completion of her thesis involved appealing to the chief executive officers of major American corporations for funding.[80] TFA's institutional gestation was paid for by a seed grant from Mobil Oil and housed in donated space from Union Carbide Corporation. One of the first-year participants testified to this duality, acknowledging on the one hand her perception of TFA as "part of the civil rights struggle . . . that wasn't finished" and, on the other, seeing quite cynically that "it was Republican people that funded the organization from a person [Kopp] whose parents were Republicans and their Republican friends."[81] Teach For America symbolized the 1980s notion of "excellence" that included both ratcheting up academic performance and addressing equity, as the project made an "explicitly egalitarian appeal to use education to raise the academic achievement and social opportunities of the disadvantaged in the United States."[82] The organization's success in capitalizing on the era's rising social conscience by borrowing the language of equity while pursuing principles of market-based competition paved a path for others to follow.

CONCLUSION

TFA offers a fitting symbol of its time. By framing teaching as a social reform effort to address inequity, TFA deployed the rhetoric, still popular among a subset of college students at the time, of the civil rights movement, and benefited from an increasing interest on the part of students in helping society. Yet the rhetoric of community service also served to undercut the argument for formal teacher training, implying that such training was less important than the elite education and idealism that recruits brought with them. And it further masked the nature of TFA as an elite, private initiative, as opposed to a grassroots campaign for change. Certainly, TFA reflects a longstanding critique of teachers and teacher education, but it also represents an important shift: TFA symbolizes the rise of private, business-model, entrepreneurial approaches to education that arose in the early 1980s and served to marginalize the role of educational credentials and expertise.

CHAPTER 2

A Mission, a Lark, a Job

Choosing Teach For America

As the 1980s transitioned into 1990, the nation grappled with the hang-over of its Reagan years and a recession, while larger global transformations at the same time stoked optimism about the power of young people to change the world. Wendy Kopp believed it was a propitious moment to call on the "brightest young minds" to help solve an intractable social problem. The nation's schools were in trouble and begging for academically able teachers, especially in low socioeconomic areas, and she thought that recent graduates and seniors at elite colleges and universities were "in the mood to help."[1] Appealing to the "most talented graduates across the country," Teach For America began its recruitment drive in the fall of 1989. Letters and promotional materials explicitly invoked the Peace Corps, presenting TFA as a novel and exciting way to harness a "common spirit" and take part in a mission-driven movement.[2] By the spring of 1990, recruiters who crisscrossed the country in search of that first TFA cohort enthused over the college students they met and, especially, how much those students seemed to want to make a difference; by June of that year, 500 candidates, chosen from 2,500 applicants, arrived in California for the first Summer Institute.

This chapter asks: Why? Why did so many graduates from elite colleges and universities apply to the unknown and untried venture of TFA? For what reasons did these young people, presumably possessed of many other options, agree to sign on? And how did the TFA participants differ from more typical teaching candidates, those who go through university-based preparation programs? Were they differently motivated? We draw on the oral history testimonies of our interviewees to examine their reasons for joining TFA and bring to bear the lens of life course development theory to analyze their reasoning.[3] From the oral histories, we glean how narrators themselves understood the interests and needs that motivated their choice to teach through TFA and we see how they had, by the time of our interviews, woven these understandings into the larger narrative of their lives before and after their TFA commitment. In turn, life course development theory enabled us to make meaning of those narratives. The thread of "life narrative," "life history," or "life course development" spans multiple disciplines, including sociology, psychology, anthropology, and social history, but across them, the "life course" idea refers most straightforwardly to the intersection of social and historical factors with personal biography.[4] As an analytic heuristic, life course development theory helped us to show the mutually informative, rich, interactive relationship that exists between our 1990 TFA participants' lives, perceptions, and experiences, on the one hand, and the historical contexts and events of the late 1980s and early 1990s on the other.[5]

Political psychologists and sociologists have used life course development to investigate how young people "come to attach their personal lives to history as a part of a generational movement, and, in turn, the effect of that experience on the course of their adulthood."[6] Even more capaciously, a life course development perspective can accommodate several significant theoretical orientations that have been used to explain involvement in youth movements. These orientations include *life cycle development*, which tracks developmental stages in the life cycle, such as the transition from college, when young people are looking to define themselves and find meaning in their lives; *political socialization*, or important influences from one's upbringing that shape political beliefs; and *generational explanations*, an orientation that prioritizes the impact of significant historical events experienced by an age cohort. In our analysis, we borrow these orientations as interpretive devices, to look carefully at the ways in which participants' stage in life, their memories of growing up, and the state of the larger world into which they graduated may have inspired their choice to join TFA.

To be clear, TFA was not a grassroots movement in the manner of the civil rights movement, for example, nor would it qualify as a youth-based political group, such as Students for a Democratic Society (SDS) or Young Americans for Freedom (YAF) in the 1960s. We compare it to such movements because of the purposeful way in which the organization distinguished the TFA experience from the ordinary work of teaching, marketing it instead through a vision of social reform. Perhaps most important, examining TFA as a movement makes sense because so many of the recruits themselves believed they were joining a youth-driven movement for social change. In its rhetoric, TFA invited applicants who were "determined to make a difference"; promotional materials stressed the need for educationally privileged individuals to "give something back" to the country and to work in the places where they were most needed, meaning inner-city and rural schools rather than management consulting or investment banking. TFA further cemented this association by evoking the "thousands of America's brightest most motivated graduates [who] travel abroad to serve in the Peace Corps."[7] In subsequent years, TFA would explicitly claim for itself the mantle of a new civil rights movement, predicated on what Kopp called her generation's insistence on educational opportunity for all Americans.[8] While the organization's branding as a movement coexisted uneasily with its corporate roots and emerging neoliberal allies, this was not yet apparent to the first cohort. In 1990, TFA sold itself as a movement and recruits were eager to buy into it. This distinction is critical to understanding who chose to join this first cohort of TFA, for what reasons, and how they diverged from ordinary teacher candidates at the time.

We consider participants' interests in TFA across the three orientations of life course development theory: first, as a result of their developmental stage in life, the transition from college to adulthood; next, as a consequence of religious, political, civic, or educational ideals and principles developed during their upbringing; and, finally, in the ways that events and the zeitgeist of their generation in the particular historical moment affected narrators' decision to join TFA. In Chapter 7, we return to this life trajectory, looking to ascertain some of TFA's effects on participants' subsequent personal and professional choices in their lives.

CHOOSING TO TEACH VS. CHOOSING TFA

For many participants and their families, teaching proved an untenable career choice, if somewhat more acceptable under the guise of a temporary foray through TFA. They struggled to reconcile the expectations associated with their undergraduate credentials with popular perceptions of teaching. For example, Caroline Sabin, who graduated from Harvard University, described her father's association of educational value with earning potential: "Work equals money . . . you can make more of it if you are well educated." Because of his beliefs, Sabin recalled, "it was really a problem for him when I decided to become a teacher. That just didn't make any sense [to him] at all."[9] Likewise, the bewildered reaction of Yale graduate Jeffrey Simes's parents to his decision to join TFA suggests that teaching was somehow an inappropriate choice: "They understood my desire to do good in the world . . . [but they wondered], 'there's so many other things you can do . . . does that [teaching] really need to be the thing you do?'"[10] Andrew McKenzie, a graduate of the University of California, Santa Cruz, described having to explain to his mother that because TFA was a "quasi-Peace Corps type of deal," he didn't necessarily have to stay beyond 2 years. "[W]hen she heard that, she was like, 'all right, you've got my support.'"[11]

For some, even the 2-year detour of TFA teaching seemed a remarkable sacrifice: Many public commentators expressed surprise at the program's success in convincing "the best and brightest from elite schools like Yale, with presumably much better-paying offers" to give up (at least) "two years of their upwardly mobile lives to teach."[12] The broader cultural understanding suggested that teaching, with its questionable social status, would interrupt that upward trajectory. Indeed, as sociologist Dan Lortie wrote in his landmark study, *Schoolteacher*:

> Teaching, from its inception in America, has occupied a special but shadowed social standing . . . [it is] accorded high respectability of a particular kind; but those occupying it do not receive the level or types of deference reserved for those working in the learned professions, occupying high government office, or demonstrating success in business.[13]

Less kindly, the occupation has been called "careerless," due to its lack of advancement opportunities, or appropriate for those incapable of doing anything else.[14] To a great degree, the low status of teaching stems from its longtime reputation as "women's work," a result of the profound historical feminization of the position and the devaluation of women's work.[15] More recently, as opportunities have opened for greater numbers of women to work in fields beyond the so-called feminized professions, teaching has suffered the loss of high-achieving women who might once have chosen to teach.[16]

In terms of remuneration, an important metric in this country for the value of work, the question of whether teaching is a poorly or well-paid position is deeply dependent upon context—from whose perspective, at what historical moment. Shrinking opportunities in the bleak economy of the early 1990s may have made teaching seem attractive to our subjects, but for well-educated young people, "choosing to teach has always meant foregoing higher-paying alternatives."[17] Indeed, some economists have concluded that the "dramatic erosion of relative teacher earnings since 1960" has served as an important disincentive to teaching, particularly among high-achievers who have other options.[18] It would seem, for the most part, that financial reward-seeking did not drive TFA participants.[19]

Traditionally, teachers have been drawn to the occupation for their love of children and of helping them grow; for gender-related reasons (as teacher education scholar Eran Tamir observes, there are "powerful social structures at play that still push primarily women with relatively low academic aptitude to teaching"); or (especially since the advent of collective bargaining) for the monetary rewards and working conditions, that is to say, the reliable salary and summers off.[20] In contrast, the choice of TFA participants to teach must be framed as the choice to *teach through TFA*, as they represent a different population than those who typically would have entered teaching at the time, and their choice involved a different set of considerations from those of traditional-entry teachers. Compared to traditional-entry teachers and even other alternate route candidates of the last 30 years, our study participants were set apart by their elite academic credentials from top colleges or universities.[21] They share this distinction with a small subset of educators trained in elite undergraduate colleges or selective graduate programs, such as UCLA's Center X.[22] Attendance at highly selective colleges and universities in America confers a special status or cultural capital, which awards graduates both a high degree of social respect and unique links to power and influence.[23] Even graduates from modest backgrounds become part of "a select group that enjoys privileged access to lucrative occupations that bestow social, economic, and cultural capital that teaching can never match."[24]

Given the stigma around teaching, and with presumably many other options from which to choose, why then did participants elect to teach through TFA? For our interviewees, the conflict between their status and the cultural beliefs around teaching meant their motives for participating in TFA differed in important ways from those of traditional-entry teachers. In large part, as indicated earlier, participants chose TFA because of how the program redefined teaching, but also because of how that redefined vision exploited the developmental moment of leaving college, key influences associated with recruits' upbringing, and the historical conditions of the time.

CHOOSING TFA: DEVELOPMENTAL MOMENT ANALYSIS

From a developmental or life cycle perspective, the choice to join the inaugural cohort of TFA would have been powerfully shaped by the life stage at which these young people had arrived. The transition from college into the larger world is a time when, according to psychologists, young people rebel against the society created by their elders and empower themselves to "'create a better world.'"[25] Scholars say this stage is necessary for:

> . . . defining self-identity, striving for independence, affiliating with peers, and for trying to find meaning in life—all characteristics likely to make idealistic young people critical of their elders [and the status quo] . . . and prone to participate in youthful movements for political change.[26]

TFA was deliberately framed in the language of social reform and appeared to applicants as an opportunity to join a mission-focused crusade aimed at social change. Accordingly, our subjects most often recalled the appeal of TFA in explicitly developmental terms as an opportunity to change society and a self-defining adventure, though they also acknowledged the venture as a pragmatic way to claim their place in the adult world. Finally, the limited commitment required by TFA seems especially apt for the early period of adulthood exploration, as it eased participants from college into the real world without requiring them to make any binding decisions about their future.

Making a Difference: Teaching as Adventure. Lortie's foundational study found that teachers in the postwar period chose their occupation primarily because they believed that teaching is a service of special moral worth. This notion of teaching as service has deep roots in the history of American schooling, where the work has long been portrayed as a special mission, guided by a sense of principle and altruistic dedication rather than learned expertise or interest in status or money. Unfortunately, the conceptualization of teaching as an altruistic service tends to undermine the idea of teaching as a profession that requires substantial training and commitment. Indeed, by pursuing candidates with elite undergraduate degrees and embracing a "teaching as service" appeal, TFA effectively downplayed the role of professional preparation in its recruitment. As Jeffrey Simes explained:

> I didn't look at it [teaching] as . . . the pedagogical profession,
> the imparting of knowledge to young minds. I viewed it as much
> more of a "let's go into the . . . toughest schools in the hardest
> neighborhoods, let's, you know, do volunteer work," basically.[27]

Beyond implications for training, however, the "teaching as service" philosophy seems to have meant essentially different things to most traditional-entry teachers than to those who came through alternate routes or elite boutique preparation programs. Lortie's work from the 1970s suggests that "teaching as service is more likely to appeal to people who approve of prevailing practice than to those who are critical of it"; few of such individuals, according to Lortie's study, enter teaching either to work with "disadvantaged students" or to change education. More recent research investigating the intrinsic reasons individuals choose to teach indicates that those who are moved to teach for altruistic or service reasons tend to frame their motivation in the language of teaching itself. That is, they wish to help children succeed, or they feel a calling to teach, in which the latter represents a distinctive and deep service ethic.[28] Where traditional-entry teachers tend to have pursued "teaching as service" as a specific kind of "helping," dedicated to supporting children's learning, many of our TFA participants (along with some other alternate route candidates and teachers who came from elite colleges or highly selective graduate programs) idealistically viewed "teaching as service" more in terms of reforming education and society than the particular act of, for example, teaching students to read.[29]

Spencer Downing, who had just graduated from the University of Chicago, articulated his thought process at the time as, "I need to do something to help my country, so the notion [of] TFA . . . the impulse was truly altruistic, if a little bit naïve."[30] Caroline Sabin had pursued teacher preparation as an undergraduate at Harvard, but by the time she got to her TFA student teaching in South Central Los Angeles she had embraced a deeply reform-minded notion of teaching as service: "Believe me, I thought I was some sort of missionary."[31] Avis Terrell also described wanting to "do something meaningful," which she recalled as unusual, compared to many of her peers coming out of Wesleyan University, for whom "the goal was to make a lot of money."[32]

Some of the recruits expressed a more specific sense of social justice, nascent though it may have been, around the work. For instance, as the first person in her family to attend college, Lori Lawson recognized her own college-going as a result of someone having pushed her to get there; as she saw it, "Teach For America kind of enabled people who wanted to give back for the opportunity they had."[33] Furman Brown channeled the founding sentiments of TFA regarding educational opportunity for all, noting that "we were going to come in and save these kids," in large part because "the public school experience that I had was great, and *it was only fair that every kid should have what I had.*"[34] Similarly, Felicia Clark described her reaction to TFA as an "inspiration, like I think that I can make a difference," and liked the "social justice aspect of making a difference in an under-resourced school." But she too related her commitment to the idea of fairness. She explained how her parents had moved when she was young, so that she would have access to a good education system: "So I always think about that, like what if I had been raised in Los Angeles versus where I went [Colorado], which, at the time, when I was in school, was the third highest state [in] education [quality]?"

As an African American, Clark recognized the disparity in the quality of education provided to Black people. When she was 8, Clark went to see her grandmother, who took her to visit some schools in Washington, DC. Recalling the experience, Clark said she "couldn't believe it. It was just . . . disorganized, yelling, no classroom control. I had never seen such a thing." In her telling, she expressed how "it just stuck in my mind," to the point that, "when I found Teach For America, and I reflected back to that experience . . . I thought, you know, I could be a better teacher than that."[35] Christina Brown, another African American woman, articulated one of the clearest social justice motives because the endeavor of bettering the education of children of color seemed more personal for her than theoretical (though she too spoke the language of "world saving"): "I wanted to give something back to my community and I wanted to help children of color to learn . . . it was all about just saving the world before I became Thurgood Marshall."[36]

TFA Teaching as Adventure. While Kathy Feeley duly noted the service aspect of her motivation—"I thought, 'this is perfect: I'll get to serve the world'"—she also added, "'I get to go to L.A. for a summer, won't that be fun?'"[37] As was the case with many of her fellow corps members, Feeley seamlessly connected the notion of service with an opportunity for adventure. In fact, in accordance with their life stage, a significant aspect of many of our participants' motives involved their desire to experience new things, rebel against perceived social expectations, and "prove" themselves by teaching through TFA. TFA, for its part, fed this appetite. For example, in a 1990 recruitment poster, a young man of color, his back to a blackboard, faces a row of students. Over his figure, the word "teach" appears; the tagline at the bottom of the poster reads "You'll be amazed at what you learn," an apt illustration of how the appeal of TFA centered on the recruits themselves and the ways that they would be challenged and rewarded. The difficulty was part of the allure: As Heather Weller put it, "It [TFA] looked like a challenge, but it seemed like something I could do."[38] Diane Brewer admitted, "There was something impulsive about it, too, that was really exciting."[39] The splashy novelty (duly noted in media at the time) of the initiative also beckoned. Priscilla Leon-Didion said she "wanted to be part of something big."[40] And Jeffrey Simes remembered that he liked the idea of taking "a road less traveled" by choosing "this kind of wild, funky new thing that no one's ever heard of, and . . . rebelling." The inaugural nature of the opportunity made it seem even more adventurous—as Simes joked, "It wasn't like . . . the Rhodes Scholarship where they've been around for a hundred years and everybody wants it. It was kind of like, you know, we're guinea pigs and we're willing to do it."[41] Brent Lyles compared doing TFA to "an adventure . . . like taking a year to go travel around the world," but he noted that "there was something very quirky and unique about those people that joined Teach For America that first year because we were all risk-takers."[42] Scott Joftus concurred: "I think that I wanted to do something where I wasn't doing the traditional going to law school or going to work at you know, a consulting firm or . . . something like that."[43] Among Harvard graduate Susanne Murray's job offers—teaching at a private school, working in a law firm, or joining TFA—she "decided on Teach For America, which felt like the gutsier decision." Pressed, Murray conflated the social reform and adventure aspects of the venture, explaining that TFA "felt like part of something social justice–oriented . . . part of something exciting and new," and that "kind of thing [just] drew me in."[44] Furman Brown colorfully described the opportunity as "crazy, ballsy, and absurd," though he also believed that TFA represented "that big kind of thinking that, you know, changed my life."[45] Finally, for Andrew McKenzie, in line with the life development stage of pushing back at the older generation and the world it created, TFA's model of the "young leading the young"—Wendy Kopp and her staff were just about the same age as McKenzie—added significant appeal to the endeavor.[46] By linking the work of teaching in low-performing schools with the notion of social-reform minded service, TFA presented educationally privileged youth of the 1980s not only an opportunity to "make a difference," but also to take a risk, rebel against social expectations, and experience something new.

Shortcut to Teaching. Given the upfront lure of an adventure, some participants found themselves surprised as they began to realize that this particular adventure actually meant becoming a teacher. Constance Bond ruefully recollected:

> I really just thought I was going to have an adventure and learn some things about myself, and maybe find something I love to do, but even then I didn't think about teaching . . . there was a little bit of a shock to me that summer of, "Oh my goodness. I really have to be a teacher. This isn't the Peace Corps. This is a full-time job and I need to figure out how to do this and do it well."[47]

Practically, TFA offered participants a shortcut to the classroom compared to the route followed by more traditionally trained teachers, who dedicated time to pre-service teacher preparation. It would have been in keeping both with the message TFA conveyed and our interviewees' life stage and elite educational position for them to believe that their attributes should allow them to elide the conventional requirements to becoming a teacher. Upon later reflection, for instance, Spencer Downing saw his decision to join TFA as colored by a "certain amount of hubris and condescension," given his then-belief that "'I have something amazing to offer and this nation really needs my skills.'"[48] For many young people, belief in the exceptionality of what they have to offer might also be traced to life stage; a sense of indomitability and possibility may well coexist with the developmentally appropriate, youthful need to remake or reform society. In turn, such beliefs would likely have encouraged corps members' assumptions that they would be able to figure out how to teach effectively, even without fulfilling the traditional prerequisites.

While TFA was designed to attract people who might not otherwise have considered teaching, some of the interviewees had thought about becoming a teacher prior to learning about TFA. In those cases, TFA's ease of entry, its promise of avoiding the typical, formal preparation program, mattered greatly. For example, tutoring at a prison during his senior year at the College of the Holy Cross planted the idea for Carlos Gomez: "I think I had it [teaching] in the back of my mind . . . it felt so gratifying to help somebody in that way that I said this might be something I might want to do."[49] Priscilla Leon-Didion had weighed taking education courses before joining TFA, as "Wesleyan had a program," though it required extra time and "it was very expensive," which discouraged her from pursuing it.[50] When she learned about TFA, Marife Ramos "thought it was a Godsend . . . because there was no way I was going to get certified without [having to go] to an education school. So TFA was the answer to my prayers."[51] And Jeffrey Simes remembered thinking that TFA would be "a fairly quick and easy way to get into the classroom compared to other routes, which I had already failed to avail myself of."[52] Because TFA required little upfront preparation, Andrew McKenzie, who had signed on to a doctoral program in Russian literature, saw it as a low-stakes opportunity to test out the work of teaching itself. Before getting deeper into academia, McKenzie hoped that TFA would enable him to "verify to myself . . . will I like teaching and am I any good?" Likewise, Spencer Downing thought teaching would provide him with skills he would need for his long-term career goal, which was to earn a graduate degree in history. He figured that an advanced degree in history might "involve teaching at some point, so I hoped that the [TFA] experience would teach me how to teach a little bit."[53]

Teaching as Transition. Finally, life stage also seemed to be at work in the way that the interviewees relied on TFA to solve the problem of what to do following college. Jan Trasen was typical, in her memory of "having . . . a senior panic. I was like, 'What am I going to do next year?'" She was doubly concerned because, at the time she graduated, there were "no jobs." Fortunately for her and her TFA alumni cohort, Trasen recalled "Teach For America coming along and being like a rescue for [those of] us . . . [g]raduating with a liberal arts degree and not having any idea of what we were going to do with our lives."[54] Diane Brewer, a theater major at Tufts, explained how she considered applying to graduate school in theater, until she realized her parents were against it. "Then I had a really, really bad experience with my thesis advisor. I literally left his office and went and took my graduate applications and threw them in the trash." For Brewer, TFA offered "two years for me to do something productive and get everybody off my back."[55] Brent Lyles, who majored in zoology and anthropology at the University of Michigan, described a similar thought process: "I was literally walking down the hall and there was a poster for Teach For America, and interviews were, like, the next day . . ." He thought it sounded "kind of cool," but just as important, he also realized that if he did TFA, "I wouldn't have to go to grad school."[56] Furman Brown, already in graduate school, found in TFA a graceful way to "get the heck out of grad school without looking like a big failure."[57] Scott Joftus entertained the possibility that TFA might help him "get some ideas about how I could form a career around doing something with kids and youth," even though he didn't really think he wanted to be a teacher. Ultimately, what pushed him over the line, as he recalled, was the "two-year commitment . . . I was like, 'Well . . . I can do anything for two years.'"[58] And though Leo Flanagan had contemplated teaching, it was as a prelude to becoming a civil rights lawyer or priest, a decision he thought he was too young to make right out of college. So, "I thought, well, I'll do this [TFA] for a while. That would be something that makes sense in either direction my life takes."[59]

Ellen Rosenstock heard about TFA from a friend who was a senior at Yale and had characterized TFA as "the Peace Corps but here in the United States." An English and Women's Studies major who graduated from the University of Maryland that year, Ellen remembered thinking, "It sounds like an interesting thing and I'm not sure what I want to do next, but I love the idea of doing something public service-y when I leave college," so she applied.[60] As Rosenstock's story indicates, a major pathway into youth movements has been through networks of peers.[61] Of course, the TFA alumni's presence on elite college campuses already placed them within an important social network, such that a couple of colleges (Colby College, Yale) ended up contributing a high proportion of first-year TFA participants. But this pattern played out on an individual as well as institutional level. Susanne Murray is a case in point: describing it as "weird," Murray noted that her "boyfriend at the time worked there [TFA]," and that "another guy I knew, Whitney Tilson . . . also went to work there, so it [TFA] was sort of . . . in the mix."[62] Mark Stephan, who had actually begun an application for the Peace Corps when he learned about TFA, said that "word [about TFA] got around kind of randomly," suggesting it was "in the ether" of his personal network. Likewise, Spencer Downing's explanation incorporates the importance of his social network in leading him to TFA, but also the fear of an uncertain future:

> There were a few of us who were sitting around kind of going, what the hell are we going to do with ourselves after we graduate? . . . And a few of us talked over the Peace Corps and a friend of mine . . . said, "Have you heard about this new thing called Teach For America? You can teach in a school that is having troubles and you can, you know, the idea is to change America by teaching kids who are at bad schools."[63]

Here again, TFA behaved like a social movement, attracting applicants through significant social capital and friend networks.

As for the reasoning behind using TFA to answer the "what next" question, many contemporary college graduates, especially those who pursue a liberal arts course of study, grapple with deep uncertainties about their postgraduate plans and careers, right up through and beyond graduation. That participants gratefully embraced TFA as a means not only of filling this void but also of putting off firmer commitments suggests several potential conclusions. Specifically, it may have been a sign of the sluggish economy and "white collar woes" faced by 1990 college graduates, which made it hard to enter a number of desirable fields.[64]

More generally, it could indicate the uncertainty of liberal arts graduates in this period about how to connect their studies to the practical world of employment, since the liberal arts tradition emphasizes intellectual development through exploration, not occupational training.[65] Or, as we argue here, it may be a factor of that common developmental stage when young people struggle to define their adult identities, establish their independence, affiliate with like-minded peers, and find meaning in life.[66] For all of these reasons, TFA served participants' purposes.

Choosing TFA: The Influence of Upbringing

When asked directly why they joined TFA, respondents' explanations tended to privilege motives associated with their developmental life stage; however, we also collected information about participants' upbringing, looking for aspects of their socialization that might have influenced their orientation toward the TFA experience. Sociologists explain that political socialization, which "reflects larger societal socialization forces such as social class, ethnicity, religion, and culture," is transmitted in large part by families.[67] Borrowing from this thinking, our interview protocol posed questions about interviewees' formative family experiences, including their religious background, civic or political involvement, and attitudes toward education, as well as about how they would characterize the neighborhood in which they grew up and what kinds of schooling they experienced before college. Few interviewees cited these influences explicitly when asked about their choice to join TFA, but we discovered a number of compelling commonalities across participants' backgrounds that may have helped predispose them to embark upon the first year of TFA.

Most of our interviewees were born in the late 1960s and grew up as children and adolescents during the 1970s and early 1980s.[68] In some ways, having grown up during these years imbued a generational mentality, though that can be a slippery concept. Others from the same age cohort made very different choices, for example, as in the large number of participants' college classmates who, upon graduation from college, headed for Wall Street. And even within this group who joined the first year of TFA, in addition to potentially meaningful similarities, we identified significant differences that defined their growing up experiences. For instance, our interviewees represented working-class to middle- and upper-middle class families; some were firmly planted in urban or suburban settings, a few grew up in rural areas, while others moved constantly, domestically or even internationally. Many of their mothers were stay-at-home moms, though others' mothers worked; professional fathers might be doctors or professors; others' fathers worked for the postal service or ran small proprietorships, such as a butcher shop. Some participants' parents divorced during their childhood. Two participants were themselves immigrants, three had at least one parent who was an immigrant, and another six described immigrants among their grandparents, making our interviewees second- or third-generation citizens; others came from families that could trace their roots in America back for generations. Some families counted educators among their ranks; others did not. A surprising number of those interviewed had attended private or parochial school for some portion of their K–12 years. All, however, testified to the value their families placed on education, whether explicitly or implicitly.

Political activism. A few interviewees—primarily those who identified as Black—could recall examples of overt political activism in their families, sometimes having occurred before they were born. For example, Felicia Clark's mother participated in community organizing and had been a member of the Black Panther Party; Avis Terrell's great-grandmother had hosted Martin Luther King while her then-teenaged parents participated in civil rights organizing and protests in Albany, Georgia; and Christina Brown's father, a teacher-turned-AME (African Methodist Episcopal) church minister, was very involved with the AME's political work, participating in a ministers' council that worked with the mayor and school boards to "push for the needs of the African Americans in the communities that he worked in."[69] Others remembered involvement in local political or civic systems—Nichole Childs Wardlaw's mother and aunt working as poll watchers, for example, or involvement in local civic associations or school board elections, as in the case of Jennifer Denino's mother or Constance Bond's father. A few, such as Mark Stephan, remembered extended family members who "might" have been somewhat politically active, but had no memories of political activity within his nuclear family: "[A]s someone who studies political science now [Stephan is a professor of political science], I thought back to my own childhood and politics and it just wasn't there. I mean I don't have distinct memories of political conversation in the family or going to political events or party activity, I mean, none of that."[70]

Many more interviewees shared examples of what might be called values-based activities, rather than political activism *per se*, that seem to have shaped their upbringing. In Jane Schneider's case, her father's occupation instilled service-oriented values in her. Coming of age, Schneider struggled against the "imperative to go into medicine" that she experienced within her family, though she also clearly had absorbed from her upbringing that medicine was worthy work because of its helping nature. For her, then, the "appeal in Teach For America [was] that it had that same sort of value to me that I saw in medicine from [my family] . . . it was helping [and] . . . doing sort of an important piece of work for the community."[71] Other families engaged in a variety of voluntary helping activities: Bill Norbert's family regularly hosted Fresh Air Fund children at their home and sent clothes to Nicaragua, Scott Joftus's family was "always hosting" families immigrating from Russia, while Spencer Downing's family hosted Vietnamese families coming to the United States. Joftus did not consider his family's hosting of immigrant families to have been "politically active"; rather, he concluded that they were "socially conscious."[72] Along the same lines, Downing explained that, in comparison to friends' families, he felt his own family's political activity to be "relatively limited," because his family's activism was "kind of broadly, you know, social welfare... there was a general sensibility . . . that if you can do something useful in the world that's a good thing to do." Downing tied this sensibility to his parents' religious and political beliefs, locating them within a "Protestant world of conservative politics that also believes you should do things to help your fellow human beings."[73] Similarly, Heather Weller's family, where "generosity was a value, . . . always had people at our house." Deeply involved in their Protestant church, Weller elaborated, her parents, who taught in the same rural school, "invited everybody who didn't have another place to go [to their home] . . . so there would be, like, stray kids from school . . . any number of non-English speaking people . . . like some African family or the Spanish-speaking families and we'd have these single people at church and people who just got out of prison and . . . had accepted Christ."[74]

Religious background. Indeed, a good number of interviewees cited religion as a prominent aspect of their growing-up experience.[75] Participants came from diverse religious backgrounds, from faith traditions as wide ranging as Seventh-Day Adventist, African Methodist Episcopalian, Evangelical Christian, and Missouri Synod Lutheran (a conservative Lutheran branch). The parents of one individual were even among the first members (and a leader) of the Unification Church in America, colloquially known as "Moonies." Fully a third of participants described a Catholic upbringing, which is somewhat larger a proportion than might be expected: Between 1970 and 1985, when our interviewees would have been growing up, only about a quarter of the American population identified as Catholic.[76] Catholicism is associated with a strong tradition of teaching and socially minded service. Catholic women made up a large proportion of early 20th-century public school teachers in the urban north and Midwest and, of course, they have long staffed the parochial school system.[77] A few of our participants directly linked their interest in "teaching as service" to Catholic values. As one example, Caroline Sabin cited her Catholicism, which exhorted her to "help people," as a driving factor in her search for "some sort of service job."[78] Lori Lawson recalled her mother, who was very active in the Catholic church, having promoted the idea that "everyone helps each other."[79]

Carlos Gomez, whose family immigrated to America from Colombia when he was 8, called his parents "very religious" Catholics. Two of his uncles were socially conscious Jesuit priests, one of them working in the urban barrios of Bogotá. At Xavier High School, a Jesuit institution that he attended in Manhattan, Gomez got what he characterized as "a very deep religious and spiritual high school experience . . . around social justice, around sort of seeing Jesus as a role model and his work with poor, with marginalized people . . ." He found that teaching through TFA offered the kind of spiritual growth he had enjoyed in high school:

> I found my students . . . had economically not much but spiritually and culturally a lot. I remember students who were just so good and their families were so good and they found a lot of . . . strength in their religion and almost as role models for me religiously. And at the same time I felt like I was giving and I was contributing but I always felt like I was, I got so much from my students and I think . . . it was almost like a real life experience where I could see, I could see sort of spirituality in religion in context.[80]

Leo Flanagan, who came from a "classic, working-class Irish Catholic ethnic" background, had contemplated becoming a priest. He likened the work he anticipated doing under the auspices of TFA to what he might have done as part of the Catholic clergy:

> I thought it was a work similar to what I might do if I went into the priesthood or the brotherhood. I'd . . . be working in poorer communities in a way that tried to help them . . .[81]

Over a quarter of our sample described themselves as part of another faith group, Judaism, though some pointed out that being Jewish meant something more "cultural" than religious to them. Considering that estimates suggest that Jews made up just 3–4% of the U.S. population in the postwar period, their high representation is either an anomaly or there is something about participants' Jewishness that impelled them toward the TFA opportunity.[82] As in the Catholic faith, teaching has historically been a mainstay occupation for Jewish women, especially in places such as New York City beginning in the interwar years.[83] In regard to the TFA "teaching as service" idea, Scott Joftus made the case for the influence of Jewish culture on his outlook, saying, "there is something to the Jewish culture" that "shapes the way you think about giving and . . . what it means to be . . . part of this world."[84]

Arthur Schuhart's decision to join TFA connected directly to what he described as the American Protestant tradition:

> [T]here's this, you know, cultural tradition in America that you owe, and you must work, and you must improve [things]. And people pick up on that . . . [and] get drawn to things like Teach For America . . . they get drawn to serve. And our society respects that and rewards that.[85]

Interestingly, though many of the interviewees expounded on the values derived from their religious backgrounds, few directly connected their religious upbringing to their choice to join TFA, even if the associated values seem to have influenced their inclinations.

The leveling influence of an elite undergraduate education.

Another important shared experience for those we interviewed lay in the fact that they all attended fairly elite colleges or universities in the late 1980s, though they arrived at those campuses from very different life (and class) backgrounds.[86] Such socioeconomic diversity offers an interesting contradiction to the link between affluence and attendance at elite institutions of higher education.[87] About a quarter of the fathers and 40% of the mothers of our respondents had not earned a bachelor's degree; for a third of our interviewees, neither parent had received a college degree. For that 30% of participants whose parents had not attended college, the path to elite higher education could seem precarious. Carlos Gomez explained how his mother, a Colombian immigrant, relied on an executive at the bank where she worked to guide Gomez through the college admissions process. Gomez ended up at the very same institution—College of the Holy Cross—that the executive had attended and described his decision as "uninformed" at best.[88] Priscilla Leon-Didion, who was already doing her family's taxes in high school, recalled that she "had no one at home to ask for help. No cousins, nobody at the time could have helped me. I was the first one."[89] Avis Terrell ended up at Wesleyan by way of the program Prep for Prep, which she described as "a program that helped minority students who they felt were academically strong get into private [colleges]"[90] Even some of those whose parents had gone to college remembered needing considerable help in making their way to highly selective institutions. So although Leo Flanagan's parents attended college, he depicted his upbringing as having been "blue collar"—his father was a butcher—and noted that "a very good guidance counselor," rather than a family connection or expectation, forged his path to Colby College.[91] In thinking about why TFA might have appealed to so many first-generation college graduates, Arthur Schuhart, himself a first generation college graduate, surmised that it had to do with what TFA represented:

> We were doing something that was more than just a job. It was more than just getting employment. It was for something. It's in the name.

And so I think the people who came from backgrounds where they were the first ones to go to school—perhaps that underneath, in their psychology, is this gratitude, you know. The knowledge of that opportunity was more important for us perhaps, because we came from families where we were the first ones to really gain an education.[92]

In sum, influences associated with participants' upbringing, including their families' political and civic activities, religious background, and college experiences, may well have inclined alumni to join TFA, especially as they perceived TFA as an extension of many of the implicit values with which they were raised.

Choosing TFA: Generational Perspective Analysis

A third perspective within life course development theory concerns the impact of "significant events and shared experiences of an age group growing up together during a certain period in history."[93] The crucial element in the formation of a generation, according to theorists, is "a generational consciousness, which occurs when an age group perceives itself as unique because of its distinct historical experiences and is at odds with older age groups," who may have had quite different social and political experiences.[94] While our interviewees would have shared some common aspects of growing up in the 1970s and early 1980s, the testimonies suggest that some of their most formative generational experiences occurred during their college years. Obviously, the historical moment—in terms of what was happening on a global and national level—would have influenced participants' constraints, possibilities, and even sensibilities to some degree. But we argue that it was the more immediate experiences at elite college campuses in the late 1980s that created a generational feeling among the TFA alumni we interviewed, even if they did not participate or react in the same ways to such experiences.

Most of our participants were college seniors during the 1989–90 academic year, a time described as "truly . . . one of those years that the world shifted on its pivot," with antigovernment protest in Tiananmen Square and events that led to the end of the Soviet Union and the Cold War, such as the fall of the Berlin Wall, the solidarity movement in Poland, and Soviets moving out of Afghanistan.[95] Many of these developments suggested the power of young people to drive global change. A few participants noted these groundbreaking developments as part of their rationale for pursuing TFA. Andrew McKenzie's background may have disposed his attention toward world affairs, as his parents both worked for the Foreign Service and he spent his childhood living abroad in countries as varied as Nicaragua, Hungary, England, and Kuwait. As he talked through his rationale for participating in TFA, he tied his interests in the initiative directly into the macro historical moment: "[I]f you look at the historical context, this is barely a year after the Berlin Wall, and Nelson Mandela is freed that year, [and] Iraq rolled into Kuwait [in] August [of 1990], so it just seemed like the confluence of all those elements made it very exciting and appealing."[96] Because TFA represented what McKenzie called "real work," work that seemed of a piece with the larger shifts in the changing world, he was all in.

As illustrated in the previous chapter, the late 1980s brought to bear a host of crucial contextual factors, though few interviewees articulated awareness of such factors in particular as having motivated their interests in TFA. For example, none of the alumni we interviewed specifically identified the politics of the Reagan administration, the immiseration of inner cities, or fears about global economic competition as reasons for their participation. Some, such as Jan Trasen, understood they were graduating into a recessionary economy with "no jobs"; others evidenced some awareness of society's growing inequality at the time, which figured into their motives for participating in TFA. Mark Stephan, for instance, recalled his interest in teaching through TFA as: "I'm going to go help those who have been left behind by this white, mostly male, upper income-dominated society."[97] Similarly, Lisa Robinson, who attended Columbia University in New York City, believed that "living in New York . . . you become especially attuned to inequities and to real unfairness . . . I realized that the depth of our problems as a country really began here [with inequity] and I wanted to do something that would help in just some small way to change that."[98]

Another significant element in the air at the time would have been the larger public conversation about education. As Chapter 1 details, *A Nation at Risk* spurred the idea that education was in crisis and, indeed, by decade's end, the public seemed convinced that American schools were failing and that teachers bore some responsibility for that failure. The case for TFA depended upon that public narrative; yet again, few interviewees articulated a clear sense or depth of understanding about the problem they had been recruited to solve as a reason for joining TFA. Kathy Feeley referenced the state of schooling in her perception of TFA at the time: "[Y]ou're going to go out there and fix all of America's public schools; there's something wrong with them." At the same, Feeley acknowledged, "I kind of knew that wasn't true because I'd been in America's public schools and I had a brother and a sister who were both teaching in them but, you know, it [TFA] sort of appealed to my vanity."[99] Both Diane Brewer and Lori Lawson zeroed in on the lack of high-quality teachers as instrumental to their attraction to TFA. Brewer expressed what appealed to her as the "idealism of going to an area that was having trouble finding teachers."[100] Lawson struggled to define how her beliefs about public schooling at the time might have contributed to her interest in TFA.

I'm trying to think, did I have a belief system around public education? Because that's really kind of what it comes back to, you know, did you believe in what TFA was ultimately trying to do? And I did. I bought into it definitely . . . [I] bought into the idea that, you know . . . let's get intelligent teachers in there who wouldn't normally be attracted to the profession.

But Lawson, like Feeley, also recognized more complexity to the situation. She went on, "there was . . . an apparent lack of a draw, to the teaching profession of, you know, very intelligent people, but that's not to say there weren't already very intelligent people electing that path to get a degree in education to teach."[101] Thus, even among those who expressed some awareness of how these larger contextual elements may have inclined them toward TFA, their conceptions of that context at the time often seem simplistic. Both Lawson and Feeley entertained conflicting ideas about the status of existing teachers and education, but it did not stop them from joining TFA (though both did end up leaving the experience before having fulfilled their 2-year commitment).

Within the broader influences of international and domestic affairs that shaped the 1980s, our interviewees' attendance and experiences at elite colleges and universities in the latter part of the decade also served to bind them as a generation. They were present during the surge of idealism that characterized the late 1980s and early 1990s on their campuses, as well as the outbreak of the culture wars and a range of student activism related to identity politics or, less contentiously, efforts to build an inclusive, multicultural democracy.[102] Many of the alumni became aware of larger global and national issues primarily as they emerged on campus, as part of learning participants did in courses or through extracurricular activities, including student protests. The campuses that displayed the greatest levels of activism at the time included the "more cosmopolitan and prestigious universities on both coasts, a sprinkling of major public universities in between, and some traditionally progressive liberal arts colleges"—in short, the very campuses attended by TFA participants.[103] Many of our interviewees recalled protests or demonstrations that took place on their campuses while they were students; though some remembered joining in, others stuck to activities better catalogued as socially conscious or service oriented. Yet among their experiences in classes, extracurricular activities, and among peers, some alumni recalled not only participating in a wide spectrum of socially minded activities, but believed such engagement was influential in their thinking about the larger world and their obligations to it. It was to these very sentiments that TFA appealed.

In his interview, Mark Stephan described his campus environment at the University of California, Santa Cruz, in the 1980s as "incredibly liberal; progressive and radical—quite honestly, I mean radical—critiques as well of the American society were just in the air, and so students, faculty, readings, all that sort of stuff was very much a part of like the life there."[104] From the other end of the country and opposite end of the political spectrum, Christina Brown found herself radicalized by a different kind of campus culture. As she explained,

> I hadn't interacted with white people who didn't know Black people before. . . . And going to school that had a lot of suburban and conservative white people—I hadn't met those kind of white people before—so that was also sort of a political awakening and just made me a little more active and militant.[105]

Others shared memories of having participated in campus protests. Jeffrey Simes, who attended Yale, was involved in the nuclear freeze movement; Bill Norbert recalled protesting CIA recruitment at Brown University in the fall of 1987, when a hundred students held a sit-in in University Hall and made demands to then-President Swearer.[106]

Many of the interviewees participated in social justice–oriented activities through campus organizations, focusing on issues that ranged from international concerns to local community or campus matters. At Tufts, Diane Brewer remembered working with a politically active campus organization focused on Central American policies. Lori Lawson participated in Emory's Oxford Fellowship, organized by the chaplain, which "was just a bunch of kids getting together to try to help influence change in a positive way." She recalled one trip, for instance, where students traveled to Calcutta to work with Mother Teresa.[107] Eric Bird pursued his global interests by participating in Notre Dame's Center for Social Concerns. While his involvement came about because of his political interests, Bird also confessed that the Center had helped him to find like-minded peers.

> I always felt different because of my low-income status . . . [m]ost of the people there [at Notre Dame] were far richer and had a far better education than I did. I always felt like the underdog. And I guess that helped push me toward, I guess, the Center for Social Concerns, trying to find a comfort zone. I hung out with a group of people who were very involved . . . and who also tended to be more liberal in their views.

Finding simpatico "liberal views" meant a lot to Bird, because, in his estimation, most Notre Dame students were Republicans. Likewise, Christina Brown used her involvement in the Black Student Union to connect with other Black people. She also recalled taking part in student government and efforts toward "larger diversity workings on campus," which included "trying to recruit [students of color]," given the low numbers of Black students at her institution at the time.[108] During his time at Brown University, along with protesting CIA recruitment, Bill Norbert participated in the Campus Democrats and the Catholic community organization, Manning Chapel, which involved "soup kitchen work or gathering clothes"; he also remembered taking a bus to New Hampshire to campaign for Democratic presidential aspirant Paul Tsongas. Given the rise in political activity on campuses at the time, it is not surprising that many of those we interviewed recalled such activities; indeed, participants attuned to larger social issues of inequity and identity politics may well have seen in TFA an opportunity to make good on their nascent political understandings and commitments.

Alumni recollected taking on less overtly political, local service work as well. Christina Brown volunteered with "at-risk" girls from the neighboring community; Lori Lawson tutored students from the local elementary school in Oxford, Georgia; and Caroline Sabin, for all 4 of her undergraduate years, volunteered with City Step, a dance theater community service program in which she taught dance to a Cambridge public school 5-grade class on a weekly basis. Susanne Murray, also at Harvard, recalled tutoring adult English language learners in Cambridge.

Beyond their extracurricular activities, some interviewees also acknowledged how important some of their college courses had been in influencing their perspectives on the world. Of 30 alumni interviewed, all but two majored in liberal arts or social science disciplines.[109] Just about a third (nine individuals) of our sample majored (or double majored) in English; other popular majors included political science or public policy, sociology, history, and psychology. Interviewees brought a variety of additional disciplinary majors to the table as well, such as African American Studies, Russian literature, philosophy, Women's Studies and, in one case, zoology. Several of the alumni made explicit connections between these learning experiences and their desire to participate in TFA.

For Scott Joftus, his concentration in public policy at Duke University—"a really, really strong program with a very sort of socially aware perspective"—represented "a major sort of factor in guiding me . . . toward Teach For America." He described his experience in Interns in Conscience, run by one of the public policy professors, in which students went to Washington, DC, to work in different types of social service agencies. Joftus participated in a "children/youth program that basically worked with first time juvenile offenders." The experience piqued his interests, but Joftus struggled to figure out how to pursue those interests: "[H]ow do you make a career out of . . . doing something with children and youth?"[110] TFA seemed to make that link for him. Diane Brewer recalled a "really inspiring professor" who had been present in Santiago, Chile, in 1973, "when the tanks rolled up to the Palace and the coup started." In Brewer's telling, she has always remembered "in vivid detail, his stories about that experience and what it was like for him." As she remembered, "that class had more effect on me politically than any other": She found learning about the "atrocities of U.S. involvement in Central and South America [to be] . . . very motivating."[111] Lisa Robinson told of an experience on the last day of a seminar class she took with Professor Edward Said, where she was asked to articulate why she planned to join TFA.[112]

> [Said] asked us to tell him what we were going to be doing after graduation . . . I told him that I was going to be teaching. And he looked at me and he said, "Why would you ever want to do that?" Which was a remarkable question, to come from someone like him, because it was . . . mockery at the same time that it was, you know, forcing me to articulate a belief. And you know, obviously I took that opportunity to express the nobility of teaching, you know, what have we been doing here for this entire semester if it hasn't been to try to improve the world in some small way, so it was exciting.

Having to defend her decision pressed Robinson to create a rationale that she saw in terms of "what . . . we have been doing here for this entire semester" and that confirmed her commitment to the venture.[113]

A few participants remarked on how some courses seemed to intersect with and inspire their lives or thinking. Mark Stephan recalled two classes that stood out to him. The first was an Introduction to Feminism course, which was "eye-opening" in that it exposed him to "literature that I just had not seen before."[114] The grounds for Stephan's interest may have been laid during his upbringing; at an earlier point in his interview, Stephan characterized the singular "political" influence he could recall growing up as his mother's awakening to feminism. The second intellectual experience Stephan mentioned involved a paper he wrote for an Introduction to Sociology class, in which he had to write about his own social demographic—where he was from and who he was, as he understood it. The paper gave him a unique opportunity to reflect on himself and his values; he shared the fact that he has gone back to that writing every so often in subsequent years, looking to situate himself then and now. Both experiences, the interview implies, tapped existing concerns Stephan had about equity and where he was personally situated in a larger social hierarchy, impulses that had encouraged him to pursue TFA. Finally, Christina Brown shared her "clear" memory of "reading *The Autobiography of Malcolm X*," and appreciating "just how school had damaged him, and reading other books about how Black people in particular have been damaged by school"; as she concluded, "it was definitely a lot of *Pedagogy of the Oppressed* liberation theology that sort of led me to want to do this [TFA]." While encountering such texts likely honed Brown's thinking, she also brought existing concerns to her coursework and her interest in TFA:

> I definitely was very race-focused in what I wanted to do and it was very much about figuring out how to help my people and not doing damage to other people's people . . . [and] just feeling like, because I had so many privileges, wanting to give back to my community.[115]

CONCLUSION

The individuals who chose to participate in the first 1990 cohort of TFA differed from more traditional teacher candidates in their elite education-al backgrounds and their reasons for and orientations toward teaching through TFA. They differed not only from traditional-entry teachers at the time, but from those of later TFA cohorts as well. There is something special about a group of young people willing to join an untested pro-gram led by their peers: When our participants applied to TFA in 1989, it was untried and unknown. The venture had been framed as a domestic Peace Corps and not yet publicly associated with the neoliberal reforms in education such as charter schools and choice. Certainly, TFA's corpo-rate roots and (as Chapter 6 illustrates) its role as a standard bearer for the upstart reforms that have characterized the years since 1990 have become more readily apparent, but this link was less visible to our partic-ipants than to subsequent cohorts.

When asked what appealed to them about TFA, interviewees' direct re-sponses concerned life-stage explanations—that is, service or reform, adven-ture, or taking a role in challenging existing social structures, for instance. We also found potential influences within the other two frames—growing up and the historical moment—even if interviewees themselves did not necessarily identify and connect such experiences explicitly to their expla-nations for embracing the TFA opportunity. Across interview testimonies, there were significant similarities in the alumni's expressed reasons for join-ing TFA, which may have had a lot to do with their common experience of elite college campuses in the late 1980s. At the same time, it's worth noting that alumni brought a range of different backgrounds and experiences to their decision to teach through TFA and, as subsequent chapters will illus-trate, many of these differences emerged, in somewhat challenging ways, at the Summer Institute addressed in Chapter 3.

CHAPTER 3

Preparing to Teach for America
The Summer Institute

As they embarked upon TFA, few participants had given much thought to the actual work of teaching or what it might require in terms of knowledge and skills. Jeffrey Simes imagined the following metamorphosis: "Come to TFA. We'll . . . fly you out to L.A., you'll spend the summer teaching there and, boom, in the fall you'll be a teacher."[1] The notion of this somewhat magical transformation was widely shared among participants and illustrates a generally shared cultural naiveté about what it takes to become an effective teacher. Recruits believed they needed to learn *something* in order to teach. TFA encouraged the recruits (and the public) to believe this "something"—a set of tips or techniques—could be acquired in the space of a few summer weeks. Indeed, this brevity of preparation and faith in what the recruits themselves brought was a key selling point of the TFA experience.

From the beginning, Wendy Kopp distinguished TFA participants as a different breed of teacher: If they "could not provide the expertise of qualified, experienced teachers," they could "provide energy, enthusiasm, and subject knowledge in positions that would otherwise be left unfilled or filled by individuals with *less training* and less support."[2] The implicit message was that, simply on their merits, TFA recruits would improve upon the status quo in many classrooms serving low-income students. This message undermined the concept that there was specialized knowledge needed for teaching, implying instead that a generally well-educated, smart person could acquire all required knowledge on the job.

Despite the initiative's premise of attracting recruits whose special qualities, rather than any professional education, would equip them to teach, Kopp did envision a need for some training to prepare Corps members for the classroom. The "mechanism for training" that would prepare Corps members to "do the best possible job during the two years they would be teaching" was the Summer Institute.[3] In 1990, the Institute consisted of an 8-week training held in Los Angeles during July and August, where year-round schooling afforded an opportunity for student teaching during the summer months.[4] For the 1990 participants, the Institute was where they came together as a unit, where they first grappled with what knowledge and qualities they would need in order to teach, and where they encountered some of the conflicts and challenges that would foreshadow their classroom teaching experiences.

Alumni memories of that first Summer Institute yield important insights about their assumptions regarding teaching and the identity politics of race, culture, and class with which they struggled. From these insights, we identified two key questions that animated participants' experiences. First, what knowledge would the TFA participants need in order to teach? And second, what characteristics would qualify them to teach children (many of whom were children of color) from low-income backgrounds? Perhaps not surprisingly, both questions speak powerfully to the larger debates around teacher recruitment and preparation that concern the identities and desired qualifications of teachers, the optimum pathway(s) to and preparation for the classroom, and the definition and transmittal of a knowledge base associated with teaching.[5] Despite its carefully selected candidates from elite colleges and universities and its new approach, TFA did not escape these enduring challenges associated with the preparation of teachers. The struggles of this first TFA cohort at the Summer Institute reflect not only their idiosyncratic experiences within a historical moment, but a larger set of persistent concerns within the field about how to attract and educate prospective teachers who can teach all children. We devote this chapter to the first question that emerged from the testimonies: What knowledge did the recruits need in order to teach? We reserve our exploration of the second question, about what qualifies an individual to teach poor children of color, for the following chapter, to be examined within the larger framework of multiculturalism in teacher education and American society at the time.

TEACHER EDUCATION, CIRCA 1990

At the Summer Institute, corps members who arrived without having thought much about what skills, knowledge, or preparation they would need to become effective teachers got a crash course in the challenges of learning to teach. Individuals who had attended a traditional, university-based teacher education program in 1990 typically would have either majored (or co-majored) in education as an undergraduate or earned a master's degree in education. Depending upon the state and institution, these programs might differ considerably in terms of credits, content, and character, as teacher education researcher Mary Kennedy points out.[6] Even so, required coursework in university-based pre-service teacher education would likely have provided for a state-specified number of credits in science, math, social sciences, and humanities, along with education classes, consisting of a combination of methods courses—to help prospective teachers learn how to teach in their content areas—and foundations courses, to introduce teacher candidates to child development and learning theory, social contexts of education and, in some cases, the history and philosophy of education. Some teacher education programs may have rounded out this study with educational research courses. In the early 1990s, many teacher education programs had just begun to respond to research calling for the addition of multicultural courses to teacher preparation. Such coursework was meant to address the demographic differences between teacher candidates, who were likely to be middle-class white women, and students who were coming from increasingly varied backgrounds. In most such programs, teacher education students would also be expected to complete a required number of field hours in local schools, during which candidates would observe classrooms and practice teaching in one-on-one, small-group, and ultimately whole-group settings. Finally, a period of student teaching, in which pre-service candidates are apprenticed to a classroom teacher (or teachers), often served as a capstone experience for university-based teacher education programs.

The vast majority of 1990 TFA participants, however, did not experience this typical training sequence—indeed, this was a distinguishing aspect of TFA. Typical among recruits would have been Lisa Robinson, who joined TFA upon graduating from Columbia University with a bachelor's degree in English literature. As with most of the recruits we interviewed, Robinson had not taken any education courses. From her perspective as a liberal arts graduate, she articulated a common perception of what the inaugural corps members believed they brought to teaching, as well as what they needed to learn:

> I wanted to feel prepared for going into the classroom and, you know,
> basically I didn't have any sort of teaching background. But I also knew
> that theory was not going to be sufficient. I felt like my liberal arts
> education was my theory base. I could figure things out. I was smart . . .
> I could be creative. [But] I needed real skills and techniques.[7]

Though Robinson recognized that she was smart and well educated, she also sensed that her general intelligence and liberal arts education might not be enough to equip her to teach. She suspected that there were "real skills and techniques" that she needed to acquire in order to teach effectively. Looking back, more than a few participants made similar comments, in which they lamented their unfulfilled wish for the Institute to have given them specific practical approaches, concrete ways of proceeding, strategies, and know-how, all of which they believed would have better enabled them to teach.

Yet participants' conceptions of *knowledge about teaching*, that is, their beliefs about pedagogical knowledge, appear to have been somewhat simplistic—boiled down to "techniques" or step-by-step strategies—or even cynical. In one example of the latter, Spencer Downing recalled that the cohort took one of the National Teacher Examination (NTE) Series tests during the first week of the Institute. According to promotional literature, the NTE is "designed to provide objective measurement of the knowledge, skills, and abilities required of teachers."[8] Downing's recollection epitomizes a popular suspicion regarding any kind of specialized knowledge associated with teaching.

> [W]e . . . are given this test, which supposedly is really hard and some of the instructors were saying, you know, this is a really difficult thing and you're having to compress four years of learning into two days and blah, blah, blah. The majority of us, I think, did really well on it . . . [W]hat that did for me was confirm [that], you know, most of this teaching stuff is pretty dumb anyway.[9]

Of course, to equate standardized test scores with teaching ability is deeply problematic. And to be fair, Downing's comments are mediated by the tone of his recollections. As he remarked in his interview, those high test scores also confirmed for him that "we are as cool as we purport to be," a tacit acknowledgment of his own hubris. Even so, both Robinson and Downing expressed widespread ideas about the nature of knowledge associated with teaching: that it consists of a set of tips, "how-to" lists, or "techniques," for instance; that it can be "picked up" on the job by smart individuals; or that it doesn't hold up as a substantive body of knowledge. Yet both could be forgiven those impressions, since the value of pedagogical knowledge has long provoked public debate and was especially robust in the years preceding the 1990 corps' entry into schools.

As both Chapter 1 and Chapter 6 establish, the 1980s saw myriad commissions and reports on the state of public education, many of which addressed perceived problems with teachers and teacher preparation.[10] Major themes of the latter included the need to expand the teacher candidate pool and to regulate teacher preparation more rigorously, to emphasize the clinical or field-based nature of teacher education, and to require teacher candidates to better master subject-matter knowledge. Such reports also provoked questions regarding the existence of a knowledge base for teaching, something that education historian William R. Johnson, writing in 1987, concluded "does not now exist in education."[11]

The TFA recruits embarked upon their Summer Institute training on the heels of these discussions and under the auspices of an initiative that, in many respects, implicitly argued against the significance of specific knowledge for teaching. On the one hand, TFA could be seen as the realization of some of the 1980s report recommendations. It constituted an alternative to so-called traditional teacher preparation, and it expanded the pool of teacher candidates, attracting those who might not otherwise have considered teaching (thanks to Kopp's targeted recruiting and strategic positioning of the experience as "selective"). In this regard, TFA represented the burgeoning trend of alternate pathways to the classroom that began in earnest in the 1990s.[12] Moreover, by targeting individuals with liberal arts and science degrees from elite colleges and universities, and by assuming that they could pick up what they needed to know about teaching from a brief Summer Institute and on the job, TFA also prioritized content knowledge, perhaps to the exclusion of pedagogical knowledge. Finally, given the short shrift accorded to preparatory education coursework, TFA embraced a "clinical" ideal, in which learning to become a teacher would occur in practice, on the job.

By privileging subject matter knowledge and learning "on the job," TFA traded on an old critique of education coursework as having little to offer to prospective teachers (who would be better served by deeper liberal arts and sciences content and more student teaching experience).[13] Put another way, the TFA model suggested that knowledge for teaching could be located within the respective areas of content knowledge (or knowledge of subject matter) and practice itself, directly contradicting the arguments of those teacher educators who wished to claim that professionalism and sovereignty of the field also required mastery of teaching competencies and a specialized body of pedagogical content knowledge, that is, the critical knowledge of how to transform one's subject matter expertise into a form that a high school or elementary student can comprehend.[14] In its outlook, TFA aligned with an important strand of developing educational thought in the 1980s (as indicated in Chapter 1), which advocated faith in the market, rather than increased regulation, to promote "greater achievement and attainment, particularly among low-income and minority students," and to develop new, less onerous pathways to the classroom that would, hopefully, attract more capable candidates into teaching.[15]

THE TFA SUMMER INSTITUTE, 1990

Though the Summer Institute embodied Kopp's concession that even the TFA recruits might require some preparation before teaching, at 8 weeks the Institute comprised a considerably shorter training period than would ordinarily be found in college- or university-based teacher education program.[16] The brevity of the TFA training drew sharp criticism on the part of some teacher educators and policymakers, who argued that corps members could not possibly be prepared to be effective teachers in such a short period of time.[17] Yet, as education historian Jack Schneider has pointed out, despite the organization's anti-"teacher education establishment rhetoric," TFA has from its inception drawn directly from teacher educators and their "best practices" to devise its Summer Institute experience.[18] In fact, in developing the inaugural Summer Institute, the novice

TFA staff relied on an "advisory group of talented practicing teachers and professors in the teacher training field [to] determine the shape of the institute and the design of the curriculum."[19] That group included well-known figures such as multicultural specialist Carl Grant, a professor at the University of Wisconsin–Madison, and Vito Perrone, then at the Harvard Graduate School of Education. Perrone, who worked with TFA in hopes of improving the teaching ranks at underserved schools, defended the "eight very good weeks" of preparation the TFA candidates would receive as superior to "most alternative route programs with no preparation at all."[20]

The instructional design for the initial 8-week training placed corps members in a student teaching placement, paired with a mentor teacher, in the morning, after which they returned to the USC campus for an afternoon of "guidance and instruction from a faculty of teachers and teacher educators."[21] The on-campus instruction took place in both large-group plenaries as well as small, discipline-based groups.

While no definitive account of that first Summer Institute exists, Deborah Appleman, a professor of education at Carleton College, paid a visit and published her observations in the *Christian Science Monitor*.[22] Appleman's motivation, as she explained, lay not only in her theoretical concerns about sending essentially unprepared young people into underserved classrooms, but in her specific anxieties on behalf of the six Carleton graduates—"young people I know and care about"—who had been selected into the 1990 corps. During her time at the Institute, Appleman noted a "variety of activities, ranging from a large group lecture on bilingualism provided by the Los Angeles Unified School District, a small group session on cooperative learning, and an afternoon session designed to introduce classroom management." She wrote hopefully of corps members who seemed "sincerely excited about the prospect of teaching," a staff of "dedicated college professors and classroom teachers," and her sense that the Institute represented a "real attempt . . . to address some major themes of teacher training, including multicultural education, professionalism, and reflective teaching." But she also judged the instructional activities to be wildly uneven, from "inspiring . . . to embarrassing," and she sympathized with participants who complained about a lack of practical instruction in "lesson planning, teaching techniques, managing student behavior, handling troubled kids, evaluating student work [and] finding resources." As a seasoned teacher educator, Appleman also lamented the dearth of "educational theory, history, and philosophy that enables teachers to gain perspective on their own teaching style and philosophy."[23] Ultimately, Appleman argued, the Institute consisted of too little time or focused instruction to help recruits develop the knowledge they would need to be effective classroom teachers.

In his assessment of TFA's training model, Jack Schneider observed that, "in its first years, TFA had very little capacity for assembling their own training program," which meant they relied heavily on a "loosely organized collection of standard teacher education materials."[24] Even Kopp, in retrospect, acknowledged that the pedagogical design of the Institute was too "loose." Teacher educators who responded to advertisements in education publications were hired as Institute Faculty on the basis of telephone interviews conducted by the young TFA staff. And while the faculty included some celebrated figures from a broad spectrum of well-respected educational institutions, TFA's direction to Institute faculty "consisted of a page-long list of topics they were expected to cover and the themes they should reinforce."[25] Such a piecemeal approach meant there was little in the way of coherent theory driving the Institute and its activities, and a wide variation in the quality of those activities.

PARTICIPANTS' RECOLLECTIONS: LESSONS FROM THE SUMMER INSTITUTE AND THEIR IMPLICATIONS

Few participants arrived in Los Angeles with clear expectations about how they would make the transformation from recent graduate to teacher.[26] But they did bring tacit expectations and assumptions about the work of teaching to the Institute and they did expect the Institute to be a legitimate, useful training experience. In the face of such expectations, the storyline about the Summer Institute that emerged from the oral history transcripts entailed several key issues. First, and across the board, participants complained about the limited capacity of the TFA organization to support and deliver a full-fledged training, organizationally or substantively. Second, and in part as a result of the Institute's disorganization, alumni also recalled their frustration with what they believed they were not getting: useful lessons in how to teach. But, finally, the most prominent recollections participants shared about the summer concerned what many referred to in shorthand as "multiculturalism," meaning dramatic conflicts over race, culture, and class that centered on the question of who was fit to teach poor children of color. Ironically, as participants told it, the Institute's focus on multiculturalism served not only to create deep rifts within the group (for which the Institute had no resolution), but also crowded out what they believed was necessary, basic, "nuts and bolts" instruction about *how to teach*.

In what follows, we examine participants' descriptions of the administratively troubled Institute. Significantly, little in the oral history testimonies is devoted particularly to how and what recruits learned about teaching at the Summer Institute. Participants' talk about learning to teach at the Institute occurs mostly in the negative—that is, what they believe they did not learn. Accordingly, we plumb those accounts for what they reveal about alumni's understandings of the work of and knowledge associated with teaching. But we also consider the few instances where individuals described having learned about teaching at the Institute. As is the case with traditionally prepared teachers, corps members generally assessed the student teaching component, which enabled participants to observe and work under the guidance of a practicing classroom teacher, as the most valuable aspect of training. But even those who praised their student teaching experiences found that teaching their own class was a far cry from the scaffolded environment of a student teaching placement. In the end, participants' experiences of learning (or not) to teach at the Summer Institute help to highlight important, persistent challenges—the ability to devise substantive, developmentally appropriate lesson plans, manage a classroom, connect with students from different backgrounds, negotiate a school culture, or reflect fruitfully on teaching practice— associated with the process of learning to teach.

Administrative and Organizational Challenges

Initially, Caroline Sabin explained, "I felt great confidence in those folks [TFA staff] . . . I was like, yeah . . . [i]t is totally organized; they know what they are doing; what a great adventure to be part of." But, she went on, by the end of the first week of the Institute, she came to the conclusion that "no one knows what they are doing" and "this is a really big mess."[27] Contrary to the faith participants may have placed in the capacity of the TFA organization, most participants recalled the Institute as chaotic and "crazy." As Christina Brown assessed, "Either they [the TFA staff] had not planned the whole summer, or they had such a terrible plan that it didn't work."[28] Participants shared instances of disorganization that ran the gamut from not getting picked up at the airport as scheduled to not knowing where they would be teaching in the fall. One corps member remembered waiting up until the wee hours of a Sunday night to find out the schedule for Monday, because the TFA staff was still planning. Nichole Childs Wardlaw, who described the Institute as "very disorganized," mused that, since "it was the first time," the TFA staff just did not know what they were doing.[29] Indeed, both the inaugural aspect of the Institute and the staff's lack of experience seem to have mitigated against a well-run, efficient Institute.

Such organizational challenges inconvenienced corps members, but some administrative oversights posed potentially more serious implications. For instance, the Institute seemed to have nothing in place to handle the emotional needs of its 488 participants. When Lori Lawson arrived at the Institute, she had lost her mother just 10 months earlier and was embroiled in a legal battle over her mother's estate. Lawson remembered thinking that it would have been useful to have access to a counselor: "I don't even recall if they had a resident psychologist, you know, out there for support, although that would have been a good idea. Not just

for me, but [for the] normal TFA crap that everybody went through."[30]
While Lawson's needs may have been unique, she recognized the need
for psychological support to deal not only with the rigors of the training,
but also with the vulnerabilities associated with this transition time in
many young adults' lives. In line with the TFA emphasis on raw material,
however, Kopp attributed the most serious difficulties suffered by a few
individuals to "poor selection decisions," thus reiterating TFA's focus on
the perceived quality of people over training and support.[31]

The disorganization of the Institute also exposed fault lines of class
and privilege among TFA staff and participants, according to some alumni. One of the critics was Christina Brown, an African American graduate
of Franklin and Marshall College, who took the TFA staff to task for their
failure to acknowledge the socioeconomic diversity of participants:

> [I]t was clear that the people that were running the program had no
> more experience than people that were in the program, and had a lot
> less experience . . . [with] what it was like for people who didn't have
> parents sending them money from home to get them through. . . .
> [T]here was one [time] where, like, they [TFA staff] lost a bunch of
> checks for our teacher tests, and they just said, "Write another one." I
> felt like, "We just graduated from college; we have no money; we have
> no jobs; we're out here with you. We don't have other checks."

As she elaborated, "There was [an] expectation that you could sort
of support yourself or write another check and it would all work out."
However, that wasn't the case for some corps members. "[A]fter people
protesting, saying 'How are we supposed to live?'" TFA did procure sti-
pends for some corps members, according to Brown, though she reiter-
ated that "people had to fight for that." In a final, stinging assessment,
Brown summarized:

> [T]hey [TFA staff] didn't know what they were doing and I guess the
> frustration is the privilege that you would think you and a bunch of
> your friends could do this without any grown-ups at the table.[32]

Brown's reference to the absence of "grown-ups" provides a shorthand
reminder that the TFA staff organizing the Institute not only lacked teachers or those with teaching experience but, for the most part, consisted of
recent graduates and classmates of Kopp's.

At the remove of 20 years, some corps members seemed to understand
and even sympathize with reasons why the Institute was so disorganized.
For instance, Avis Terrell saw that "they [the TFA staff] weren't fully
prepared," but she thought perhaps this was because the whole endeavor
was still "like an idea, you know, a thesis or something."[33] Recognizing

both how hard the TFA staff was working and the magnitude of their challenges, Heather Weller was also willing to cut them some slack. "I mean, I felt like they worked their tail off above and beyond what is humanly possible. . . . But they had to learn as and invent as they went along."[34] Furman Brown, who subsequently founded his own startup organization, could identify from his experiences what it must have been like for the fledgling TFA organization to try to put on the Institute. "[Y]ou don't have all the pieces in place that you know you need, but you['ve] got to demonstrate enough success to be able to get the pieces."[35] In fact, though many participants could see the reasons behind the disorganization of the Institute, their understanding coexisted with persistent memories of the summer's discomfort, a discomfort that ultimately arose less from organizational inconveniences than from the unresolved questions around what they needed to know and be to teach.

The Nature of Summer Institute Instruction: TFA Coursework

Collectively, the alumni transcripts described the Institute as too "theoretical" and, specifically, too focused on developing multicultural competence at the expense of providing participants with more "practical" training that they needed (though some individuals found real practical value in their student teaching experiences). We approach participants' perceptions of their Summer Institute learning in two parts, first addressing memories of the TFA-provided preparatory coursework and next exploring descriptions of their student teaching experiences. Assessing the overall package, Jane Schneider reported, "There was a lot of sort of didactic theory, but there was very little that was practical."[36] Of course, the complaint that teacher preparation involves too much theory and too little of practical value represents a common, persistent gripe on the part of teacher candidates from many different program types. Given the lead role played by established teacher educators in shaping and conducting instruction at the Institute, it is possible that the training provided by TFA was, in the end, not so different in substance from what teachers in some university-based preparation programs might have encountered.[37]

In the case of the Summer Institute, it was not "theory" in general, but discussion of multiculturalism specifically that participants believed distracted them from learning how to teach. As Furman Brown characterized the Institute, it "was a lot about, sort of, social justice . . . but very little about pedagogy or practice."[38] Jeffrey Simes seconded this sentiment, explaining that the Institute "was much more about multicultural studies and much less about, 'Let's talk about the science behind child development and like how, you know, verbal skills develop.'"[39] Scott Joftus attested to a focus on multiculturalism that "completely spiraled out of control to the point where there was very . . . little training and talk around things like classroom management and . . . formative assessment and, you know, things that actually will help you become a good teacher."[40] The Institute's debt to the ideas and practices of existing teacher educators might also explain the emphasis on multiculturalism, as the early 1990s witnessed a growing emphasis in the field of teacher education on teachers' multicultural competence.

From another perspective, however, Leo Flanagan, whose professional trajectory included years as a principal in East Boston, surmised that the Institute's imbalance between multicultural theory and practical skills occurred not only because of the heightened attention to multiculturalism at the time, but also because the TFA staff lacked a deep understanding of what was involved in teaching and learning to teach.

> [E]ven at its most rigorous, it [the Institute] was very theoretical . . . [it was] very concerned with notions of racial and gender and multicultural [issues]. I think that the number one concern was that people [i.e., the TFA teachers] would be culturally sensitive when they went into the classroom, and I think the sense was that the teaching in and of itself is a relatively easy thing to do and these smart people will figure it out. So, let's almost skip over that and make sure we spend most of our time in making sure that they are appropriately culturally sensitive before they get into the classroom.[41]

Flanagan's perception of TFA's stance—"[T]eaching in and of itself is a relatively easy thing to do"—speaks volumes. The initiative's implicit faith in people (i.e., the particular TFA candidates) over training, the fact that the TFA staff had little experience of or knowledge about teaching, and even the disjointed nature of the Institute faculty (i.e., they may have been teacher educators, but they were hired to provide discrete pieces of a larger whole designed by the inexperienced young staff) suggest, at the very least, some skepticism about the significance of specialized knowledge associated with teaching.

As a consequence, many alumni sensed that they had missed something valuable. Avis Terrell frankly recalled that, when she got into her own classroom, "I definitely felt unprepared," because the curriculum of the Summer Institute was "horrible."[42] Scott Joftus was equally negative, if more explicit: "[T]he problem was that I . . . came out of that Institute . . . knowing nothing about *teaching*." In hindsight, he could identify some of what he didn't know then. "I knew nothing about managing a classroom, teaching reading . . . Dealing with—what do you do with second language learners!?"[43] Similarly, Brent Lyles could see in retrospect, after his experiences in the classroom, some of the lessons he did not get in the summer of 1990. "Looking back, the critical skills are, what does it mean to be a teacher, and what does it mean to have to manage a classroom of 30 kids, and what does it mean to have goals and teaching objectives that you need to hit over the next six months, 12 months?"[44] For Constance Bond, "the Institute did not prepare me for what to expect," particularly, as she recalled, in terms of practical, day-to-day operational aspects of teaching. Somewhat humorously, Bond marveled that, "[I] didn't know how to do a bulletin board. I didn't know it was our job . . . to do that. [I] didn't know really what to do the first day or the . . . second day or how to set up the attendance roster."[45] Again, Bond's complaint echoes those of many traditionally trained teachers who wished to have learned more about the practices and expectations of a particular school or system where they end up teaching. These complaints suggest a highly procedural idea of teaching, in which conforming to a set of behaviors or routines, unmoored from a sense of how such activities correspond to pedagogical aims, passes for "teaching."

Lisa Robinson, on the other hand, recollected having picked up "whole language approaches to teaching," as well as "a lot of conceptual approaches" and "practical elements" through the Summer Institute. But she found herself unable to operationalize that knowledge:

> What we lacked, which we soon found out [that] we lacked, was understanding how important it is to kind of set down the rules of your classroom early on. I think that's the one experience we all had once we got to [the classroom] . . . was that discipline became our number one priority, because you couldn't teach until you had the control and respect of your class.[46]

Quite a few interviews featured the theme of classroom management—also an oft-cited complaint among more traditionally trained teachers.[47] Mark Stephan told of his struggles with classroom management. "[O]ne thing that really stands out is both personal, but also is a larger structural question . . . is the *classroom management issue*." He shared an anecdote to illustrate his point.

> I was getting some hints that I needed to work on this [classroom management], but I just wasn't fully seeing it. [But a student I was teaching] said to me . . . "Mr. Stephan," she said, "you're too nice. You're too nice. You've got to be tougher. You're going to have to be meaner." . . . I kind of nodded my head and I was like, "Yeah, you're right. I am too nice." But I mean, looking back, that was the writing on the wall that I wasn't fully seeing . . . she was so completely right.[48]

Stephan linked his struggles with classroom management to his very identity as a teacher, an observation echoed by research. The process of becoming a teacher is, in part, a process of developing a professional identity. This development occurs over time and "involves gaining insights of the professional practices and the values, skills, knowledge required and practiced within the profession."[49] Recent research suggests that a professional teacher identity—that is, an identity that is "based on . . . core beliefs about teaching and being a teacher"—is an essential "intellectual dimension" of teaching, one that enables teachers to become flexible, confident practitioners.[50] But if Stephan's memory is a guide, it seems that TFA recruits found little within the Institute instruction to support the process of developing their teacher identities.

While most of the testimonies focused on participants' feelings and perceptions of missing out on important knowledge, several individuals also observed how, at the time, their own ignorance compounded the problem. As Lisa Robinson remarked, "We didn't know what we were getting into, so we didn't know what we needed."[51] Looking back to his uninformed self, Scott Joftus remembered, "[T]he most dangerous thing, definitely, was not knowing that I didn't know it. . . . I wasn't even smart enough to, like, start running around and asking people, you know, 'What should I do?' And reading books and stuff like that."[52]

Against the testimonies' vast silence around substantive pedagogical instruction, several participants juxtaposed their memories of practical learning that occurred in the small, discipline-based groups. Andrew McKenzie recalled encountering "workshops and classes that were very practical on, you know, leading a language arts lesson or, you know, various things about classroom practice."[53] Lisa Robinson summoned up a memory of learning "whole language," a progressive approach to teaching reading popular in the early 1990s:

> We had these veteran teachers who were coming in from these, you know, fabulously homogenous, [what] we imagined to be homogenous, like, schools in Ohio or something like that, just teaching whole language approaches.

Robinson made fun of the "beautiful, white, blond teacher" whose lessons were unlikely to be appropriate for what she called "our kids," meaning the students that the TFA corps would find in their placements. At the same time, however, Robinson acknowledged, "the idea of *whole language* was what I could take away from it." Even if the "white bread experience wasn't going to be particularly valid," Robinson believed, she could still take out of those lessons "something of value and significance . . . exciting for our students." In a promising way, Robinson saw these lessons, especially "relating all of the different disciplines to that idea [of whole language as] . . . absolutely crucial to kind of beginning to carve out a teaching philosophy."[54]

Within one of the social science content groups focused on high school history, both Spencer Downing and Arthur Schuhart recalled one instructor who really helped them. "Phil" (who they recalled having a Greek last name that neither could remember) was a social studies teacher in New York City and one of the experienced educators working at the Institute. As Downing recounted,

> . . . both in terms of the curriculum and the way that they taught us, [the veteran educators] were extraordinary . . . I thought they were really good at explaining things that I hadn't thought about in terms of how you present content to kids. And I thought they were really good at saying, "Here are innovative ways of teaching the basic stuff that you're going to have to teach."[55]

Veteran educators such as Phil helped recruits to figure out their teaching philosophy and exposed them to "actual pedagogy" and classroom management, in contrast to what Schuhart termed the "other crap" they encountered at the Institute. More specifically, as Schuhart described,

> Phil would make us sit down with him every afternoon after dinner and . . . write our next day's lesson plans. And then he would critique them, and he would write them up, and he would make us type them up. And then he would make us practice them. . . . It was him . . . making us think about what does it mean to teach? What is your obligation? Who are you, what are you going to do, why are you in front, and what gives you that right? And you know, rely[ing] upon this methodology that [was] very, very straightforward. And that was the most important part of that experience.[56]

In Downing's narrative, Phil "came in with this big binder of stuff . . . and said, 'Here you go. Take it. Take what you need.' And it was good, it was really good stuff." He gave the example of how Phil's curriculum suggested using "local activism to get students to learn social studies, how government works." Despite Downing's admiration, however, he qualified his praise in a way that still undercut the significance of pedagogical knowledge: "[I]t was cool in one of those ways . . . like, wow, that was a fun learning annex class."[57]

Given the dearth of specific commentary about the process of learning to teach, these small examples loom large. They suggest that the Institute offered some instruction that would have been relevant and significant to developing recruits' understanding of teaching, but that it was offered sporadically, idiosyncratically, or without enough anchoring context for the cohort to absorb it. As noted, the oral histories only represent what participants deemed significant enough to remember 20 years later.

Apparently, the pedagogical instruction that took place under the auspices of the Institute did not impress recruits enough for them to call up much in the way of cogent instances or examples.

On the other hand, according to the oral history testimonies, most participants believed that their student teaching placements represented the greatest learning opportunity of the Institute. Their views would not have differed much from those of traditionally trained teachers at the time; a 1990 review of literature on student teaching found that teachers consistently rated student teaching as "the single most beneficial segment of their teacher education program."[58] Today's call for more "clinically based" teacher preparation builds on this presumption that student teaching constitutes a "key component—even the most important component of—pre-service teacher preparation."[59] Yet as scholars of teacher education warn, while student teaching may offer powerful opportunities for learning, if it is not well structured and supported, student teaching may in fact impart a host of misunderstandings about teaching, especially teaching in high-needs schools.[60] Researcher Catherine Cornbleth argues, "It is one thing to place prospective teachers in low-income schools with diverse student populations; it is another to study and reform what occurs there."[61]

A 1990 literature review on student teaching contends that, while the general esteem for student teaching might suggest it possessed a "sound theoretical foundation, with general agreement concerning its structure and activities," in reality, critics claimed that "student teaching . . . has not developed a sound theoretical basis and has no uniform structure." While many institutions require fieldwork hours, including student teaching, they do so "without examining what occurs during these experiences."[62] As a result, student teaching experiences vary widely in quality from one placement to the next; moreover, the lessons teacher candidates learn through student teaching may also depart in significant ways from what they have learned in their education coursework.

Given the "unevenness" associated with the Summer Institute instruction, it seems unsurprising that TFA's first-year student teaching placements seemed to follow a similar pattern; that is, placements varied in quality and the degree to which they aligned with the goals and philosophies that the Institute was meant to promote. TFA's internal confusion around goals and philosophies made any such clear philosophical alignment challenging. And the loose coupling that characterizes universities and their field placements (in traditional teacher education) also showed up in the TFA recruits' narratives of their experiences. Indeed, the testimonies demonstrate just these sorts of variations.[63]

TFA alumni viewed their student teaching experiences as more meaningful and useful than the poorly facilitated and more "theoretical" work they encountered at the Institute. They confronted the powerful influence of community ecology, many participants remarking upon the particular frustration of trying to figure out how to apply what they learned in one context to other, different contexts. They also experienced, according to their testimonies, a range of cooperating teacher models and mentoring, as well as a wide variety of activities and levels of engagement in their student teaching placements. In what follows, we examine each of these issues that emerged from alumni transcripts, with an eye toward how these experiences influenced participants' preparation for and understanding of classroom teaching.

Perceived value of student teaching. The alumni's nearly uniform acknowledgement of the student teaching portion of their training suggests that student teaching was, for most, a memorable and significant aspect of their summer training experience. Jeffrey Simes offered an eloquent case in point, in his claim that, "The student teaching was great. I mean, it's really amazing, like five minutes of the student teaching was equivalent to like five hours of the [TFA-led] . . . stuff." He elaborated:

> [T]hey [the cooperating teachers] were extraordinarily professional, like they just, they knew their stuff . . . [In contrast to] professors from wherever who are talking about the importance of multicultural education in a very abstract way . . . here's these people [the cooperating teachers] who just, you know, it's no nonsense: How do we get it done? How do we control the classroom? Okay, here's the book we're going to be reading today. How are we—what's the lesson plan? Let's talk about that. Very, very no nonsense, nose to the grindstone, practical, you know, useful stuff, and it had a real result, right? Kids were learning, they were on task.[64]

Arthur Schuhart concurred. In characterizing his student teaching, he argued, "To me, that [i.e., the student teaching] was really what Teach For America was about." He "blew off and ignored" the discipline-based group work and plenary sessions, because "[i]t was the experience with the cooperating teachers that to me was really what it was about."[65] In speaking for many in their cohort, Simes and Schuhart expressed both the satisfaction with "real" work they enjoyed during student teaching and also implicitly indicted the Institute coursework for its failure to support them in developing what they understood to be practical or relevant skills. While the recruits' vexation may indeed suggest an overemphasis on multiculturalism and theory, it may also indicate the Institute's failure to convey successfully some of the significant theoretical ideals that underlie teaching or to help participants connect such theory meaningfully to the practical work of teaching. Consequently, for most alumni, the "experiential, craft-oriented process" that they experienced as student teachers seemed more valuable—it was "real"—and only tangentially related (if at all) to any guiding theory that could have helped to explain their own or their students' behaviors.[66]

The ecology of student teaching mattered. The ecology of a community and school, as well as the attitudes of cooperating teachers, exert a "major influence" on the skills and attitudes acquired by student teachers.[67] In arguing how this context matters, researcher Catherine Cornbleth proposed that most student teachers in urban schools tend to have encountered their schools, to their detriment, before they actually enter them. The portrayal of urban schools in local media and university course readings tends to be "largely negative, highlighting violence . . . low test scores, or high dropout rates." According to Cornbleth, teacher candidates get the message that teaching in such schools will be difficult, given the "low socio-economic status and racial-ethnic-cultural diversity" of the students.[68]

From the scenarios set up in the TFA interview process to the painful dialogue around multiculturalism that consumed much of the Institute instruction (addressed in Chapter 4), the 1990 TFA alumni had been primed to think about the schools where and the students whom they would be teaching as dramatically *other*—poor, of color and, often, violent—but not given tools to learn about the actual community where they would teach. While several participants alluded to these themes in describing their student teaching placements, the lack of preparation for and understanding of the communities in which they taught emerged powerfully once alumni began their full-time teaching placements.

Varying quality of cooperating teacher as model and mentor. Participants' experiences were anchored not simply in neighborhoods and schools, but in specific classrooms helmed by particular teachers. Traditionally, the quality of the student teaching apprenticeship has relied greatly on the cooperating teacher and supervisor, in conjunction with the ideas, aims, and knowledge associated with the preparation program and state requirements.

Of course, though cooperating teachers and student teachers are meant to work together toward a common purpose, their relationships are often fraught with unclear expectations and differing assumptions, and further undermined by a lack of training and experience regarding teacher learning as well as too little dedicated time for substantive mentoring.[69] These pitfalls showed up in participants' oral histories, which described cooperating teachers who ran the gamut from wonderful to "crazy." In fact, despite TFA's professed faith in innate, individual virtue, the selection of cooperating teachers seems to have been a matter of exigency—managing to find placements for Corps members—rather than careful choices of like-minded, exemplary teachers. Kopp herself admitted there were "significant inconsistencies among the 500 master teachers."[70] But because the instruction that alumni received at the Institute seemed to them so lacking, the cooperating teacher became a central instructional figure. For some, this meant a mentor to emulate; for others, it meant an example of the kind of teacher they did not want to become.

Interestingly, many participants employed only rudimentary criteria to distinguish good from poor teachers. Even in adulatory descriptions of "good" cooperating teachers, many of the 1990 corps members drew on general, even vague, descriptors, not allowing for a clear understanding of exactly what qualities they believed distinguished the cooperating teacher as so helpful. For example, Lori Lawson thought Ms. DeMarco was "wonderful"; Scott Joftus's cooperating teacher was "fantastic" and "brilliant"; and both Nichole Childs Wardlaw and Jeffrey Simes pronounced their respective cooperating teachers "awesome."

Some participants fleshed out their admiration in somewhat more precise terms. As Priscilla Leon-Didion remembered: "My master teacher . . . was wonderful. . . He was a calm, older man." In her opinion, because he was "this master . . . like a magician," he enabled her to bond with the students, "absorb all of this," and have a "really good experience."[71] Both Kathy Feeley and Lisa Robinson remarked on the value they saw in their cooperating teachers' years of experience. Of the "veteran teacher" with whom she worked, Robinson observed, "She [had] been teaching for over 30 years. She so had it down. Her systems were so deeply rooted in place and those kids knew it. Like they came into her classroom and they were at home."[72] Though Robinson may not have pinned down all the contributing elements, she conveyed her appreciation of the way in which her cooperating teacher had created a particular kind of classroom climate conducive to safety and learning. Another somewhat more specific portrayal came from Leo Flanagan, who remembered how his cooperating teacher "modeled really good talking to the kids" and conducted "a lot of really fun cool activities with the kids . . . in a way that was really deeper [than just the activity level]."[73] Bill Norbet found himself wondering how long he would have to teach in order to "control the classroom" in the manner of his cooperating teacher. "[T]he kids pay attention and seem to learn."[74] And Diane Brewer noted the way her cooperating teacher managed to "really connect with the students," which then enabled the teacher to encourage them and help them with their English skills.[75] Most of these more specific accounts contain the seeds of pedagogical knowledge, but of an arguably formative nature. Because alumni did not expand on these ideas, it is impossible to know if they eventually gained a more sophisticated understanding or if these aspects of pedagogical knowledge remained nascent.

One of the alumni, Andrew McKenzie, was able to articulate a detailed and informed description of how his cooperating teacher supported his instructional development. As it turns out, McKenzie was one of few alumni still deeply engaged with teaching (though at the time of his interview, as an instructional coach rather than a full-time teacher), which may account for the specificity of his description.

> One of the best things that she [the cooperating teacher] did for me is . . . when I got up and tried to teach . . . she had this yellow legal pad and she would just write furiously . . . The first time that was happening, she didn't tell me she was going to do that. I thought, oh man, I am blowing it because these are all criticisms or . . . things I needed to correct . . . [S]he would write down, as best she could, things I said, things the kids would say. . . . She'd make observations about, you know, who was raising their hand and not being called on, you know . . . and it was really, really beneficial because we would go over these notes, and she'd hand me like eight pages, you know, like, every lesson, and it was, basically, a transcript of everything that had happened in there.

From McKenzie's report, it also seems that he responded productively to the cooperating teacher's help: "I would take whatever she suggested and enact it immediately, like, the next day. So, I was very open to her feedback, and very grateful that she gave such detailed feedback.[76]

If McKenzie offered an eloquent best-case scenario of what a cooperating teacher could contribute to the cultivation of novices' teaching abilities, other recruits depicted their cooperating teachers as archetypal bad teachers, lazy and exhausted or unstable and incompetent. In Mark Stephan's case, his cooperating teacher "was pretty burned out," which meant that Stephan "was just kind of helping him do some paperwork, basically." In his ultimate indictment of the situation, he proclaimed that, "Everyone was just sort of killing time."[77] Jan Trasen's cooperating teacher similarly provided a negative example: As Trasen remarked, "I sort of learned from her the way I didn't want to be." The teacher, as Trasen remembered, "wasn't particularly creative"; she was older, "exhausted," and made choices with which Trasen disagreed: "I still remember some of the things she did that I was pretty horrified by." Perhaps most unfortunately, Trasen remembered the cooperating teacher using the student teacher as relief.

> She saw my presence as a little 2-hour vacation for her. I got to sing and dance in front of her kids so she got to relax . . . I got to experiment on her kids and use some of the tricks that we were learning in our [TFA classes], and she got to have an extra cup of coffee.[78]

Bad as those stories were, other alumni portrayals depicted cooperating teachers who were stunningly lacking in competence and even, in one instance, potentially dangerous. Such examples ranged from Spencer Downing's cooperating teacher, who he termed "really, really nice," but "an awful teacher," to Caroline Sabin's cooperating teacher, about whom she said, "There was something wrong with her . . ."[79] According to Sabin, the teacher could not engage the students and, even worse, seemed to lack basic mastery of teaching and content herself. As Sabin recounted in one egregious example:

> The worst moment was . . . the final exam . . . [which] she gave . . . to the two of us [student teachers] to administer. Class has already started; she hands us handwritten sheets, like 37 handwritten questions, which she now wants us to go write up on the board, and that is how the kids are going to take their exam. They are going to watch us handwrite 37 questions on the board and then they are going to take the exam.
>
> [Meanwhile, the set of questions on the paper] is completely misspelled. So, as I am writing up the questions, I am correcting the spelling. And [the teacher] is now correcting *me*, "No, it is spelled like this," and what can I do? I can't undermine her authority . . . [and tell] her, "Really, it is spelled like this," and I just started thinking, wow, this is so unbelievably sad.[80]

Avis Terrell suspected that her cooperating teacher might have been a "drug addict." As she remembered, "[H]e would just leave me in the class by myself. . . . He was just very erratic, and not helpful . . . I think he was crazy."[81]

Variability of activities in which student teachers engaged. Addressing another important aspect of prospective teachers' experience within the student teaching arrangement, researchers suggest that many student teachers are offered control over a limited scope of classroom activities, and that the teaching they are able to do depends on the idiosyncrasies of individual classrooms and teachers. As a result, their interactions with students may remain at a superficial level, their teaching equated "with moving children through prescribed lessons in a given period of time."[82] Alumni testimonies revealed a range of activities in which they engaged during student teaching. Many student teachers, as cited earlier, find that they are allowed to manage only a closely circumscribed set of activities and responsibilities with students, to the degree that their interactions with students are brief, routine, and mechanical in nature.[83] Several of the alumni recalled their student teaching stints as limited in just such a way. For instance, Constance Bond was placed with a "great teacher" for student teaching, but one who rarely allowed Bond to participate: "She really wouldn't let me teach." As a result, Bond remembered, "I watched her, but I never really got to reflect to see what it [actually teaching] was like."[84] Similarly, Brent Lyles complained that, during his student teaching, "I didn't even actually teach much. I mostly observed other teachers teaching."[85] Kathy Feeley also recalled that she "did a lot of sitting and watching" during her student teaching.[86]

Others recalled a much broader opportunity—if not necessarily more support—for trying out their teaching. Thus, even if Jan Trasen's teacher used her as respite from teaching, at the very least, the teacher "had her class under control enough" that Trasen could "teach them and use some of the things we learned [through the TFA and small-group instruction]."[87] Better still, Nichole Childs Wardlaw recalled how her cooperating teacher not only "let me do as much as I wanted to do," but he also "encouraged" her and "was very supportive" when she taught lessons. [88]

Another common critique of student teaching, that it only exposes students to "situation specific phenomena" of particular classrooms, also emerged in the TFA participants' experiences.[89] More than a few of the alumni referred to the futility of being prepared for a particular context and grade level, only to find themselves teaching in a different grade in a vastly different environment. As Brent Lyles quipped, his student teaching in a 4th-grade classroom of mixed gifted and special education students located in East Los Angeles did little to prepare him for teaching 8th-grade math in rural North Carolina. Teaching children at 4th- and 8th-grade developmental levels certainly would have required pedagogical adjustment but, as Lyles pointed out, the difference in context flummoxed him as well.

> On some level, we could all make the case for, "Yes, that actually did prepare me in some ways," but it is kind of funny to just put it in those terms, because man, it was worlds away from what I was doing. It's a very urban school that I [student] taught in.[90]

From student teaching in that very urban context, Lyles then went to teach in the tobacco town of Henderson, North Carolina, with a population he estimated at about 17,000. As Lyles joked, "our second year there we got a Blockbuster video [store]. Very exciting." Plenty of other alumni shared this dissonance, which Constance Bond flatly summarized, "The school I had student taught in was nothing like this school I was placed in."[91] This would have been true for many who attended university-based preparation programs as well; what might have made a difference, however, would have been for TFA to provide recruits with tools for approaching and understanding a new community, something that did not occur. [92]

Jane Schneider had hoped to work with "little kids." Student teaching provided that experience: The group hug she received from her young students—"tiny little affectionate beings"—on the final day provided her enduring "image" of what she thought teaching would be. But for her permanent assignment, Schneider found herself teaching an overcrowded 6th-grade classroom in Inglewood, a "tough group of kids" where the school "couldn't hold on to a 6th-grade teacher."[93] Particularly in terms of classroom management, Schneider felt the mismatch between her student teaching placement and her assigned grade and class. Diane Brewer student taught in an ESL classroom in Hollywood, California, where most of the students came from Central America. She had what she called a "great experience," primarily because she could work "one-on-one" and "connect with the students," because it was a small class. Though she loved that experience, "It did absolutely nothing to prepare me for teaching Spanish in rural Georgia"—as she explained, her student teaching experience "was like tutoring versus teaching."[94] And finally, Marife Ramos's inclination was to squeeze all of the relevant information she could from her cooperating teacher: "What resources do you have or what can you tell from your experience, your years in the classroom, to let me know about what resources I can reach out to?" Unfortunately for her, the cooperating teacher taught in L.A., whereas Ramos began teaching in New York City. She asked, indignantly, "Honestly, am I going to reach out to someone in L.A. when I'm teaching in [New York City]? No. I mean my phone bill at the time would have been gargantuan." Her distance from her cooperating teacher left her isolated or, as she put it, "out on an island," because she couldn't access him for support. "I think they [TFA] should have put you with a [cooperating teacher] in your destined territory." That didn't happen, Ramos suspected, because "Teach For America did not know where we would teach until the latter part of the summer."[95]

Lisa Robinson, who student taught in a bilingual kindergarten in Watts ("and I was not bilingual!"), got a job teaching 4th grade at the Thomy LaFon Elementary School in New Orleans. As she recalled, her student teaching offered little to help shape realistic expectations of what she would encounter in New Orleans.

> I think I imagined teaching . . . you know, Cajuns . . . I had
> never been to New Orleans, so I really didn't have a realistic
> understanding of where I was going and I think that somehow my
> imagination led me to understand that I was going to probably be
> in a more rural part of Louisiana . . . I didn't think that I would be
> having inner-city kids.

In reflecting on the Institute, Robinson recognized that everyone—including TFA staff and others responsible for the training—"was flying by the seat of [their] pants," but she still criticized the training for having taken so little account of the particular contexts in which the recruits would eventually teach. "[S]houldn't we be really learning specifically about the kids who we're going to be teaching?"[96]

Robinson's point is a valid one, which has been debated within the field of teacher education—do you prepare teacher candidates for particular environments or for the general work of teaching with the assumption that they will figure out how to adapt? Yet even if candidates had been prepared in contexts similar to those where they eventually taught, the variability among student teaching experiences meant that participants walked away with vastly different models and understandings of teaching in action. Finally, as many alumni also recognized, even when they were exposed to significant and meaningful learning opportunities, they were not provided the time and frame of reference to absorb and capitalize on such opportunities. But again, this is hardly unique to TFA; the issue has dogged traditional university-based teacher education as well. How can teacher educators help prospective teachers develop the larger understandings, perspectives, and knowledge of schooling that enables them to make sense of what they are learning in productive ways that they can act upon, even in different environments?

Vision of teaching. Referencing his student teaching, Furman Brown knew that "what was good . . . was that I got to see how a teacher launches [a class]." In other words, Brown got to witness the process by which a teacher created a climate for effective teaching and learning in her classroom. But, he recalled, at the time, "I didn't realize how important setting the tone and standards and sort of positioning yourself as a person in charge [was]," in large part because "I wasn't really . . . understanding what she was doing."[97] Many of the alumni had embarked upon TFA with a simple, inexperienced, and consequently unsophisticated vision of what effective teaching looks like and consists of. As a result, it was often only in retrospect that participants began to understand the strengths of their cooperating teachers. For example, after describing how good his cooperating teacher had been, Scott Joftus admitted that, "my problem was I didn't appreciate her brilliance until it was too [late]." Joftus explained his conflation of teaching with performing, having learned the difference through hard experience. As he summarized,

> I thought she [the cooperating teacher] was really strict, and I
> was like, "Oh, I can't be like that, you know, I need to be more
> engaging and entertaining." But she was . . . a great, great teacher.
> And realizing, I mean the way she managed a classroom. She taught
> those kids so much it was really impressive.[98]

Likewise, Eric Bird struggled to reconcile his untutored beliefs of what teaching should look like with what he observed during student teaching.

> I remember the [cooperating teacher] explaining to me . . . about
> discipline and keeping the kids in a line and keeping them quiet—
> how important that was. And my thought at the time was, "My
> God, let's just teach these kids!" . . . Now I realize that . . . you need
> to set a structure and that was what she was trying to teach me.[99]

Alumni grappled with how to make sense of what they thought teaching should be and what they saw that seemed to be "successful" in their student teaching classrooms. Of course, we don't know how they understood success in the classroom, especially given their likely preconceptions about teaching, since the Institute had not been able to support them in thinking about and understanding teaching in ways that departed from what they may have remembered from their own student experiences. What comes across clearly in the interviews is the absence, on the part of recruits, of a larger picture of what good teaching involved and required. For example, Susanne Murray remembered having thought that her student teacher had been "decent" or useful, only to realize later that her perception came from the fact that "I had nothing . . . [and] he gave me something to work with." Indeed, as she gained teaching experience, Murray believed her positive assessment probably came about because "the bar was so low" and that, in fact, the cooperating teacher probably hadn't been all that effective. As she recalled, "[W]hen I became a better teacher, I was like, you know, what was he doing?"[100]

Looking back from the perspective of someone who stayed close to schools following his TFA experience, Furman Brown suggested the inadequacy not just of the student teaching he did under the auspices of TFA, but of student teaching itself as a preparatory practice. "I can't imagine learning much in a couple of weeks' worth of student teaching . . . I've always felt that was kind of an exercise more than a real experience."[101] And even though Jeffrey Simes felt that student teaching comprised the most valuable aspect of the TFA training, he too found fault with the practice of student teaching:

> You can sit in the back of the class, you know, for a year, and it's
> just not quite the same as getting up there and being in charge of it
> [the class] . . . [Y]ou got a flavor for it [teaching], but I think until you
> actually get there and do it, it's, you know, *you just got to do it.*[102]

CONCLUSION

The alumni found themselves woefully unprepared once they got into their own classrooms and many blamed the Institute. Unfortunately, the perceived failures on the part of the Institute planted the idea for many of these first-year corps members that pre-service preparation itself doesn't matter and that, in fact, to learn to teach, "you just got to do it," as Simes said. Participants complained that the Institute focused too much on the "theoretical" at the expense of the practical. But on the basis of their statements, as well as the accounts from journalists and educators, there is little evidence that the alumni received instruction in developing relevant theoretical frames that would have helped them to connect significant understandings in the field (about cognitive development, learning theory, or specific disciplinary pedagogies, for example) to so-called practical actions within the classroom. Even the perceived value of student teaching was undercut by the absence of a theoretical frame that would have allowed participants to make sense of what happened in those placements. Because participants missed out on a larger conceptual vision of what teaching is, many left not just the Institute, but their TFA tenure, with a superficial understanding of instructional practice. Twenty years after the fact, many alumni held fast to the mistaken impression that teaching is technocratic, a matter of mastering the "tricks" or techniques that would have allowed them to "deliver" instruction.

To be fair, the frustrations described by the TFA cohort differ from those expressed by more traditionally trained teachers less in substance than in degree. Though they may have greater opportunity (by virtue of their fuller roster of coursework) to develop a meaningful theoretical frame for teaching, teachers prepared then and now in conventional university-based programs also complain about a lack of preparation for the practical realities of teaching, such as classroom management, lesson planning, teaching techniques, and dealing with cultural differences. That teachers from more conventional preparatory pathways experience many of the same frustrations as our participants points toward two important takeaways. First, this confluence in criticism suggests real shortcomings in how the field has operationalized teacher training—so far, neither university-based programs nor the alternate routes seem to have figured out how to effectively prepare teachers to be ready for what they will face when they take up their own classroom. But perhaps these persistent complaints should also indicate just how difficult it is to prepare individuals to teach effectively, especially in underserved communities. That is, contrary to popular opinion, teaching is actually hard to learn and perform well. The inauguration of TFA presented an opportunity to address these issues in novel and effective ways. But by placing its bet on the quality of the recruits rather than on a serious rethinking of how to develop effective teachers, TFA missed that opportunity.

CHAPTER 4

"Multiculturalism Run Amok"

Identity Politics at the Summer Institute

The Summer Institute was meant to prepare the TFA recruits to take on their classroom teaching responsibilities. As Chapter 3 illustrated, alumni retained powerful memories of how, under the auspices of Institute instruction, they struggled to learn what they believed they needed to know in order to teach effectively. The oral histories suggest that, generally, participants found the Institute too "theoretical" and, specifically, too focused on developing multicultural competence, at the expense of providing the recruits with more "practical" training they thought they needed. And though participants discussed (often in response to some probing) recollections of how they learned (or did not) to teach at the Institute, by far the greatest share of memories that emerged about the Summer Institute involved activities and conflicts around what participants referred to as "multiculturalism." Instruction toward multicultural competence certainly made up some portion of the summer's curriculum —within the overall scope of the summer training, Appleman noted the Institute's attempt to address "major themes of teaching training, including multicultural education," Schneider acknowledged the Institute's use of works by Lisa Delpit and Jonathan Kozol (staples of social foundations and multicultural courses in university-based programs), and Carl Grant, a noted scholar of multicultural education, had been hired to conduct lectures.[1] But for participants, multiculturalism came to define their experiences of the Institute.

Scott Joftus arrived at the Institute from Duke University. A white man from an upper-middle-class background in the Midwest, Joftus had found Duke to be "segregated racially and conservative socially," but was able to major in a public policy program that he described as having a "socially aware perspective." Joftus studied the civil rights era, interned for a social service agency focused on juvenile offenders, and learned about "grassroots type of organizing." As part of what he termed a "very enthusiastic, progressive. . . talented group of folks [i.e., the 1990 TFA recruits]," Joftus found the Institute's "preaching to the choir" on multiculturalism perplexing.

It was PC [political correctness] run amok . . . [Y]ou could not have a conversation, at least in sort of a formal training session, that didn't end with talking about multiculturalism and the importance of understanding race and gender . . . it just completely spiraled out of control.[2]

As participants described their impressions of multicultural instruction and dialogue at the Institute, it became clear that, for many, the basic question of what *knowledge* they needed was often superseded by questions of identity. For much of the history of schooling in the United States, teachers have been judged more by qualities of their "character"—often a proxy for race, class, and gender—than their pedagogical knowledge.[3] At the TFA Summer Institute, participants depicted a more contemporary struggle around character that arose from the hotly contested question of who was fit to teach low-income children of color.

Alongside their common focus on "multiculturalism," however, the transcripts also suggest an intriguingly wide variation in individual perceptions. Alumni's recollections of the contentious events associated with the Summer Institute exposed a range of vantage points and perceived group memberships. Oral history is ideally suited to revealing such inconsistencies in perception, and to making sense of the different meanings that these individuals attached to their common experiences. Attending to both the consistencies and differences, we observed that participants' accounts of the Summer Institute dealt less with the mechanics of learning to teach than with the deep fault lines of race, class, and culture—even within the elite group that made up this first TFA cohort—and how those fault lines were understood to intersect with the work of teaching.

MULTICULTURALISM IN 1990 AMERICAN SOCIETY: A DEBATE "OLDER THAN THE NATION ITSELF"

Carl Grant, a well-known scholar of multiculturalism in education at the University of Wisconsin, addressed the Institute several times on the topic of multiculturalism in American society and schools. He introduced what many alumni recalled as the "salad bowl" metaphor for multiculturalism, which Carlos Gomez remembered as "many cultures living together . . . the idea of teaching values and cultures and trying to keep everyone's culture, but sort of everyone thrown together [like a tossed salad], as opposed to a melting pot where all these cultures blend into one."[4]

The "melting pot" metaphor, popularized in Israel Zangwill's 1908 play of the same name, was meant to reassure Americans of their country's unity despite the diversity of its populace. But the "melting pot" metaphor always had its critics. By the early 1960s, the ferment of the civil rights movement, along with the evolving ideas of thought leaders (Nathan Glazer and Daniel Moynihan published *Beyond the Melting Pot* in 1963), offered a strong rebuttal to the paradigm of cultural blending. This new emphasis on preserving distinct cultural identities met with a backlash in the conservative climate of the 1980s, igniting the culture wars. According to intellectual historian Andrew Hartman, "the culture wars are just a new name for a debate older than the nation itself: . . . the struggle to define a normative America."[5] In the late 1980s, this struggle erupted intensely on college campuses across the country. In the opinion of English and Education professor Gerald Graff, the academic curriculum became "a prominent arena of cultural conflict because it is a microcosm . . . of the clash of cultures and values in America as a whole"; this clash, Graff averred, arose from bringing historically excluded groups "into the educational citadel."[6]

One offshoot of this struggle was the phenomenon of "political correctness." As conservative cultural critic Richard Bernstein defined it, political correctness (or PC, as commonly abbreviated) constitutes adherence to "the view that Western society has . . . been dominated by what is often called 'the white male power structure' or 'patriarchal hegemony,'" and that as a result, "everybody but white heterosexual males has suffered some form of repression and been denied a cultural voice."[7] Journalist Joan Beck identified the goal of the PC movement as "laudatory"—"to end prejudice against minorities, make college curricula more multicultural and loosen the grip that elitist whites have had over higher education and its gateways to jobs and power." But, she added,

> . . . the lengths to which some students, faculty (many of them former 1960s campus radicals) and administrators are going to ferret out prejudice and discrimination are mind-boggling. Groups of PCPs [politically correct persons] have disrupted classes, prevented speakers from being heard, burned controversial publications, bullied professors into changing course content.[8]

Bernstein criticized the PC trend as having the effect of "intolerance, a closing of debate, a pressure to conform," such that views considered insufficiently sensitive to multicultural differences could not be articulated. This kind of conflict around political correctness animated many of the higher education institutions attended by TFA participants, by way of highly publicized battles over "speech codes," curriculum, and identity politics. As this chapter illustrates, many of the same conflicts animated the Institute training. Indeed, as one corps member reminisced:

> [I]f I were going to write a history of what came to be derisively known as "politically correct culture," that Summer Institute might be a highlight.[9]

MULTICULTURALISM AND TEACHER EDUCATION

Conflicts over multiculturalism or political correctness that emerged at the Institute did not spring solely from participants' campus experiences. In conjunction with the more general cultural phenomenon of ideological conflict over multiculturalism, the early 1990s also witnessed the beginnings of a multicultural movement in education.[10]

Teacher educators' focus on multicultural competence at this time emerged as part of the larger cultural zeitgeist, but also as a specific consequence of more teacher educators of color attaining positions of relative power. For example, James A. Banks, an African American teacher educator, became a prominent advocate for multiculturalism in teacher preparation. He cited the demographic realities of schooling—in which the student population was growing increasingly diverse while the teaching force remained relatively homogeneous—as an impetus both to recruit more teachers of color and to "help all teachers—especially white, mainstream teachers—to acquire the attitudes, skills, and knowledge needed to work effectively with students of color."[11] By the early years of the 21st century, teacher educators Villegas and Lucas argued that "preparing teachers who are culturally responsive is a *pressing issue* in teacher education."[12]

In a 1990 review of scholarly literature on preparing teachers for diversity, Grant and Secada criticized the "paucity of research" regarding demographic diversity and teacher preparation: They suggested that, while the issue of teachers' cultural competence had been recognized since the 1966 publication of the Coleman Report, researchers and teacher educators had been slow to respond.[13] Indeed, according to the National Center for Education Statistics, by 1990, 40% of the national K–12 school population consisted of children of color, while nearly 90% of teachers were white.[14] (This trend persists; by 2014–2015, children of color made up more than half of the national K–12 population, but the percentage of teachers who are white has remained close to 85%.)[15] The demographic divide also encompasses class differences and a growing language gap. In 1989, for instance, 15% of white children, 44% of African American children, and 36% of Latinx children lived in poverty, nearly half of them in urban areas, whereas most teachers hailed from lower-middle- or middle-class homes, having grown up in suburbs or rural areas.[16]

Such differences between American teachers and their charges acquire meaning because, as educational researcher Mary Louise Gomez argues, "[T]he race, social class, language backgrounds, and sexual orientations of prospective teachers affect their attitudes toward 'Others,'" including beliefs about whether "'Others' can learn."[17] As John Goodlad established in his 1990 study on teacher education, many prospective teachers are "less than convinced" that all students can learn.[18] Gomez's influential research, carried out in the late 1980s, along with Grant and Secada's review, further shaped the field's emphasis on multicultural competence, which prevailed at the Summer Institute.

Digging into the differences between teachers and their students, Gomez examined an AACTE study from 1990, which relied upon questionnaire responses from 472 prospective teachers (60% white, 40% persons of color). She found:

> [N]early all of the whites surveyed grew up in white neighborhoods, attended institutions of higher education also mostly populated by whites, and reported spending most of their time at school with other whites. Their counterparts who were African American, Latino, and Asian were more likely to live near, go to school with, and spend time with other people of color—especially those who were members of their racial or ethnic group. [19]

Such segregation meant that many white teachers were unfamiliar with cultures, races, and backgrounds different from their own. As a result, they saw the learning and achievement challenges encountered by children from such backgrounds "not as outcomes of teachers' beliefs about and behaviors toward children in school," but as a consequence of those children's identities and upbringing. [20]

As Gomez determined, many prospective teachers lacked the basic skills, attitudes, and knowledge for teaching diverse learners. According to one widely shared view, responsibility for helping teacher candidates to acquire such skills, attitudes and knowledge lay with the professors and other instructors who prepare teachers.[21] But by 1990, teacher education had not risen to the challenge. As one education researcher observed,

> Teacher educators continue to assume that teacher education students will pick up the necessary knowledge, skills, and attitudes that will help them teach classes of socioculturally diverse students without any direct instruction and planned experience.[22]

Gomez castigated both the Carnegie and Holmes reports that appeared in 1986 for their failure to articulate "a coordinated vision of how successfully teaching 'Other people's children' is tied to all aspects of teacher education."[23]

A few years later, drawing together a broad body of research, teacher education scholar Kenneth Zeichner outlined minimal cultural competencies that teachers should possess. These included knowledge about children's development, how they acquire second languages, and how their learning is influenced by variables such as "socioeconomic status, language, and culture." More specifically, teachers would need to learn about the "languages, cultures, and circumstances" of the particular students in their classrooms and use such information to devise relevant curriculum and teaching approaches. They would also need "a clear sense of their own ethnic and cultural identities" in order to be able to understand those of their students and families.[24] Finally, Zeichner warned of the difficulty of carrying out these tasks well, pointing out that knowledge about other cultures may shade into stereotypes, leading prospective teachers to form views based on cultural deprivation or to apply a fixed set of group characteristics to the unique individual before them.[25] Many teacher educators agreed that undertaking this work during teacher preparation could only begin the process of "critical self-inquiry" needed for prospective teachers to effectively teach diverse learners. [26]

In concluding their 1990 review of the literature on preparing teachers to teach diverse learners, Grant and Secada lamented both the "vagueness associated with multicultural education," which made it challenging to relate such lessons to "the real world," and the nascent state of knowledge about developing teachers' multicultural competence.[27] As they wrote,

> There is much that we do not know about how to prepare teachers to teach an increasingly diverse student population. We think that new responses are called for in teacher recruitment, pre-service education, and in-service education.[28]

Certainly, TFA represented a radical departure in teacher recruitment and the Summer Institute offered an opportunity to refashion pre-service preparation. Moreover, the emphasis on developing multicultural competence among the recruits, whatever its failings, constituted an attempt to incorporate cutting-edge sensibilities of the field with a new format and audience.

TFA PARTICIPANT EXPERIENCES OF "MULTICULTURALISM" AT THE SUMMER INSTITUTE

For all the time and attention allotted to multicultural competence, however, many TFA participants weren't sold on the version of multiculturalism they encountered through the Institute. As participant Leo Flanagan suggested in retrospect, the Institute training in multiculturalism could have helped the recent graduates to figure out their identities and grapple with cultural difference—"It was a time when people really were kind of pounding out" their understandings—and to explore how those identities meshed with the work of teaching low-income children of color.[29] But according to the transcripts, the way in which multiculturalism was defined and presented—simplistically, divisively, and with little practical connection to the environments or classrooms in which the recruits would teach—along with corps members' disregard for some of their instructors and the ineffectual instruction around multiculturalism, grievously undermined that opportunity.

The Institute's Conceptualization and Presentation of Multiculturalism

Scott Joftus, a white male, reflected that he didn't want "to discount the multiculturalism and stuff . . . because, you know, I think that is part of being a good teacher." But he also expressed frustration with how poorly the Institute managed the dialogue about multiculturalism, so that "almost all of the activities sort of devolved . . . to the point where I think . . . there was a lot of discomfort."[30] Jeffrey Simes, too, protested the simplistic nature of their instruction in multiculturalism.

> [T]here was [practical] stuff I felt like I needed to know and [instead] I was just getting this sort of, "We should be sensitive to all people," which I kind of agree with anyway and I don't really need to be told.[31]

More baldly, as Flanagan remembered, the training treated each participant as "a person who is completely culturally ignorant and who will fall victim to the worst sort of tendencies of the dominant culture if we [TFA] don't intervene."[32] Both Joftus and Simes reflected a common perception among the TFA participants that the multicultural work of the Institute related little if at all to the "practical" work of teaching. As Joftus explained, the heated conflicts and strong feelings provoked by the Institute's treatment of multiculturalism meant that recruits did not receive "a lot of quality training . . . *in the types of skills that I think we needed to have* [to teach.]"[33] As many of the testimonies substantiated, the uproar associated with sessions on multiculturalism sucked both time and attention away from what recruits believed would have been more practical, useful learning. Many traditional route prospective teachers struggle to relate poorly defined and delivered multicultural programs effectively to the day-to-day work of teaching, but the TFA recruits' complaint was broader: they received neither a coherent multicultural program nor satisfactory exposure to the techniques and strategies that would have served them in day-to-day teaching.

The critique was not limited to white recruits. In fact, those corps members who had already grappled with multiculturalism in their own lives found the Institute's conceptualization to be especially lacking. For example, as a high-achieving African American woman, Christina Brown had plenty of experience as a minority within a larger white context. She found Carl Grant's salad metaphor "ridiculous." "I don't think salads have to worry about class and power and oppression in the same way that people do . . . Salads don't have legacies of historical baggage." She remembered her anger at the time, that "[t]hey [the TFA staff and instructors] were figuring out what multiculturalism meant . . . while working with us and having us work in the schools."[34]

In addition to criticizing the Institute's conceptualization of multiculturalism, recruits also condemned its delivery of the multicultural training. Much of the instruction on multiculturalism occurred in plenary sessions, held in a large auditorium and presided over by Institute faculty. Ostensibly, the aim was to deliver a lecture and engage the corps in discussion, but with nearly 500 passionate, highly educated, and opinionated individuals in the room, such a structure made little sense. More than once, the sessions turned into free-for-alls, degenerating into battles over identity politics and what qualities were required to teach poor children of color.[35] Diane Brewer was one of several participants who described the experience as being "like the *Donahue Show* [where] someone was running around with a microphone giving everybody opportunity to talk"; Jane Schneider just remembered "a lot of people bursting into tears and screaming at each other."[36]

Participants blamed some of this disorder on the quality of the instructors, accusing them of underestimating their audience and poorly facilitating the sessions. Caroline Sabin, who is white and who characterized herself as sympathetic to the multicultural conversation, recalled "not being impressed by Carl . . . our multicultural guru."[37] Eric Bird also complained, particularly about instructors' ineffectiveness in managing the large sessions.

> Even while [a] professor [was] trying to lead the class, somebody would disagree with one thing . . . and then that would lead into a half hour debate . . . We would get off topic anywhere and everywhere. We would have, you know, all 500 of us together in the same auditorium. Then we'd spend a huge amount of time arguing over semantics."[38]

As many participants recalled, large group exercises meant to engage participants in substantive dialogue about thorny issues of race and class often had the effect of silencing, offending, or segregating individuals according to perceived group status. For example, some alumni remembered an activity in which they were divided into groups that represented different races, cultures, and religions. Participants described feeling uncomfortable with the experience, though for different reasons. Ellen Rosenstock, who is white and Jewish, remembered white corps members feeling uneasy about speaking freely in these situations.

[H]ow can I speak up and say what I think? . . . [I]f I speak up, whatever I say is going to be wrong because there was a lot of anger . . . I know that a lot of the people I was hanging out with were feeling like, "I can't say anything. If I speak up, then I'm the bad white person."[39]

Nichole Childs Wardlaw, who is African American, had a different response, which was incredulity that her experiences or opinions should be taken to "represent" the race. "I was like, 'What? So now I'm supposed to speak for everybody in my culture?'"[40] Marife Ramos lamented the way that, instead of bringing the group together, these plenary conversations around multiculturalism created deep rifts: "It became an ostracizing, divisive forum and many times I just wanted to skip out of it because it polarized [us]."[41]

Leo Flanagan shared several trenchant memories of how political correctness was exercised during the large-group sessions at the Institute. For example, he described, when "this real big shot [instructor] was talking about Hispanic culture," a young woman stood up, took the microphone, and announced in the middle of his talk, "'I am not Hispanic; I am not Herpanic; I am nobody's panic; I am a Latino.'" For Flanagan, even though he recalled knowing better than to call the woman "Spanish," he also "didn't think [at the time] there was a big difference [between] Hispanic and Latino." In another instance, Flanagan recalled corps members "hissing" at a purportedly sexist instructor.[42] But rather than providing teachable moments, such incidents were regarded by participants as unresolved issues, which worked to divide and discomfit the group.

Because Christina Brown went on to facilitate diversity training in her subsequent professional work, she brought an especially critical eye to the way in which the Institute failed to structure and support the work around multiculturalism. As she pointed out in her interview:

You can't have a whole group session with 500 people. . . That's not how you do diversity work. It should have been small groups. It should have been structured. It should have been talking about where you'd come from and what your orientation is to this work [teaching]. That's not what was done and so it was a set up for everyone in terms of how it was structured.[43]

Generally, participants remembered those large sessions as the main site of strife over race, culture, and identity. Cultural unease and arguments over multiculturalism also spilled across instructional forums at the Institute, to the small groups and student teaching, and even into social spaces. Thus, continuing the theme of inept instructors, Avis Terrell told of a young Black man who, as she remembered, did not get along with his small-group leader. According to Terrell, the recruit "was always talking about her [the group leader] . . . like he was being treated unfairly . . . he felt like she was racist." Though Terrell, a Black woman, did not necessarily agree—"I just felt they [the instructors] weren't prepared"— she did convey the degree to which conflicts at the Institute seemed to be refracted through the lens of race or culture.[44]

Spencer Downing, a white man who came to the Institute from the University of Chicago, described himself as having arrived full of hubris about the work of teaching and with a good dose of cynicism about political correctness. He remembered curriculum debates within his social studies group that turned on cultural differences over knowledge, describing a particular disagreement in his group about how to approach instruction in sensitive topics, such as slavery. "I distinctly remember a moment where I said that I could see no problem with students play acting a slave auction and my thinking at that time was, you know, the more you make things real, the more they [students] can understand the past." Downing's thinking angered an African American woman "to the point of crying, that anybody would contemplate such an idea . . . she was incredibly upset at the idea and upset at me." Though he saw no problem at the time with his stance, looking back, Downing acknowledged, "I've come to realize how idiotic that was for me to say."[45]

Lori Lawson's experience in her small group both cut to the heart of her identity and impugned her potential teaching abilities. In her interview, Lawson described herself as having "some ethnicity about me"; one individual who picked up on Lawson's "ethnicity" was a self-identified Latino recruit, with whom she recalled having the following conversation about multiculturalism:

> He said, ". . . you're Hispanic, aren't you?"
> "Well, my mother was Spanish, yes."
> "And you cannot speak Spanish?"
> "No."
> "And your mother never embraced the heritage and shared it with you?"
> "No, she was trying to assimilate in a small Southern town that was largely racist."
> He ripped me a new one, ripped her a new one. I'm like, "She's dead." He was like, "Oh, sorry."

Beyond being personally upsetting, the comments also indicted Lawson's fitness to teach: "He said essentially that I would not be able to embrace it [culture] with kids that I teach if I didn't embrace it myself."

As Lawson bitterly reflected, "I was 21, my mother had been dead for ten months . . . and he was . . . calling her a bad mother for not teaching this to me . . . I thought it was unfair."[46]

Some participants also described having witnessed cultural conflict in their student teaching experiences. In most cases, the alumni who reported such incidents had a clear sense of being culturally enlightened compared to the teachers, whose behavior they criticized. Such instances could have provided opportunities for multicultural instruction: Alumni made uncomfortable by what they observed might have been offered a supportive space or forum for reflecting on what they had seen, exploring other ways they might have reacted, or devising strategies for dealing with such occurrences in the future. Avis Terrell recalled the case of "a Mexican boy . . . [whose] name, I think, was Pepe . . . [that] the teacher was calling him, 'Peter.'" When she asked the boy whether that was his name, he said no. Terrell remembered thinking, "'His name is not Peter.' And that's not even a nickname. So I felt offended." She told the boy, "'Don't ever let anybody call you something other than your name.'"[47] Similarly, Jan Trasen remembered her surprise at having "a bunch of Chinese and Korean kids named John and Billy" in her student teaching class, but that was before she realized that her cooperating teacher would "invent an American name for her foreign students and say, 'Oh, he likes being called John.'" As Trasen recounted, "I'd be like, "Isn't his name 'Shao'?" And the cooperating teacher would respond, 'Oh, but he loves "John." . . . and I can't say Shao anyway, and Shaw and Chi, and how do you keep them all straight?'" Trasen found the teacher's behavior "horrible," but attested that she "learned from her the way I didn't want to be."[48]

Lisa Robinson recalled the uncertainty and racial discomfort she felt at how her lead teacher, who was African American, handled several "problem" students. In dealing with one Black boy, the teacher, "who appeared to be . . . this angelic, wonderful teacher who everybody loved," showed a very different side. "[S]he became . . . kind of physical and she raised her voice and she took on a whole different persona with him." The teacher explained to Robinson that this child "came from a different background and this [kind of treatment] was what he responded to." As Robinson commented, because the teacher was also African American, "there was a way in which . . . she [the teacher] felt like she kind of understood" what the disruptive African American student needed. Robinson remembered finding the teacher's behavior inappropriate: "[W]hile that may have been an effective technique to kind of train the boy to . . . succumb in the ways that she wanted them to, I didn't feel that was the only—I didn't feel like that was the most honorable way to achieve that."[49]

Caroline Sabin also shared powerful memories about the cultural insensitivity of her cooperating teacher. Raising the specter of historically troubled relations between Black teachers and Latino students, Sabin portrayed the teacher, a Black woman, as having "hated the Latino students."[50] As Sabin remembered, however, the Latinx students "didn't care, because she was so stupid . . . [but] the Black students were battling with her all the time." Sabin narrated her memory of daily roll call in the class:

> She never learned to pronounce any Latino kids' names. She had no idea how to pronounce [them]. They didn't care . . . [but the] Black kids hated it when she mispronounced their names. I can remember there was this one girl; I think her name was Sheila, but [it] was a completely crazy spelling of Sheila. So, the teacher would, sort of, pronounce it maybe phonically [sic], or whatever, every day, and every day, Sheila would say, "It's Sheila," and then the teacher would argue back about, "How can it be Sheila? Look at the way it is spelled." Every day, they would have this debate about how, really, your name is stupidly spelled and it shouldn't be the way you claim it [is].[51]

At the same time, Sabin recalled coming face to face with her own cultural limits in trying to work with students whom she literally couldn't understand:

> [W]e were doing a lesson on heroes and so we were asking the kids for heroes and [the] Latino kids were offering up Pancho Villa . . . Between never having heard the name but also their [the students'] very thick accents, we were having a hard time . . . They repeated it like 12 times and we didn't know what—finally, we had them spell it. So, we were writing it; I remember standing back from the board, "Oh, Pancho Villa."[52]

On the evidence of such testimonies, it seems that recruits encountered multicultural conflict across Institute learning forums, conflict that influenced both their sense of personal identity and their beliefs about pedagogy. Perhaps more important, these recollections also illustrate the degree to which training that was meant to help corps members acknowledge, understand, and work through multicultural issues essentially exacerbated those issues. As a result of the Institute, participants indicated greater isolation within their perceived group identity, rather than greater understanding across group identities. In participants' telling, the Institute provided them with few means to resolve the issues that emerged or to connect those issues or resulting understandings fruitfully to their work as teachers. Even understanding how difficult it is to facilitate successful diversity training, Christina Brown remained critical. She blamed the Institute's approach to multiculturalism for setting participants up "not to be helping each other to prepare and not to function in the ways that we were renewing our commitment to the work [but instead were] feeling our frustration with each other."[53]

Uncommon Memories of Common Events

Across the participants' varied accounts of the Institute, certain watershed moments were recalled time and again, though notably in different ways by different participants. Indeed, these events, which took place during the large-group sessions, became a kind of Rorschach test, reflecting widely divergent personal perspectives, which were, in turn, shaped by individuals' understandings of their own race, class, and culture. We argue that participants' descriptions of such events are especially meaningful in their capacity to reveal critical assumptions on the part of different corps members regarding race, culture, class, their own positionality in such debates, and the connection of such issues to teaching. At the core of these debates lay a fundamental question: Who was or was not fit to teach students of color from poor families?

Fear of Black People. One incident reported by several participants concerned the confession of a white woman, during a large-group session, to her fear of Black people. Caroline Sabin, a white woman herself, recalled the speaker as having wept about being raped by a Black man. Avis Terrell, a Black woman, remembered the story otherwise. In her version, the woman said she got "beat up by a Black boy." Christina Brown, also an African American woman, recounted the woman's admission as having been "mugged by a Black person once, [so] I'm afraid of Black people.'" Looking back, Brown recognized that whites and Blacks at the Institute "were in different phases of . . . racial identity and development." In her experience, this meant that white people at the Institute "often need[ed] to be forgiven and congratulated for doing this [TFA]."

> That was their need, their internal need . . . to feel safe like, isn't it great you're here and you're going to do this? . . . And you're not responsible for slavery or you're not responsible for oppression. Because that's what they needed to hear in order to be able to move on. And they wanted to be told, "You are so brave for coming here in spite of the fact that you're afraid of Black people." That's not something that a Black person is going to be able to tell them, so it [was] a real mismatch.

During the Institute, Brown herself associated with what she described as an activist group of corps members of color, united by their keenly felt racial differences from the majority of Corps members and the TFA staff.

> I remember one time Wendy [Kopp] sitting down with us . . . a bunch of Black women [and explaining the genesis of TFA] . . . "Anybody could do it; I just wrote this proposal and I asked people for money and they gave it to me, and I started this." I remember after she got up to leave, one of my friends said, "If I knocked on the same people's doors and said, 'I have a proposal I'd like to try out,' they'd be like, 'There's a maid out here and she wants some money.'"

As Brown noted, "The level of access that [Kopp] had from the world in which she grew up . . . is not a level of access that would have enabled a Black person to go and collect money in the same way."[54]

The Institute was not Brown's first encounter with such disparities. At Franklin and Marshall College, she found herself among a lot of "suburban and conservative white people." As she acknowledged, "I hadn't met those kind of white people before, so that was also sort of a political awakening and just made me a little more active and militant."[55] Her experience as one of a small group of people of color on a primarily white college campus influenced her concerns at the Institute about how recent white college graduates who had little experience with ethnic diversity would handle their future work in urban classrooms.

> [W]hen you go to college, you hear white people say stupid things about people of color . . . and ask you questions about your music, or your hair, whatever. But it's not their job to teach you and to understand who you are, so you . . . could ignore them, but it just seemed really unfair to put these same people in classrooms with people [K–12 students] who couldn't defend themselves.

Brown believed that her academic studies also profoundly affected her stance at the Institute. She credited her views in part to the Government and Sociology major and coursework (including a Sociology of Education class in which she read Freire's *Pedagogy of the Oppressed*) that had informed her thinking, and that fed her frustration at the Institute with "people's sense of being ahistorical," and the fact that many of the recruits "just didn't get power and privilege and poverty and those issues that really were my main [reasons] for being there."[56] Worse, though, than their ignorance, according to Brown, was the idea that these individuals would be set loose on students of color.

> [B]ecause I'm coming from a *Pedagogy of the Oppressed* liberation philosophy, it becomes even more oppressive to see what I see as

the oppressor pretending to play in this realm where it shouldn't be okay to play because real damage is being done.[57]

In retrospect, Brown described herself as a "militant" at the Institute, part of a small band of activists bonded by their race identity and understandings of racial politics. As she said, "It felt like I was in a community [that] appreciated the importance of culture in our work and had the sense of 'these [future urban students] are *our* children.'" It was a sentiment, she believed, that the small community of Black and Latinx corps members shared.

"Don't fuck up our kids." Christina Brown, unlike most participants interviewed, did not explicitly recall an incident in which a Latina corps member took the microphone during a whole-group forum to angrily warn the group, "Don't fuck up our kids."[58] Her incendiary statement suggests that, in accordance with Brown's sentiments, some Black and Latinx recruits deeply suspected the white TFA participants' motives and ability to relate to and teach ethnically and racially diverse students in underserved schools. Carlos Gomez, a recruit whose parents had emigrated from Colombia to America a few years before his birth, was one of the alumni who admired the Latina's message. He remembered the tension within the corps around the woman's speech, but he mostly recalled feeling "awestruck" at the speaker's connection to her identity and her righteous intensity. Indeed, the speaker's strong claim to her ethnic identity struck a chord with him; as Gomez reported, the Institute occurred at a moment in his own life when he "sort of came into touch with my own Latino identity." It had been difficult, he remembered, to be Colombian in the 1980s, given the country's negative association with drugs. He recalled feeling a bit like a man without a country during his upbringing, marginalized in the United States for his Colombian roots and in Colombia as *"el gringo."* In his telling, he only began to really embrace his Colombian heritage at the Institute, in part as a result of the opportunity to be around other "Latinos and Puerto Ricans and Mexicans and Cubans." As a result, Gomez found the Latina speaker's staunch ownership of her ethnic identity thrilling.

Gomez also understood the Latina speaker to have come from a neighborhood like those where the corps members would soon be teaching, which accorded her and her message additional authenticity.

[It] was like she loved being Mexican American and she grew up in these neighborhoods and she care[d] deeply about the kids in her neighborhood . . . [W]ho could speak . . . with more authority than she?[59]

Because he recalled that the speaker had attended Princeton, she was a "model," in Gomez's estimation, of someone who had succeeded despite her background. Consequently, he believed, she had important knowledge and perspective to offer to the group, given that "her teachers did something right, her family did something right, she did something right," and he thought the group should learn from her.

Though Gomez identified deeply with the positive aspects of recognizing and claiming an ethnic identity, he also noted his confusion around the anger he perceived in the Latina's words.

> I don't think I fully understood where . . . her anger . . . her, sort of, feelings were directed. Were they directed at the people out in the audience who were going to go ahead and be teachers in East LA where she was from? Or was her anger towards Teach For America?[60]

As Gomez's views indicate, the perspectives expressed by recruits of color were hardly monolithic. Other alumni from minority groups articulated their impatience with the Latina speaker's message and the larger racial politics of the Institute. While Marife Ramos, who is Filipina, steadfastly believed in the value of having a conversation about cultural competency, she adamantly opposed the notion that people could not teach students from cultures other than their own.

> [I]t was maddening. I hate that stuff. . . . "[Y]ou're not going to be able to teach my kids, you're not going to be able to teach my culture, because you know nothing about it" . . . [I]t just robbed me of time we could have been learning about these cultures rather than telling me that I can't teach your kids because I'm white or I'm this, or I'm not Asian, I'm not Latina.[61]

Another recruit, Priscilla Leon-Didion, who immigrated from Ecuador as a child, expressed disdain for such "politics." Going back to her formative years, she recalled how her parents' activism in Ecuador "really put me off politics," and how she avoided rallies and other political activities at Wesleyan. In particular, Leon-Didion disapproved of the way that minorities at the Institute drew attention to their differences and the bias they had experienced, calling it "annoying" and "immature." She described a blonde woman from Puerto Rico, who "complained of all the discrimination that she had faced." Because the woman was "half white . . . European," Leon-Didion argued that if the woman "would just quiet up, no one would hear [her] accent, nobody would know [her ethnicity]."[62]

Though she described herself as having been an "apolitical" nonparticipant in the racial politics of the Institute, Leon-Didion recalled "being recruited to be with the militant Latinos," to no avail, and evoked in detail the efforts of activist recruits of color to position themselves in relation to minoritized children, as a means of gaining greater legitimacy as teachers of such children.

"Race and *my kids*," you know. "You're not going to do this to *my* kids." So whenever a person of color would get up . . . [that] was the message. . . . [I]t was just such a litany that I was so tired [of] . . . . I just felt so fed up. I mean, I'm like, "Give me tools to learn and work with any kid. I'm not ready for the political discussion from the, you know, self-proclaimed experts who knew nothing."[63]

Leon-Didion questioned here the connection between cultural identity and the ability to teach. Rather than trafficking in the "political discussion" of cultural "experts" who "knew nothing" about *teaching*, Leon-Didion found herself begging for the "tools to . . . work with any kid," conceptualizing pedagogical knowledge as something apart from the discussions about multiculturalism that had monopolized corps members' focus at the Institute.

Another important set of perspectives emerged from white participants who found themselves stunned by the anger they encountered from some corps members of color. These alumni struggled to understand why their good intentions were so vehemently questioned. Jane Schneider, for example, had expected everyone to be "accepted," whatever their background: "[Y]ou're trying to do something that you think is helpful." Instead she recalled feeling blamed for simply endeavoring to teach underserved children of color, noting the "divided, angry split" that arose among corps members.

[S]he came up to the podium in front of all 500 of us [and] sort of pointed at us and said, "we don't want you to fuck up our kids." . . . [T]hat was a really core moment, you know, of just . . . how split and fractured everything was.[64]

As Schneider recalled, the Latina "was definitely distinguishing herself from someone like me," with the implication that Schneider's white identity detracted from her ability to teach underserved students. Schneider struggled to deal with the resentment, which she found "incredibly painful."

I felt like, you know, yes, I'm from a very privileged background. And you know, yes, I'm white, and yes, I've had everything handed to me . . . I recognize all of that . . . [But] I felt like I probably represent[ed] maybe 90 percent of the people who were there, which was, I guess, part of the problem, that it [TFA] was so white and so privileged . . . [there was a] very vocal minority that resented how white it was, and resented . . . every single one of us, you know, for having that background.

As Schneider said, she wasn't naïve enough that she expected to be "appreciated," but she did want to be "accepted."[65]

Like Schneider, Andrew McKenzie found the wholesale dismissal of white recruits puzzling, particularly since, as he remembered thinking, "We are all [here] for the right reasons." He too recalled the instance of the Latina speaking out: "[B]asically, her comment was, you know, 'You—meaning people who are not Hispanic—don't know what it is like to live in those neighborhoods, so you will never be able to relate to the students there.'" McKenzie granted the point that "if you're not born and raised" in a specific environment, "you are not going to know it as well as someone maybe who was." But he also pointed out that different ethnic neighborhoods contain "many nuances"—implying that it would be difficult for anyone to fully know a neighborhood. And he pronounced it "presumptuous and premature" for those outspoken critics to dismiss all the recruits "who are there . . . with the best intentions and with open minds and a willingness to, you know, roll up their sleeves and do hard work and good work," just because they were white and had privileged backgrounds. [66]

Though they may have disagreed with the hostile views expressed by vocal recruits of color, both Schneider and McKenzie made efforts retrospectively to understand those perspectives within the bigger context of racial politics. For a few, such as Heather Weller, a white woman raised as an Evangelical Christian, those views seemed not only unaccountably antagonistic, but deeply threatening to the values and beliefs with which she had grown up. She could not fathom either the depth of people's anger, or the reasoning behind it.

> I had never been around so many angry people in my life. . . . [A]ll of the homosexuals felt like people were prejudiced against them, so they threw fits. And then all of the Black people felt like everybody was prejudiced against them their whole life, so they threw fits. And then all of the Asian people felt like they weren't getting any representation, so they threw fits.

Weller told of "physical symptoms," such as "shaking and crying," that she experienced in response to this anger. For even though she claimed to like the variety of perspectives she encountered, she also recognized that she "didn't have an easy way of processing . . . the intense stress" of being surrounded by those "who were very much yelling and screaming that they were absolutely right [even though] it contradicted my values."[67] She remembered thinking: "I'm so sorry I'm white, I so sorry. I don't even know you. I didn't do anything and I didn't beat your grandma and I'm so sorry . . . I was just going to do the same job they did.[68]

Other white corps members questioned whether, in fact, they were fit for the work they had undertaken. So while Scott Joftus believed much of the conversation about race and multiculturalism amounted to "political correctness run amok," by summer's end he acknowledged powerful doubts about his ability to teach in underserved schools.

> I remember sort of always feeling, I don't know how to say it, but sort of "less than." The fact that, you know, that I was white, and I'm going into . . . a, you know, mostly minority population and feeling like . . . that was not the right thing to be doing.[69]

As he characterized it, there was "a lot of white guilt going on" and, in response, Joftus recalled, "I kind of feel like I withdrew a little bit."[70] Kathy Feeley, a white woman, remembered the Latina's admonition as a question: "Who are you people to be teaching my children?" As Feeley recognized, "it was this challenge and . . . it was, you know, those sorts of moments that really made me think, like, yeah, who am I?"[71] Spencer Downing remembered not only how "politically engaged" the conversation around race got over the summer, but also "how many white guys were going around feeling like they were the new oppressed people." Affirming Christina Brown's sense that whites and Blacks at the Institute were at different stages of development in their racial understandings, Downing explained such feelings by observing that "The whole question of people of color came into the lexicon for many of us there [at the Institute]." Consequently, while many recruits arrived having "thought we were part of some progressive thing that would change American education," the white recruits found themselves cast as "benighted dinosaurs" that were going to "ruin new kids' lives."[72]

Certainly, as most participants narrated their experiences of the Summer Institute, race became a major issue across different racial and ethnic groups, albeit for different reasons. But several alumni were astute enough to also notice the way in which class operated, sometimes in ways that countered a simple racial narrative. For instance, in contrast to Carlos Gomez's account, when Jane Schneider described the Latina who spoke about "our kids," she characterized her as "from a very privileged background"—not from a poor neighborhood in East L.A.—even though she was "identifying as this, like, angry Latino [sic] woman." Other alumni corroborated Schneider's account, identifying the woman who spoke out as having come from economic privilege and implicitly suggesting that, given her class background, it was disingenuous for her to identify with the students they would be teaching.

Whether or not the Latina came from an upper-class background—indeed, whether she was Mexican or Puerto Rican, whether she went to Princeton or not—all of these details derive from participants' perceptions and ultimately seem less important than how those perceived details mattered to recruits at the time. Some, such as Gomez, found the Latina's

credibility enhanced by the perception that she was speaking from experience. Others, such as Schneider, found her speech hypocritical, given
what Schneider understood to be her false identification with children
who came from very different backgrounds, socio-economically, than
that of the woman herself.

The corps members were acting out some of the very conflicts which
the multicultural curriculum was meant to help them analyze and understand. But according to interviewees, there was little support or
infrastructure to help them deal with these rifts and the conflicts they
represented. As Leo Flanagan remembered, things got so bad that the
TFA staff intervened dramatically.

> They [TFA staff] stopped the whole Institute for like three days and
> just had an intensive session in a workshop about the whole cultural
> or multicultural [thing], and then I think after that there was an
> emphasis on trying to . . . put it back together again . . . But it was
> too late at that point.[73]

As a result, many participants left the Institute with unsettling and
unresolved feelings about multiculturalism, their identity, and their ability to teach children different from themselves. Some alumni, such as Andrew McKenzie, remembered how getting into classrooms and beginning
student teaching helped shift their attention to the "concrete challenges in
front of us, day in and day out."[74] Thus, in addition to questioning what
qualities would best equip the recruits to teach low-income children of
color, participants also began to raise rather urgent questions about what
tangible skills and knowledge related to teaching, *per se*, they would need
to take command effectively in any classroom.

CONCLUSION

The rationale for providing multicultural training has been to help teacher candidates address what contemporary researchers describe as the
"demographic divide," or the "marked disparities in educational opportunities, resources, and achievement among student groups who differ
from one another racially, culturally, and socioeconomically."[75] According to this line of thinking, basic teacher competencies such as classroom
management, knowledge of content area, and pedagogical knowledge are
necessary but not sufficient to ensure that all children have an opportunity to learn; teachers must also be attuned to students' backgrounds and
cultures if they are to teach them successfully. But theorists suggest that
in order for teachers to build a repertoire of teaching strategies that work
with diverse children, they must first inquire into their own backgrounds,
presumptions, and attitudes; then, with this self-knowledge, they must

learn about the backgrounds of their students and connect what they discover to decisions they make about curriculum and pedagogy.[76] Ultimately, while the Summer Institute may have succeeded in provoking general awareness of significant multicultural issues among the alumni, it lacked the theoretical wherewithal necessary to help participants deal with unsettling issues or connect their cultural awareness to classroom teaching in ways that went beyond the mere assertion of identity.

The conflicts that emerged at the Institute reflected a particular time and place in American history. Ideas and social actions associated with multiculturalism swept through elite campuses in the late 1980s and early 1990s, and the newly minted graduates who joined TFA had often studied oppression, colonialism, and social activism in their academic coursework or joined campus movements driven by identity politics issues. Yet while in many cases their passions had been awakened, they still engaged these issues in the style of heated campus debate, without achieving a more constructive understanding of either themselves or what would be their new professional surroundings.

If the Institute's emphasis on multiculturalism aligned with the historical moment, it was misaligned with participants' life stage. As argued in Chapter 2, alumni would have come to the Institute during a significant transition in their developmental trajectory; in late 20th-century American society, the passage from adolescence to the early 20s marked a time of intense identity formation. Because they would have been in the throes of working out their adult identities, participants were vulnerable to the destabilizing effects of the Institute's unruly multicultural debates. Indeed, the way that participants recalled these particular Institute experiences, still with deep emotion and in vivid detail 20 years later, suggests the primacy of those experiences at that time in their lives. This phenomenon raises a larger question about the appropriateness of framing young graduates as an ideal pool of teacher candidates. In the opinion of Martin Haberman, a pioneering educator of teachers for underserved populations, "Those still engaged in the struggle to develop their own identities are the last people we should seek to place as teachers with children and youth who need confident, competent role models."[77]

More than participants' state of mind, however, the Institute staff was ill-equipped to handle the highly sensitive topics associated with multicultural training. But the alumni would not necessarily have fared better by way of traditional, university-based preparation. If, as the broad review undertaken by Grant and Secada claims, multicultural awareness represented a new dimension of teacher preparation in 1990, teacher educators' (including those who led Institute sessions) understanding of how to teach multicultural sensibilities was not very well developed. Research at the time indicated the challenge of diversity training in the context of pre-service education, particularly when such training was offered (as is still often the case) as a single, standalone course.[78] At a deeper level, some questioned the very feasibility of shifting individuals' cultural perceptions. Haberman, for instance, wondered whether appropriate cultural awareness can even be taught in a classroom. Answering his own question, Haberman argued that "The short answer is 'no,' if we define cultural awareness as one's sensitivity to issues of cultural diversity . . . and the commitment to educate in ways which will enhance human diversity and provide equal opportunity." Softening a little, he added that: "The longer answer is 'possibly,' if schools and colleges of education markedly change the ways in which they normally operate."[79]

TFA presented an opportunity to implement some of the changes that Haberman encouraged. But, at least insofar as the oral history testimonies indicate, it was largely a lost opportunity.

At the most basic level, the organized training provided at the Institute failed to help alumni link their theoretical or personal understandings about multiculturalism to the actual work of teaching. Even corps members such as Christina Brown, who came to the Institute with a sophisticated multicultural critique of society, had no idea how to bring her ideas to bear within the context of classroom teaching. Exercised effectively, multicultural considerations might have enriched participants' understanding not only of cultural concerns, but also of good pedagogy. Indeed, in the classroom, multicultural awareness serves as a foundation for culturally responsive teaching: a pedagogical approach that insists teachers know their students well and recognize the cultural wealth they possess. Such awareness, then, is fundamental to devising the kind of effective instruction in which teachers and students together construct meaning out of content. As advocates of culturally responsive teaching have argued, this kind of "collaborative, interactive model suggests . . . that curriculum and pedagogy [are] connected in direct and intentional ways with the lives of children," which, in turn, can lead to better learning outcomes.[80]

The TFA alumni we interviewed decried the Institute's efforts at raising their multicultural awareness not because such topics lacked relevance to actual classroom practice, but because they suspected it did matter, a good deal, and thus demanded more substantive treatment. As Mark Stephan characterized the gravity of the Institute conversations about multiculturalism, "It wasn't just a bunch of students . . . jabbering in a dorm lounge. It was now something that was going to impact what we did."[81] In other words, campus-style exploration suddenly became quite real. As the next chapter illuminates, the alumni's first-year experiences in the classroom filled in that reality and, in so doing, gave specific form to their criticisms of the Institute and the ways they believed it had shortchanged them.

CHAPTER 5

Ordeal by Fire

The 1990 Corps in the Classroom

"We were all, like, in hysterics every day, like, oh my God. It was very 'baptism by fire.'"

In August of 1990, following the Summer Institute, the TFA participants dispersed from Los Angeles to teaching placements in five different TFA sites: New York City, Los Angeles, New Orleans, and rural towns in North Carolina and Georgia. There they had to fend for themselves for the first time, finding housing, figuring out transportation and, in some cases, even securing their own teaching positions. Of course, on top of these new adult challenges, they also had to teach. Alumna Ellen Rosenstock called this experience a "baptism by fire,"[1] but this chapter, with its focus on participants' classroom experiences, is titled "Ordeal by Fire," because *baptism by fire* implies that participants got through a hellish experience and were saved in the end. Over the course of their initial year as TFA corps members, the participants interviewed described their trajectory from hope and idealism about teaching to concern and even despair about whether they could do the job to which they had committed themselves for 2 years. Although many of the participants we interviewed described becoming better teachers by their second year in the classroom, the majority did not leave their 2-year teaching stint feeling "saved." Instead, participants recalled feeling inadequate, exhausted, ashamed, and even traumatized as a result of their efforts to teach.

While our focus is on our participants' experiences, and not their students', it is important to note that these troubled first years of teaching are particularly significant when they occur in the context of economically disadvantaged schools and communities, such as those in which the alumni were placed. As scholar Lisa Delpit explains, children from privileged backgrounds can perform well despite poor teaching because of the resources they have outside of school, but "for children of poverty, good teachers and powerful instruction are imperative."[2] Unfortunately, students of the TFA cohort had to make do with teachers struggling to get through their first year of teaching.[3]

This chapter draws on participants' narratives to explore the teaching challenges that provoked their feelings of inadequacy, exhaustion, and traumatization. We consult scholarship on novice teachers and learning to teach to set the stage for and help explain the alumni's struggles, which included difficulties in assuming authority in the classroom, managing students, and helping them to learn, given the TFA alumni's limited knowledge of curriculum, instruction, and the social contexts of the schools in which they worked. As the testimonies illustrate, such issues were exacerbated by participants' high expectations for their own success, especially as those expectations were fed and shaped by the TFA recruitment process and Summer Institute. We trace the ways that many alumni responded to the obstacles they encountered and explore the fact that many seriously considered quitting. The decision to stay or leave was fraught; either staying and leaving could be construed as a statement of integrity, depending on the narrative. With the perspective of 20 years, many of those interviewed also had strong feelings and opinions about what might have helped them at the time, such as better preparation or in-service support from TFA. Much of the current research on how to support novice teachers underscores the validity of participants' beliefs.

In identifying and exploring corps members' memories of their initial classroom experiences, we arrive at key areas of criticism of TFA, including the program's truncated course of preparation before recruits assumed their own classrooms, its resolute reliance on "smart people" rather than on rigorous and deep preparatory experiences, and its focus on placing new teachers into the most difficult classroom environments. But in so doing, we also identify and acknowledge some of the challenges that are inherent in preparing all teachers to teach effectively in schools that serve poor or disenfranchised populations, problems that have dogged the enterprise of teacher education since long before TFA. These challenges include, for example, how to bolster teachers' capacities to work with culturally diverse communities or how to provide new teachers with the kind of ongoing support they need, especially if they are working in under-resourced or dysfunctional schools.[4]

"SURVIVAL AND DISCOVERY": THE BEGINNING TEACHER'S EXPERIENCE

In order to analyze the alumni's memories of first-year teaching, we begin by situating their experiences within the understanding that teaching is complex and that learning how to teach is a challenge. An abundant body of literature addresses the major transformations and associated struggles that teacher candidates confront in becoming "real" teachers. Contemporary scholars have conceptualized such struggles within a developmental process or career trajectory and identified important benchmarks that define that trajectory, such as the transition from simplistic perceptions of teaching (informed by novice teachers' experiences as students) toward a deeper understanding of what teaching actually is; the construction and assumption of a "teacher" identity; and the challenge new teachers face in negotiating the complexities of teaching.5 Such conceptualizations offer a useful heuristic for considering the plight of the first-year TFA participants. However, it should be noted that these constructs were not necessarily available at the time the alumni entered the classroom. An accounting of the literature at the time suggests that scholars had only recently begun to "systematically frame and study" the issue, so that "much of the work on teachers' knowledge and learning to teach was in an early, formative stage."6 More current research and robust conceptualizations of what is involved in crossing the divide between a novice and a competent teacher can help to make sense of the TFA alumni's experiences in the classroom.

New teachers—of any degree of preparation—often struggle during their first years in the classroom to master and exercise the knowledge, skills, and dispositions they need to teach well. Perhaps this should not be so surprising: Regardless of the field, starting a new career is a daunting process that demands the development of new competencies, behaviors, and attitudes, and the restructuring of identities.7 In Huberman's (1989) classic work on the career cycles of traditionally prepared teachers, he devised a taxonomy of what teachers can expect over the trajectory of their career. He christened the early career period of beginning to teach "Survival and Discovery," and described it as a stage marked by "reality-shock, especially for teachers with no prior teaching experience, in confronting the complexity and simultaneity of instructional management." According to Huberman, challenges of this phase include

> the preoccupation with self ("Am I up to this challenge?"), the gulf between professional ideals and the daily grind of classroom life, the fragmentation of tasks, the oscillation between intimacy and distance with one's pupils, the apparent inadequacy of instructional materials given the diversity of pupil characteristics—the list goes on.8

The early years of teaching have been described as "a time of intense learning . . . [and] intense loneliness."9 New teachers struggle to develop and exercise their professional identity and to adapt to the institutions where they teach, often without the benefit of the supports they need— manageable assignments and access to experienced mentors—and, in under-resourced schools, with the additional burden of larger classrooms, more difficult student populations, and fewer classroom resources.10

As Huberman's construct suggests, this progression occurs over time—some estimates suggest that it takes at least 5 to 7 years to cultivate the competencies needed to teach well. Even when novice teachers have been exposed to teaching tools and techniques, it takes a proficient teacher to actually deploy them organically and effectively. Likewise, where new teachers tend to focus primarily on themselves—that is, how they control the classroom—more competent teachers tend to "focus on student welfare and learning to drive their teaching decisions."[11] In the former case, new teachers may develop "techniques of teaching that 'work,' that . . . get teachers through the day," but such methods generally "do not result in high levels of learning for students." Interrupting this pattern, and moving teacher candidates toward student-driven teaching "appear[s] to be related to teachers' preparation," specifically, the provision of strong, purposeful learning experiences under the right circumstances.[12]

As new teachers, the TFA participants fit squarely into the novice stage, but without adequate preparation or support, they struggled to move beyond those techniques that got them through the day. And though their struggles echoed the anxieties of traditionally trained teachers that appear in the literature, the alumni had less to guide them than the traditionally trained teacher. Because their education and leadership experiences (rather than preparation or teaching experience) supposedly equipped them to teach, the TFA alumni did not have access to the basic theoretical and practical foundation that a good teacher preparation program might have provided.

CHALLENGES: AUTHORITY AND MANAGEMENT

The majority of our participants across the five placements admitted that teaching was much harder than they had ever expected. Participants described their struggles to develop a teacher identity and to become an authority in their own classroom as well as how classroom management problems disrupted their planned lessons. In their interviews, many participants reflected that their management issues may well have been connected to gaps in their understandings about teaching and learning.

A teacher's professional identity is shaped by the influence of professional contexts, "the teacher's own personal characteristics, learning history and prior experiences," and by teaching experience, as that teacher identity continues to evolve over time.[13] The process is also understood as dynamic and relational, situated in "one's biography, present circumstances, deep commitments, affective investments, social context, and conflicting discourses about what it means to learn to become a teacher."[14] A significant initial challenge for interviewees relating to the development of a "teacher identity" lay in what alumnus Spencer Downing called "the transformation from being the student to being the authority figure."[15] As professor Megan Trexler explains, the role of teacher requires one to develop authority, a process that poses a common obstacle for teachers of varying identities and teaching methodologies and one that may prove more difficult for those assuming positions of authority for the first time.[16] Trexler notes that pre-service experiences in classrooms have the potential to provide teacher candidates important opportunities to interact with children and other teachers; these experiences then offer grist for teacher candidates to examine their roles and negotiate authority in relation to students and their new identities as teachers.

At the outset of the 1990 school year, most corps members were 22 or 23 years old; some recalled looking—and even feeling—more like adolescents than adults. Ellen Rosenstock described her own internal confusion when, within the first weeks of school, the administration assigned a paraprofessional who was in her 50s to assist in Rosenstock's classroom:

> I remember being on the stairway [with] the class and the kids screaming, like screaming, as I was walking them . . . And she [the paraprofessional] screamed from behind the class and all the kids got quiet and she said, "Get in line." And she said it like that, like, "Get in line." And I myself got in line.[17]

Rosenstock "forgot that I was teacher for a moment" and had to remind herself, "That's right, I'm the teacher." Recruits generally found the work of taking charge and developing a "teacher identity" to be exhausting. As Mark Stephan said, "[T]hinking about establishing authority when I didn't know how to establish authority just taxed me, just knocked me down, knocked me down."[18] More in-depth student teaching experiences in K–12 classrooms prior to being the teacher of record, as Trexler notes, might have enabled these new teachers to think through their relations with teachers and students, perhaps even with the guidance of an informed mentor, and thus to become accustomed to what it meant to be "the teacher," what was appropriate, and what the pitfalls would likely be when these boundaries were not clear.

Classroom Management

A critical part of taking on a teacher identity and exercising authority, as participants discovered, was learning to *manage their classrooms*. Classroom management has long been a central concern of teacher candidates and new teachers.[19] And no wonder: Classroom management is crucial to teachers' early careers. If they are to engage students in substantive learning, teachers must be able to effectively manage their classrooms.[20] In urban settings, where students' diverse languages, experiences, ethnicities, religions, and abilities may differ from those of the teachers, anxieties around classroom management are often heightened. [21]

According to the novice TFA teachers, classroom management presented one of the greatest obstacles they encountered in their teaching. Many alumni recalled their naïve belief that, if they were "reasonable," their students would listen and respond favorably toward them. As Brent Lyles recalled, he "expected that I would get respect from my students automatically."[22] Lisa Robinson remembered initially "just trying to be logical and talk to [the students]," though she soon saw the folly of her thinking. By the end of the second week, she reported, there were "chairs thrown . . . Hair pulling, kids punching on each other, those kinds of things . . ."[23] Other interviewees offered explicit examples of how classroom management challenges interrupted their instruction. Bill Norbert recalled his annoyance at not being able to get through a carefully planned lesson. "I remember being frustrated that first year . . . [f]eeling like I had a lot that I wanted to offer . . . You know, I planned these lessons carefully and, basically, I found that the day didn't go exactly according to plan."[24] Lisa Robinson concurred, "We would make these lesson plans that were incredibly detailed with all these incredibly creative ways of teaching math or teaching whatever and, you know, they just [fell] apart."[25]

Both now and in the past, "classroom management" has been rather simplistically understood by many would-be teachers as "organizing classroom routines and dealing with misbehavior."[26] Indeed, many of the participants we interviewed struggled to understand classroom management beyond their role as authority figures or disciplinarians, and even in their assumption of authority.[27] For example, the novice TFA teachers did not know how to enact an authoritative stance conducive to a well-run classroom. Even if many alumni suspected a significant link between classroom management and good teaching, they had little guidance at the time in developing a fuller conception or practice of classroom management, such as that described by teacher education researchers LePage et al.:

> Classroom management encompasses many practices integral to teaching, such as developing relationships; structuring respectful classroom communities where students can work productively; organizing productive work around a meaningful curriculum; teaching moral development and citizenship; making decisions about timing and other aspects of instructional planning; successfully motivating children to learn; and encouraging parental involvement.[28]

Without that fuller understanding, many alumni continued to struggle for what they described as a basic level of control over the class.

The alumni did not begin teaching without some guidance, however. Prior to entering their own classrooms, the TFA participants had been introduced to a set of classroom management techniques at the Summer

Institute, by way of Lee and Marlene Canter's book, *Assertive Discipline*.[29] The book featured a behavior management technique, introduced in the mid-1970s, which argued that teachers could achieve positive behavior management by developing a three-part discipline plan consisting of (1) rules to be followed at all times; (2) positive support for students who follow those rules; and (3) corrective actions to be consistently implemented with students who choose not to follow the rules. The Canters' book continued to find a market years after the Summer Institute, though some education researchers consider it a "behaviorist" method, representative of rote conditioning that does not account for more complex explanations of behavior and learning, and have documented widespread criticism among educators themselves, who found the approach "damaging and ineffective."[30] Interestingly, few participants mentioned the book or its ideas in their testimonies.[31] Whether it did not conform to their beliefs about teaching or did not end up being useful in practice, *Assertive Discipline* did not seem to have been helpful in shaping participants' thinking about classroom management in ways that they were able to recall in their interviews. (The choice of that particular book, however, may imply something about teacher educators' beliefs at the time, or at least the beliefs of those who staffed the Summer Institute.)

TFA participants' experiences might be written off as a failure of TFA's style of preparation, except for the fact that traditional teacher education programs may not have served them much better. In the past, most teachers learned how to manage their classrooms on the job, because university-based teacher education has rarely included coursework on classroom management. A 2011 review suggested that fewer than half of college recommending teacher education programs required classroom management coursework; increasingly, however, it seems that high-quality teacher preparation programs are incorporating explicit attention to developing prospective teachers' understandings and practice of the elements that make up classroom management and are being encouraged to draw on research-based approaches to do so.[32] The lag in offering explicit instruction in classroom management may well be rooted in teacher educators' belief that strong pedagogical methods can ameliorate classroom management issues and that fundamentally strong teaching obviates the need for more superficial training in management techniques; it may also be that, in some programs, classroom management strategies are integrated into other coursework.

Management Within Difficult Conditions: School Culture

Our participants' efforts to manage their classrooms did not occur in a vacuum, but rather within school cultures, many of which modeled and prioritized a control and compliance ideal of "management." Some of our participants discussed the public humiliation of not being able to properly line up their students to walk down the halls of the school. Kathy Feeley, who left her placement after only 3 months, remembered spending "all day . . . lining them up to leave the cafeteria or something." On one occasion a student got her arm stuck in a banister, ". . . so I'm trying to deal with that and my entire class is going, like, hog wild around me and it was just . . . other teachers are kind of walking by and sort of like grinning a little bit, right, but nobody's really helping me." The principal finally freed the child's arm from the banister, but Feeley characterized the experience as "being the last straw" in her TFA career.[33] Likewise, Eric Bird described taking his class to the bathroom on the first day of school, focusing on how hard he tried to keep his students in line and quiet: "I remember the assistant principal walking by and I was saying, 'I am trying.' I just remember about crying right at that moment because I just felt like it was totally out of my control."[34]

Figuring out their own practices of classroom management also seemed especially challenging for some TFA participants because other educators at the schools could be heavy-handed with discipline. As Lisa Robinson remembered, "the teachers that seemed to have the greatest control over their classes were tyrannical."[35] At the time of his interview, Leo Flanagan was working as an elementary school principal. He attributed his failure of management in part to the methods of the other educators in the school: "The things that I saw people doing were so out of bounds of appropriateness that I could never have succeeded in that school." When he struggled to keep his 3rd-graders in line, he asked the children what a fellow teacher did to get them to behave so well. "The kids said, 'Oh, she would hit us.' She would tie three rulers together and just give the kids a whack if they misbehaved." Flanagan also recalled the building principal's particularly startling threat to a child: "I'll throw you down those motherfucking stairs and tell them you fell if you don't start behaving."[36] Tellingly, Flanagan said that, even now, after years of teaching and "being a very, very good teacher," he didn't think he could teach successfully if he were plunked down in that original TFA placement.

The level of physical control over the children in some of the schools, although generally not as violent as in Flanagan's description, seemed oppressive to alumni. Christina Brown described substituting for the physical education teacher in her New York City school and being told not to allow the children to run around or move. The administration set many restrictive rules to avoid "control issues," for example, limiting children's activity during their PE period to "walk[ing] slowly around."[37] Lisa Robinson remembered being mystified by all of the rules governing students' conduct, down to how students were supposed to walk in lines, and described an authority on the part of school faculty and administration that seemed "aggressive."[38] The fact that classrooms were enormously overcrowded made management that much more difficult. More than a few alumni had similar stories, all of which spoke to the schools' efforts to control children.

CHALLENGES: INTEGRATING INSTRUCTIONAL KNOWLEDGE

> Children in urban areas, like children everywhere in the world, do not come to schools with empty heads, devoid of ideas, knowledge, skills, experiences or dreams. Like other children, they engage in complex reasoning, have the ability to problem solve and use logic, and have no shortage of imagination or creativity.[39]

One of the great challenges of teaching is that it requires bringing together multiple kinds of knowledge in an integrated way in relationship to diverse groups of children.[40] Many of the alumni, upon reflection, connected their classroom management issues to gaps in their understandings about the broader processes of teaching and learning. Without knowing how to set up routines and classroom rules, develop and implement a strong academic plan, effectively use knowledge of child development, draw on the strengths of the students' home experiences, or appreciate the challenges arising from students' lives outside of school, corps members had few means of understanding or handling the management issues they faced. For example, one shared misconception lay in participants' insufficient appreciation for the importance of setting up effective learning environments and routines during the initial weeks of school. Research suggests that well-organized classroom structures, procedures, and routines ensure that students understand their roles in the classroom and what is expected of them, which together have the potential to quell management issues and provide space for purposeful instruction.[41] This would have been a routine topic of most teacher education programs; it would also have been modeled in many of the TFA recruits' student teaching placements. But it was something that participants tended to value only after they had attempted to preside over their own classes. Scott Joftus, for instance, estimated that 90% of his management problems had to do with the fact that he "didn't have the right sort of structures and system in the classroom."[42] Furman Brown recalled that he did not recognize at the time how important it was to be "really organized on all kinds of levels." [43]

Consistency and Predictability in the Classroom

Creating clear classroom rules and applying consequences uniformly for breaking those rules is a vital element to setting up a viably functioning classroom.[44] Through trial and error, some corps members learned the value of consistency in their interactions with students, but it was a consistency that differed from the behavioral, public, and sometimes humiliating *Assertive Discipline* method. As Spencer Downing explained, "You know, be consistent about making people remove their gum from their mouths; these kind of little things that creates [*sic*] a sense of order and discipline in your room."[45]

Forms of Organization, Planning, and Assessment

Beyond the parameters of setting up their classrooms to maximize instructional possibilities, these new TFA teachers possessed scant understanding about the basics of teaching and learning, pedagogy, and curriculum. They didn't know how to develop lesson plans, create units of study, or assess their students' learning. Eric Bird said that he understood the message at the Summer Institute that, "having kids sit in their desks, filling out worksheet pages was not a good way to teach kids." But he wasn't sure what *was* an appropriate experience. Bird explained, "[U]nfortunately, for me, while I agreed with [a policy of no worksheets] and I tried to stay away from worksheet pages, I didn't have anything to fill it in with."[46] The overarching plans and learning objectives that went missing in many of these corps members' classrooms, in turn, contributed to their failures to discipline the classroom. Constance Bond explains:

> I did not have an academic plan. They [my students] basically knew it and to them it was just a free-for-all. So it was behavioral problems that were killing me, but now I know it was because I had nothing. I was not going in prepared . . . for them to learn. They just were running me into the ground and they knew how to do it.

Bond said at the time she was "asking anybody for classroom management strategies, which, of course, are all empty because . . . [i]t's not about 'managing' them."[47]

Bond later came to understand that a strong instructional plan would have alleviated many of her management issues. Teacher educator scholar Karen Hammerness supports Bond's realization when she writes that "Classrooms function best not only when students are well-behaved and have activities consistently available to them, but also when students are involved in intellectual work that they find interesting and challenging."[48]

As their descriptions suggest, corps members had not mastered a general understanding of effective instructional methods that might have helped them to make schoolwork accessible to the students. Nor did they have at their disposal more specific strategies for teaching very particular skills, such as reading. Learning to read is not necessarily a natural process and teaching students to read represents a complex endeavor that, in the best cases, draws on deep knowledge of literacy and a broad repertoire of instructional strategies. Christina Brown remembered being stymied because she had no pedagogical knowledge for teaching children to read: "I didn't know anything about teaching kids how to read. I literally knew how to read and loved to read but that has nothing to do with teaching it."[49] Though Brown quit her commitment with TFA after the first year of the program, she later earned a master's in literacy education, perhaps a testimony to her frustration. Likewise, Jennifer Denino felt uncomfortable teaching children to read because she felt she was "making things up as I was going along," which was why she too decided to go to graduate school in education after her 2 years with TFA.She recalled saying to herself, "'I just screwed a bunch of kids . . . Like, I can teach the math . . . I was really comfortable teaching math, and science, and stuff like that, but it was like the reading part that I was like, 'I am doing a disservice here. I don't know what the hell I'm doing.'"[50]

Dealing with Academic Variation

Some corps members recalled not knowing how to handle the many different academic levels in the classroom, something contemporary teacher educators refer to as "differentiation." Avis Terrell discussed the challenge of teaching new immigrants who were learning English at the same time they were expected to learn the same content as the rest of the class.[51] Felicia Clark was shocked by the vast differences of ability in her classroom: "I had two languages, and two grade levels in one classroom, and very limited resources. Just all of that, I hadn't ever experienced a school like that."[52] At the time of her oral history interview in 2009, Lori Lawson was still unclear about exactly how teachers are supposed to know to what level to aim their teaching: "Do you teach to the lowest common denominator and how in the world do you figure out what that is? How do you really assess to what level you're supposed to be teaching?" She did not recall learning anything about how to address differences in students' abilities and achievement levels during the Summer Institute.[53]

In the mid-1980s, discussions about how to meet students' different educational needs, beyond simply "tracking" them into homogeneous classes (an approach criticized for exacerbating inequalities) had begun to stir in the field of education.[54] These discussions took off in the 1990s, in large part as a result of increasing diversity within the student population, buoyed by the mainstreaming of special education students and growth in numbers of English language learners. By the early 1990s, teachers were encouraged to present material in ways that varied according to students' learning styles, which might be auditory, visual, or kinesthetic, for example.[55] Because the first-year TFA participants we interviewed were missing knowledge—about setting up the classroom, teaching reading, and supporting bilingual learners, for instance—that was central to teaching, they were unable to support the diversity of student abilities, learning styles, and experiences that they encountered in their classrooms.

STRUGGLING WITH THE SOCIAL CONTEXT

Difficult Environments

By design, TFA placed corps members in some of the most difficult teaching environments in the nation. At the close of the corps' first teaching year, the *New York Times* published an article taking stock of their experiences. Reporter Susan Chira wrote that, despite some success stories, many participants "spoke of anguish and frustration" as they confronted the "realities of difficult classrooms and the blighted neighborhoods around them."[56] Our oral histories reveal in painful detail the struggles that participants faced both in the classroom and communities where they worked. Participants taught in schools that were located in economically disadvantaged neighborhoods and communities, places where children frequently have "unmet needs for adequate housing, health care, nutrition, and even safety."[57] Consequently, the larger social context of participants' classrooms intensified the challenges of first-year teaching, particularly since alumni received little in the way of useful training to prepare them and so few corps members had experience working in such communities.

Participants shared memories of working with students whose most basic needs were frequently unmet, including some who were homeless and hungry. They remembered specific instances when they did not know how to work with children who had been abused, had a parent in jail, or, for example, had stolen something from the classroom. Brent Lyles, whose school was located near a military base during the Gulf War, taught students whose brothers and sisters were fighting in the Persian Gulf and who, in turn, feared that bombs would be dropped in North Carolina. In his interview, Lyles recollected not knowing how to quell his students' anxiety and, as a result, feeling unprepared to meet students' emotional needs.[58]

Given the crack epidemic that raged in many low-income urban communities in 1990, more than a few alumni told of crack vials that littered sidewalks or playgrounds at their schools. Lori Lawson, who remembered bullet holes in her classroom windows, recalled being told not to go outside the schoolyard after 11:00 a.m. because "that's when all the drug dealers wake up in the neighborhood."[59] Caroline Sabin recounted finding a bullet casing on the floor of her classroom; she also shared the plight of a fellow participant assigned to a school in Compton, California, who struggled to teach over the sound of police helicopters hovering overhead.[60] Lyles remembered arriving some mornings at the "very urban school" where he student-taught 4th-graders in East Los Angeles to find that "the whole school had been trashed by gangs; graffiti everywhere, broken windows." Despite the fact that "gang kids [had] gotten into the classrooms and torn shit up," he reminisced, "you just had to go in and do your best teaching."[61] The violence, drugs, and distress of poverty in the economically disadvantaged environments that were home to the schools in which our participants taught created stressful experiences for families and children that influenced the classrooms and generated issues that the alumni did not know how to address.

Preparing new teachers to work in schools serving low-income communities represents a very particular set of challenges. Since at least the early 1960s, researchers have documented the ways in which schools serving so-called disadvantaged students present different conditions and difficulties than typical middle-class or suburban schools; such observations led to calls for specialized preparation of those teachers who plan to teach in urban schools.[62] Consequently, over the last 30 years, many teacher preparation programs have incorporated either discrete urban-facing programs or infused across existing programs efforts to deepen their candidates' knowledge of the student diversities typically found in low socioeconomic areas. More recent iterations of these efforts include coursework on multiculturalism, culturally relevant pedagogy, and funds of knowledge; fieldwork in urban school settings; and community-based learning experiences, all of which are meant to develop candidates' abilities to address a variety of student needs.[63] Despite such programmatic changes, however, "concerns still remain about transforming programs and practices in order to affect teachers' capacities to work with culturally diverse communities."[64] The difficulty of preparing new teachers to teach in schools that serve low socioeconomic communities, the conditions of those schools, and the high rates of teacher turnover present serious issues, especially when coupled with the need of the children in such schools for excellent teaching.

The TFA participants' descriptions of the communities in which they taught align with reports at the time, such as Jonathan Kozol's portrayal of overcrowded and understaffed schools in poor communities that appeared in his book *Savage Inequalities*.[65] Kozol bore down on the ways in which communities' fundamental socioeconomic struggles manifested in schools, through a lack of funds and resources, poor leadership, and ineffective institutional practices, many of which emerged in the alumni's recollections.[66] For example, alumni referred to the dearth of textbooks in their schools, to overcrowded classrooms without enough furniture to accommodate the students, and to the transience of children, who moved in and out of the neighborhood so often that it was difficult to keep track of who was in the classroom. They recalled the poor physical condition of their buildings. Jeffrey Simes taught in an elementary school in Bedford-Stuyvesant, Brooklyn, named after Ronald E. McNair, "one of the astronauts who blew up in the Challenger," which Simes sardonically suggested was "actually kind of a fitting metaphor for the whole school."[67] The top floor of the four-story building couldn't be used, because the roof leaked so badly; Simes's own classroom had a "horrible vermin problem . . . [with] roaches everywhere all the time," along with a sink that continuously dripped hot steamy water and never got fixed. As Arthur Schuhart depicted his school: "It looked like Berlin, 1945. Desolation. It was desolation."[68] Between the struggles associated with the schools' communities and, often, the lack of resources or leadership at the schools themselves for dealing with the challenges that students brought to school with them, corps members recalled feeling overwhelmed at the magnitude of the task they had undertaken. In turn, this overload made it difficult for the alumni to appreciate the strengths and funds of knowledge that did exist in those communities.

High Ideals, High Expectations

Although the first cohort of TFA participants faced many of the same difficulties as most beginning teachers, particularly teachers working in low socioeconomic communities, the high expectations that accompanied TFA members into the classroom compounded their challenges. From its inception, the TFA organization championed the notion that recent graduates from top colleges and universities could solve problems deeply rooted in the educational and social systems of the nation. When presenting TFA to college seniors in 1989, Wendy Kopp framed the program as an opportunity for recent college graduates "to address the inequities in our country" with hard work. As she wrote, "They would throw themselves into their jobs, working investment-banking hours in classrooms instead of skyscrapers on Wall Street. They would question the ways things are and fight to do what was right for children."[69] Kopp's articulation of her vision implies that traditionally trained teachers who were already in classrooms didn't work "investment-banking hours" and didn't "fight to do what was right for children." Additionally, she seemed to suggest that the new TFA recruits would bring something special and exclusive to the table—their idealism, their elite education, their talents—to replace "the ways things are." However, beyond the Wall Street work ethic that Kopp assumed to be characteristic of the graduates of prestigious colleges, it is unclear that the idealism, elite education, and leadership experiences of recent college graduates who lacked any background in education could radically improve the status quo of American urban education.

Nevertheless, the combination of their background characteristics and their willingness to work hard implied, for Kopp and for the TFA pioneers, an extraordinary potential to effect change. These unrealistic expectations set the group up for the feelings of inadequacy that suffused their testimonies.

The first-year TFA recruits entered teaching pumped up by the media's coverage of them as the "best and the brightest" and by the messages they read in their recruitment letters, which asked them to "give something back to America" and promised them that their smarts would allow them to fix the "dilapidated" education system.[70] Many of the 22- and 23-year-old recruits got the message that participating in TFA was something they could do to fulfill their social responsibility as privileged members of society. Yet the experience turned out to be quite different.

ALUMNI RESPONSES TO CHALLENGES

Feelings of Inadequacy

Many of our participants encountered a serious disconnect between the idealism that TFA used to recruit them, on the one hand, and their day-to-day experience in their classrooms, on the other. They had been celebrated in a variety of forums as the best and the brightest and yet they could not get through a lesson plan. For some, the failure to accomplish what they had imagined themselves doing provoked great disappointment. Jane Schneider described her idea of teaching before she entered the classroom as a "fantasy of going in and being, you know . . . sort of ultra-competent and ultra-kind." In the end, she said, "it was a very naïve, young, idealistic picture."[71] Failing even to come close to accomplishing the original fantasy was particularly challenging for individuals like Schneider, a recent Harvard graduate, who was not used to falling short of expectations. Lori Lawson, who quit during her first year, remembered confronting her limits, thinking, "my best is not good enough for this group of kids."[72]

Other participants indicated their surprise when they realized that fixing a "dilapidated education system," as their recruiting letter had said, was not going to be so easy, or even possible. Ellen Rosenstock recalled thinking that if more people in power knew how bad it was in the schools, they would help resolve the situation: "I remember feeling like if only . . . the first George Bush [President George H.W. Bush, who was president at the time] . . . if only he could see, or if [First Lady] Barbara [Bush] who was so into reading, if only they could come into my classroom, or I could get Oprah into my classroom, nobody would let this happen."[73] Christina Brown noted, "I just didn't realize how horrible it could be and how much kids could suffer in school. So it was definitely like the whole Save-the-Children, Save-the-World thing . . . you couldn't sustain that kind of idealism in that environment."[74] In the end, Jeffrey Simes said, the experience made him more mature and tempered his idealism. He explained, "You go in there thinking . . . [that] goodwill will change the world, and you leave realizing that that's necessary but not sufficient . . . that's a valuable lesson."[75]

Anxious and Exhausted

As a result of the alumni's teaching struggles, many of our participants described feeling extremely tired or anxious within the first few months of teaching. Preparing lessons at night and then working to engage their students all day, day after day, left many participants exhausted. Kathy Feeley said that she was too embarrassed about the problems she was having in the classroom to ask her brother and sister, both teachers, for advice and help. Instead, she dealt with the stress by smoking cigarettes and skipping meals. The alumni were astonished by their students' energy, especially in comparison to their own fatigue.[76] In Bill Norbert's recollection, "I just remember being, like, tired from talking and hoarse from, like, raising my voice."[77] Scott Joftus added, "My throat was just always really sore. I was often discouraged. I knew I was doing a terrible job. I actually at one point in the spring said, 'I don't think I'm doing anyone any good.'"[78] Mark Stephan remembered feeling like "kind of a zombie" by the end of his first week of teaching.[79]

Such feelings of anxiety in the initial years of teaching are hardly unique to these TFA corps members. Teachers who enter teaching through more traditional routes can also experience what Huberman calls "painful beginnings." Traditionally trained teachers in Huberman's study described "role overload and anxiety, difficult pupils, heavy time investment, close monitoring by teacher education staff and isolation inside the school."[80] In many respects, the disorientation, frustration, and challenges faced by TFA recruits mirrored what many traditionally trained teachers also experience. Yet the latter group of teachers, by virtue of their more conventional training sequence, would likely have been introduced to a range of coursework and experiences over time in schools (such as fieldwork and student teaching) that would have at least exposed them to the realities of teaching and possibly even given them a rudimentary repertoire of skills that the TFA recruits had not developed in their 8-week Summer Institute, which included just 5 weeks of half-day student teaching. Perhaps the 1990 corps members felt failures more acutely precisely because they had been touted as the best and the brightest and were, by the logic of the program, supposed to be able to succeed, especially given the belief that "smart" people could "pick up" teaching on the fly.

Torn About Continuing or Quitting

The teaching experience was so difficult and demoralizing for participants that many of those we interviewed considered quitting teaching during their first year. Plenty of interviewees remembered having friends who left the program during the first year. Some participants recalled the TFA organization trying to convince the corps members not to quit the program during its inaugural year. Lori Lawson said that, after she decided to leave, a representative from TFA spoke to her roommate, also a corps member, about the importance of remaining in the program.[81] Scott Joftus explained that he also discussed his thoughts about quitting with someone from the organization: "I felt . . . miserable and all that stuff . . . they just convinced me to stick it out. And honestly it wouldn't have taken that much [to convince me to stay] because of that guilt of not wanting to quit."[82] Some, like Mark Stephan, who eventually quit the program, felt pressure from the organization: "They didn't want TFAers leaving, you know . . . They needed us to stick it out so they [could] continue as a program. So there was some pressure of, you know, you really need to make this work and do everything you can."[83]

The participants we interviewed who did quit (see Appendix A), like Stephan, described being so unhappy that they could not conceive of an alternative to leaving. Stephan recollected having panic attacks, seeing a counselor, and barely being able to get himself to school. His friends and family reassured him that it would be okay if he quit the program. Stephan said the 3 months he spent teaching in North Carolina with TFA "was one of the more traumatic periods of my entire life."[84] As Kathy Feeley recalled, "It was so bad that I was *forced* to quit."[85] And though Jane Schneider felt like a "bad person," she believed that she "had sort of gotten to a place of pain where I just, I needed to leave."[86] Finally, as Lori Lawson recollected, "I just could not bear going in another day and it was hard to decide . . . I did feel a real deep dedication to trying to help those kids, but I also felt that it was not, I was not doing them any great service."[87]

Deciding whether to quit the program was complicated. Most of those we interviewed who did not leave during their 2-year commitment said that the reason they did not quit was because of their sense of commitment: to the organization, the school in which they were teaching, or the children in their classrooms. Marife Ramos said that she didn't quit because of both a sense of commitment to the middle school children she taught, and "the commitment I made to Teach For America and if I let Teach For America down then I let my school down."[88] Bill Norbert said simply he didn't quit because "I'm not a quitter."[89] Of course, not being a "quitter" would have been familiar territory for the recruits, many of whom had been rewarded in their lives for their hard work and perseverance. Accordingly, the TFA organization presented the choice to remain in the program as the ethical decision, precisely because corps members who remained would not be abandoning the schools or their students.

But for some participants, staying in the program began to seem like an unethical decision. For instance, though Eric Bird fulfilled his 2-year commitment, he regretted not quitting: "I should have quit that very first day and, to this day, I believe that." He said that he "thought about it [quitting] all the time" and now thinks that leaving would have been the right choice. "What would I have done if I would have quit? I probably would have gotten my master's in education and pursued being a teacher that way."[90] Together, these accounts underscore the inanity of expecting the unprepared recruits, no matter how "bright," to function successfully in the circumstances in which they found themselves, much less to fix a "dilapidated education system" as the recruitment letter advertised.[91]

CONCLUSION

Contrary to popular belief, learning to teach well is a tremendous challenge, and the circumstances of the 1990 TFA cohort made it even more arduous. We considered participants' difficulties under the auspices of their efforts to assume authority in the classroom, manage students, and actually support student learning, a tall order given how little the alumna understood about fundamental aspects of instruction, schools, or high-poverty communities. And all of publicity and pressure for success only intensified these challenges for the interviewees. Perhaps the most salient issues to emerge from the oral histories included the lack of adequate preparation before and support for corps members during their teaching and, closely aligned with that, participants' recognition that their attributes and elite education were not an adequate counterweight for their lack of preparation. They also found themselves sorely ill-equipped to deal with the context of the communities and conditions in the schools where they taught. All of these issues not only had a powerful bearing on participants and their subsequent professional choices; they also have significant policy correlates, which we take up again in Chapter 7 in our assessment of the legacy of TFA, and have animated many of the battles over university-based teacher education, which we address in the next chapter.

CHAPTER 6

University-Based Teacher Educators in the Crosshairs

Responding to TFA and the New Reforms

TFA was just one of many challenges to the educational status quo that roiled the field beginning in the 1980s; together, those challenges and the critiques they represented galvanized a range of responses on the part of teacher educators. This chapter takes a close look at the ways traditional teacher educators have, since the 1980s, sought to assert the credibility of their work against a broad and varied chorus of naysayers, leading to a fertile, if contested, period of change in teacher education. Between mid-century and the 1980s, teacher educators were able to withstand the drumbeat of criticism, more or less conducting business as usual. But beginning in the 1980s, a confluence of factors threatened university-based teacher educators' control over their field. Primary among such factors were so-called alternate routes: essentially programs where preparation occurred on the job rather than, as in the model of university-based programs, before assuming a position as teacher of record.

Teacher educators answered their critics in different ways. Some, pointing to the many obstacles that make preparing teachers difficult, essentially "circled the wagons," defending the status quo of university-based teacher preparation. Others, acknowledging some validity to the critiques, looked to improve teacher education through a variety of avenues, including efforts to shore up the professionalism of teaching, deepen the context of practice, and increase requirements for entering and exiting teacher preparation programs. Still others sought to marshal proof of teacher educators' effectiveness, developing lines of research to identify and assess how teacher educators make a difference in the teachers they produce. This last approach has intersected with a larger agenda of accountability, advocated by both internal and external sources, as well as the right and the left, which has increasingly informed education writ large over the last 3 decades. And yet another response on the part of university-based teacher educators has been to join forces with or at least provide preparation credits and courses for the very alternate pathways (and even providers) that have sprung up to challenge traditional university-based teacher preparation.

Before investigating these responses in detail, this chapter first casts a brief look back, situating the current moment within a longer arc of history, so as to understand more clearly just how teacher educators got to this point and why they have come under fire. We examine the kinds of criticisms that have dogged teacher education over time and see how, in the 1980s, criticism crossed the line from rhetoric and reports to the development of competing pathways to the classroom. On that foundation, the chapter then builds a case for the impact of the 1980s reforms on the larger endeavor of teacher preparation and also identifies the persistent constraints that have made deep and abiding improvement in the preparation of teachers elusive.

MIDCENTURY CONSOLIDATION AND NEW CHALLENGES

As surprising as it may seem today, teacher qualifications have not always depended upon formal education. It wasn't until the mid-20th century that formal teacher education became firmly established within colleges and universities in the way we recognize today.[1] Before the advent of professional preparation, when the job of teaching required no specialized training, teachers were often hired as much for their character and religious devotion as their knowledge of content and pedagogy.[2] Formal preparation began to emerge in the early 19th century, within a hodgepodge of institutional contexts, initially including female seminaries, teachers' institutes, and normal schools and, from the late 19th into the mid-20th century, teachers colleges, state colleges, and a gamut of university settings. Though these types of institutions would eventually sort themselves into a pecking order, it is worth noting the incredible institutional variation that characterized teacher preparation well into the 20th century.

The 19th century bequeathed another enduring influence on teacher education: the feminization of teaching. As historian Nancy Hoffman writes, "By the end of the 19th century, the profession of teaching had moved to the position that it would hold for the next century and beyond: less than equal in status to male professions, and a source of satisfaction and power for women."[3] The accessibility of teaching as a "semi" profession also presented an opportunity to members of other social groups— the working class, immigrants, and, later, African Americans—effectively barred from higher-status professions. These gender, class, and race characteristics led to a view of teaching as "second-rate" and powerfully shaped the status and nature of the evolving profession and its training.[4]

Postwar Consolidation of Teacher Education

By the early 1960s, the variety of teacher training institutions associated with the 19th and early 20th centuries had all but disappeared in favor of general college- and university-based schools and departments of education; during the same period, states had raised certification standards, requiring a bachelor's degree as a matter of course and adding hours and requisite coursework to preparation programs.[5] But just when things seemed to be settled—"when the nation had moved to require a college degree of every future teacher and when the programs that offered these degrees had been consolidated into one basic form"—critics attacked.[6]

The postwar baby boom renewed the nation's focus on matters of schooling and, in revealing the purported shortcomings of K–12 education, heightened scrutiny of teacher preparation as well.[7] But teacher preparation was never an easy fit within multipurpose colleges and universities. For one thing, the university did not seem to share the same needs and concerns as K–12 schools. As a result, educational study was increasingly isolated from practice and, at the same time, cut off from other branches of scholarship within the university.[8] The kind of practical, vocational learning associated with older institutional models of teacher preparation stacked up poorly in a university environment that privileged abstract and theoretical knowledge. And the absence of a clear and viable knowledge base for training teachers meant not only that teacher education programs lacked currency within the university structure, but that they had little evidence for the effectiveness of their approach.[9] These general complaints, along with other familiar criticisms—low standards and lack of rigor, the preponderance of boring and easy pedagogy courses (protected by state requirements) at the expense of liberal arts study, the "inferior intellectual quality" of teacher educators, and too little opportunity in K–12 school classrooms to practice teaching real students—persisted over decades.[10]

Some criticisms reflected the social preoccupations of particular historical moments. Much of the conflict in the 1950s and early 1960s revolved around the academic shortcomings of teacher education. The 1957 launch of Sputnik reoriented the national dialogue about education away from alleged progressive extremes of the 1940s toward a focus on academic excellence; in this scenario, teacher educators were characterized as misguided anti-intellectuals responsible for undermining academic rigor in the schools.[11] Critics, including arts and sciences faculty (few of whom could be bothered to participate in what they considered the pedestrian job of preparing public school teachers), derided education classes as "puerile."[12] Many such detractors proposed eliminating mandated pedagogy courses altogether in favor of a solid liberal arts education plus practice teaching.[13] In response to such critiques, the Ford Foundation put money behind a series of 5th-year programs at select colleges and universities.[14] Designed to lead from the top, these Breakthrough programs were established in elite institutions of higher education, with a concerted focus on attracting academically talented candidates (who had completed 4 years of liberal arts study) into teaching. Thirty years later, TFA would capitalize on many of the assumptions that underwrote the Breakthrough programs, including the belief that selecting academically elite candidates would obviate the need for serious or ongoing pedagogical training.

1960s–1970s: Focus on Teaching "Disadvantaged" Students

Another set of concerns moving into the 1960s and 1970s, however, targeted the inability of teachers produced by typical university-based programs to effectively teach so-called disadvantaged students. In 1964, the President's Panel on Education Research and Development concluded dismally that "the majority of urban and rural slum schools are failures"; the Dean of Fordham University's School of Education in New York City suggested that the problems of urban education would simply go unresolved "until the schools get an adequate supply of skilled and understanding teachers."[15] As one critic pointed out, however, the "pedagogic tasks which confront the teachers in the slum schools are far more difficult than those which their colleagues in the wealthy suburbs face."[16] A novice teacher concurred, begging, "please to God, if you are going to send . . . [new teachers] into urban schools, prepare them a bit better than I was prepared."[17] Complaints also came from the suffering, underserved communities themselves. Buoyed by the civil rights movement, community control initiatives of the 1960s and 1970s arose to protest the poor quality of education provided to children of color by predominantly white teachers, repudiating both the teachers and the system that produced them and demanding a more diverse teacher pipeline and population that could teach a diverse curriculum.

Pressure to prepare teachers specifically for urban schools—the popular euphemism for schools serving poor and minority populations—in the 1960s resulted in dedicated programs and summer institutes at a handful of universities, including Hunter College, Syracuse University, and Antioch University; other experiments took hold under the auspices of the Council of Great Cities, for example, while professional associations and journals devoted meetings and special issues to the subject of how to better prepare teachers for urban schools.[18] Distinctive training and approaches included, for instance, sensitizing teacher candidates to the culture of their students, developing special instructional methods and materials designed for the particular needs and backgrounds of such students, and assigning prospective teachers to urban schools for practice teaching; there was also discussion of using non-professionals from the community in the classroom, as well as creating school–community liaisons.[19] While these experiments failed to catch on widely in universities at the time, many of the ideas formed a seedbed for awareness and forms of multiculturalism or culturally responsive teaching that appear in university-based teacher education programs today. As we have seen, the first Summer Institute training for TFA revolved largely around the subject of multicultural sensitivities, endorsing cultural responsiveness as a central tenet of urban teaching.

The 1960s emphasis on producing teachers specifically for underserved schools also brought about the Great Society's National Teacher Corps (NTC) program in 1965. Trading on the image of the Peace Corps, the NTC was a federally supported program designed to recruit social reform–minded, liberal arts graduates into teaching at schools in poor communities and to spur the development at universities of the kind of specialized teacher education courses and experiences described above, so as to prepare Corps members to meet the needs of their "disadvantaged" students.[20] Much of this will seem familiar: Teach For America borrowed liberally from the design of the National Teacher Corps, from its packaging of teaching as social reform to its targeted recruitment pool of high-achieving college graduates who wouldn't otherwise have gone into teaching. But important distinctions separate the two programs as well. The NTC engaged universities as partners, with the explicit aim of making university-based teacher education more relevant and effective. TFA, on the other hand, largely ignored university-based teacher preparation, doubling down on the idea that training mattered less than the quality of the recruits. And in a telling contrast of time periods, where the 1960s NTC was a government-sponsored program, the 1980s TFA operated as an autonomous nonprofit organization, funded by corporate and philanthropic gifts. Much as the 1960s context shaped the nature of the National Teacher Corps, so the historical moment of the 1980s influenced the development and operation of TFA. In spite of their similar missions, each belongs squarely to its time.

Despite the vociferous piling on, criticism of and attempts to reform teacher education between the 1950s and 1980s did little to fundamentally change the enterprise.[21] The Ford-funded 5th-year MAT programs were planted in a tiny minority of elite institutions in the late 1950s, with negligible effects on the larger field of preparation. Efforts to prepare teachers specifically for "disadvantaged" children resulted in only a smattering of specialized so-called urban programs, and the competency-based teaching efforts of the 1970s, which attempted to define and teach discrete teaching skills, were sparsely implemented.[22] To be sure, the 5-year MAT model (a 4-year liberal arts course of study followed by a 5-year of professional coursework), the importance of an internship or residency in a school classroom, closer university–school partnerships, deeper understanding of school and community contexts, and the participation of liberal arts faculty in teacher education—all ideas that arose in response to complaints during this period—persist as ideals for teacher education today, recognized in theory if not always in practice. Ultimately, however, the denunciations of teacher education between the 1950s and 1980s achieved only limited change.

THE 1980S: UNLEASHING CHANGE

By the 1980s, however, change was afoot. The shifting political and cultural values of the era led to new approaches to old dissatisfactions with teachers and their preparation. Capitalizing on antibureaucratic and entrepreneurial impulses and mimicking trends in the larger society, reformers in the 1980s embraced the nascent neoliberal critique of education, ramping up the narrative of failure around teacher education, carving out alternate pathways to the classroom, and devising ways around existing bureaucratic impediments.[23] For the first time in 30 years, university-based teacher educators and their programs found themselves not just on the defensive, but actually encountering significant competition in their authority over the production of teachers. Though the new alternate pathways initially served only a tiny minority of teacher candidates, they represented the possibility of breaking with the status quo and, as a result, commanded both attention and resources.

In the spring of 1983, an insider to California's teacher education and licensing committees and *Education Digest* editor named Alan Jones predicted that the 1980s would be a "watershed decade for teacher education in the United States."[24] Little did he know how right he would be. In his prediction, Jones articulated several critical concerns of the time regarding teacher education that read like a roll call of greatest hits. First, he noted the challenges of supply and demand, wondering how an adequate supply of "qualified and committed candidates" could be attracted into the field and trained to meet coming demands. He probed the issue of teacher candidate "quality," weighing the call to raise teacher education program standards against the need for flexible standards that would allow for a wide array of candidates, including minority applicants. Jones further recognized the difficulty of meaningfully connecting university-based teacher education to the needs of the schools, and he conceded the problematic role of education faculty, unloved on their own campuses and uncertain about the role they ought to play in "giving leadership" to the larger field. Finally, he pointed out teacher education's resource problem. In a climate of scarcity, what level of support existed for teacher education and what level of resources would "allow teacher education programs to function in a quality manner"? Ultimately, Jones figured that such problems would only be solved if the public could be made aware of the magnitude and complexity of the issues, and thereby persuaded to support a "large-scale redirection of public resources" toward higher teacher salaries that would, in turn, justify investment in high-quality teacher preparation. "[W]ill the public," Jones asked, "value education as a staple of the American way of life, and value it adequately to make teachers' salaries and teacher preparation programs competitive with other professional careers"?

It would be hard to imagine Jones's commentary appearing any later than it did, or the decade being more of a "watershed" for teacher education, given the explosive release of A Nation at Risk at the very same time. Many of Jones's concerns and his call for public attention showed up in A Nation at Risk and the many other reports that followed, though such reports failed to garner the investment and supports that Jones had envisioned. Instead, as presented in Chapter 1, A Nation at Risk and the reports it unleashed sounded an alarm that, in the fears stirred, set the course for a particular set of reforms, reflective of the era's values. One of the report's most powerful effects was its influence on public attitudes toward K–12 education, in which it established a narrative of failure around teachers and their preparation.

As discussed in Chapter 1, reforms of the period tended to follow one of two conflicting trajectories: either ratcheting up standards and regulations to ensure higher quality or, on the other hand, working to strip down the bureaucratic barriers presented by the web of regulations and requirements, making room instead for entrepreneurial and market-based solutions. These polarized approaches have come to define the contemporary debate about teacher education in terms that have pitted the university-based model where "all of the initial teacher preparation is completed before individuals assume full responsibility for a classroom," against "early entry" or alternate route programs, in which teachers essentially learn on the job.[25] Critics have derided the university-based model, which typically provides a combination of courses and field experiences culminating in student teaching, as hidebound, ineffective, too theoretical, and lacking requisite "brass-tacks classroom experience"; in contrast, they have framed the nontraditional "early entry" programs as an innovative, "desirable and inevitable replacement" for the university-based model.[26]

Starkly pitting one design against the other, however, elides important particularities. For example, not all alternate pathways are created equal and, as many teacher educators themselves would admit, existing university-based programs exhibit wide variation in quality.[27] Nor does all teacher learning rely solely on the specific pathway of entry. Some research suggests that the preparation program may matter less to teacher learning than that first job.[28] And, finally, many alternate pathways draw on university-provided coursework to enable their candidates to become certified. Despite such nuances, however, debate in the field has tended to coalesce around differences in the two preparation designs as a critical inflection point for the field. Teacher education scholar Ken Zeichner has framed this debate about how and where to prepare teachers as two radically different visions for the future of teaching: a professional ideal of teaching, supported by professional education, versus a vision of teachers as "technicians," who only implement scripted curricula.[29]

While *A Nation at Risk* and its narrative of failure certainly accelerated the emergence of the alternate routes, concerns about the quality of teaching predated the 1983 report; indeed, such concerns had already stirred efforts toward reforming the preparation of teachers well before TFA came on the scene.[30] For example, the state of New Jersey initiated one of the earliest alternatives in 1985, setting a pattern that many other states followed; while not a precursor, the New Teacher Project (TNTP), started in 1997 by a TFA alum, has since sponsored TFA-like "Teaching Fellows" programs across the country.[31] Early iterations of alternate pathways were often developed to fill existing teacher shortages and attract a greater diversity of candidates, including candidates of color, not unlike Wendy Kopp's stated goals in her thesis for a "teacher corps."[32] But over time, the growing chorus of failure along with expansion of privatization across society reoriented the aims of and dialogue around alternatives toward supplanting rather than complementing university-based programs.[33] Today, a variety of reformers and stakeholders, including conservative think tanks, private advocacy organizations, and the federal Department of Education, promote the view that "universities [have] had a monopoly on teacher preparation even though programs were ineffective [and] certification procedures were cumbersome and unnecessary"; these stakeholders accordingly advocate alternate pathways as "a superior policy model."[34] Even some teacher educators, looking back, have suggested that "[w]e brought it upon ourselves."[35]

SINCE THE 1990s: ALTERNATIVES TAKE OFF

As such alternatives have expanded since their advent in the mid-1980s and early 1990s, they (as well as more recently created programs that operate completely outside of established systems of university-based preparation programs) have prepared an increasing proportion of those entering the field.[36] By 2006, all 50 states and the District of Columbia had authorized alternate routes to the classroom; of the 3.8 million public school teachers who taught in the school year 2105–2016, nearly one in five came from an alternate route program.[37] As might be expected, the inception and growth of these alternatives resulted in a "tumultuous" few decades, from the early 1990s through the present, for university-based teacher education in this country.[38]

Increased regulations. Of course, the struggles of university-based teacher educators have not occurred in a vacuum; a number of contextual factors have exacerbated the challenges they have faced. In line with the "raising standards" reform trajectory, college and university teacher education programs found themselves subject to increasing regulation at both the federal and state levels.[39] Whereas the 1966 Coleman report established for a generation of researchers the overriding salience of family context over school factors, the early 2000s saw the popularization of research that argued instead for the centrality of the teacher and teacher quality to student achievement.[40] Indeed, a primary feature of the 2001 No Child Left Behind Act required every child to be taught by a "highly qualified teacher." States set guidelines as to what constituted "highly qualified," relying heavily on certification (along with a bachelor's degree and some kind of indicator of subject matter knowledge) to attest to quality, meaning that teacher educators were at the mercy of their state certification systems. In terms of program quality, as teacher education expert Linda Darling-Hammond noted, those regulating entities and the institutions of higher education that housed teacher education programs were hamstrung by "lack of consensus" within the profession about "internal quality control," and so largely failed—despite more regulations— to "drive weak programs toward stronger, more successful models."[41] Moreover, as Darling-Hammond elaborated, the fact that the profession itself doesn't control licensure has further complicated efforts on the part of university-based teacher educators to improve their programs.[42]

New forms of accountability. In addition to university-based programs' struggle to comport with increasing regulations, such programs have also been subject to new forms of accountability, as part of a broader embrace of accountability measures across the field of education over the last 30 years. Perhaps the most well-known of these, value-added measurement or value-added models (VAM), emerged as a purportedly objective way to measure the quality of teacher education programs: Using the test scores of K–12 classroom students, VAM would evaluate the quality of those teachers and, in turn, assess the teacher education programs from which those teachers graduated. Psychometricians declared the process unsound for the uses to which it was put, but that did not stop many education reformers and policymakers from inserting VAM into state policy and federal grant requirements.[43] Many teacher educators, for their part, found such measures to be punitive and have argued instead for what they believe are "other more reasonable and valid ways" to strengthen accountability in teacher education.[44]

Resource shortages. In his 1983 article, the aforementioned Alan Jones lamented a shortage of resources to support high-quality professional teacher preparation. Dwindling resources have continued to shape the efforts of university-based teacher educators to offer strong programs. Public universities, which still prepare the majority of American teachers, suffered substantial defunding over the last 3 decades, a downward trend that worsened following the 2008 recession.[45] Over the same years, funding priorities on the part of the federal government and many private foundations shifted to favor alternatives over university-based programs. The resulting lack of investment has meant fewer dollars for improvement of university-based programs and, according to many teacher educators, anxiety that the disappearance of funding represents a larger effort to "break up the system and try to replace it with greater market competition."[46]

Many alternate route programs have had to toe some of the same regulatory lines as have the university-based programs. Because teachers require certification to be hired, alternate routes have had to find ways to provide requisite coursework and experiences for certification. TFA teachers, for example, may have begun as teachers of record immediately after completing their Summer Institute, but dating back to the first cohort, they have had to complete required coursework toward certification, as some of our narrators recalled in their oral history testimonies.[47] Early on, the provision of such coursework occurred most often in conjunction with existing university providers; more recently, alternate routes such as TFA and local Teaching Fellows programs have contracted with some of the independent providers that have sprung up. But independent providers also face the same accreditation pressures as institutions of higher education: Relay Graduate School of Education, for example, is institutionally accredited by the Middle States Commission on Higher Education (MSCHE), just as traditional universities would be, and by the National Council for the Accreditation of Teacher Education (NCATE), for their preparatory program. Though accreditation remains voluntary, that process along with state-defined certification requirements continue to influence the shape of teacher preparation. Then again, some alternate route programs are subject to the control of districts (for example, city-based residency programs are managed by those cities' superintendents) or of the charter networks for which they supply teachers.[48]

Over the past 30 years, as teacher educators have faced these challenges to their authority over teacher preparation, they have been pulled into the larger debate about different models of teacher preparation.[49] Their responses, as suggested at the outset of this chapter, have varied. As several teacher education scholars have framed it, the field seems to be currently divided into three camps: defend (the university-based stalwarts), reform (the alternatives seeking to displace the university), and transform (including those university-based teacher educators looking for substantive change).[50]

Defense of the Status Quo

In response to critics who have argued to replace rather than reform university-based teacher education, many university-based teacher educators have doubled down in defense of their work.[51] These teacher educators have sought to reframe the narrative of failure associated with university-based programs within a broader understanding of social and political changes that have undermined such programs, condemning the values, motives, and quality of "evidence" behind what they deemed to be a "larger neoliberal 'ed reform' movement" designed to "radically disrupt public education (and teacher education) to make room for 'innovative' market-based reforms."[52] Many proponents of this view have focused on the money trail, as resources gravitated from university-based programs to non-university programs, underscoring the debased support for traditional models of preparation. Like Alan Jones in the 1980s, today's defenders of teacher education have pointed out how teacher education is strained from many sides: University-based programs are expected to do more with less (accomplish more in terms of accountability with fewer resources), educational researchers are poorly funded for their work, and many tenure-track teacher educators are burdened with more administrative work than peers in other departments.[53]

This group has protested the larger shift toward individualism, free markets, and private goods, and decried the way that many so-called reformers of university-based programs have held teachers, schools, and teacher education responsible for failures they believe are rooted in structural factors such as poverty and systemic racism. Recent defenders of teacher education have argued that inequality and poverty, more fundamentally than the quality of teachers and teacher education, impede students' educational achievement.[54] Finally, in her summary of university-based teacher education defenders' views, teacher education scholar Marilyn Cochran-Smith noted teacher educators' frustration at being excluded from key discussions and networks as well as at what seem to them to be exaggerated claims of success on the part of alternate pathways and "intentional misrepresentation" of research on university-based preparation.[55] As Fraser and Lefty summarized, perhaps we should not be surprised, given the constraints on university-based programs—the different pressures exerted by universities and K–12 systems, their perilous status in higher education, the onerous requirements of accreditation—that they have not changed more quickly. Yet while many of the defenders' arguments may be valid, Fraser and Lefty nonetheless find that "too many schools . . . have reacted defensively to the criticism without engaging in the hard, self-critical work that would create a different kind of education school."[56] Or, as Oxford University's Harry Judge sadly commented on the 1990s Holmes Group's attempts to implement reforms in teacher education, "The effort stalled when the colleges and schools of education had to think seriously about reforming themselves. They will change only when they really wish to, and not enough yet do."[57]

Reaction: Making University-Based Teacher Education Better

Still, some teacher educators *have* taken up this difficult task. A broad coalition of teacher educators have both endorsed the importance of expertise and training provided by university-based teacher education and acknowledged the challenges and weaknesses of such programs. For example, Ken Zeichner and Hilary Conklin assert, "There is no dispute about the need for improvements in the dominant college and university system of teacher education," while Darling-Hammond declared (on behalf of university-based teacher educators) that "getting our act together— finally, seriously, and collectively—is essential to the nation's future."[58] The field has actually displayed an impressive history of self-critique over the last 40 years, though it has too often seemed to lack a shared vision and common language, that would enable teacher educators to "engage substantively with each other about the problems that plague the field and about the criticisms leveled against it."[59] According to those who wish to transform rather than jettison university-based programs, "traditional" teacher education *has* improved over the last 30 years, even if the field continues to struggle with "constraints that haven't been fully resolved," including feeble connections to the field, status issues in the university, the expertise of education faculty (particularly in translating disciplinary knowledge into good teaching), poor program coherence, and the role of such programs as money-makers for institutions of higher education.[60] Two primary lines of reform have emerged out of these conversations, a powerful professionalization agenda and an agenda based on social justice.[61] Though the professionalization agenda provided the more powerful organizing principles, the field has also marshaled the social justice argument in pushing back against the incursion of alternate pathways, which have had a greater influence in those schools and districts serving low income students of color. And sometimes the two agendas have been linked.

Professionalization Agenda for Change

Tighter regulation. In operationalizing the professionalization agenda, university-based providers have advocated for more and stricter gates as well as elevated standards for teachers. Early critics such as Darling-Hammond stressed the harm caused to urban schools and students by the incursion of inadequately trained recruits, suggesting that

TFA in particular presented a "direct challenge" to those who would raise standards for teaching.[62] But even before TFA, many teacher educators as well as policymakers had already been involved in the efforts to design professional standards for teaching and strengthen teacher education and certification requirements.[63] In the wake of *A Nation at Risk*, nearly every state passed education "policy packages" that included raising teacher education program requirements, such as minimum grade point averages and admissions standards.[64] On a federal level, the 1998 reauthorization of Title II of the Higher Education Act added accountability measures that required states to report every year on quality indicators related to teacher preparation programs; both the George W. Bush and Obama administrations sought to tie funding for teacher education programs to accountability.[65]

Clinical Focus. Another aspect of the professionalization agenda aimed to knit university-based programs more closely to actual practice. The first decade of the 2000s saw a new focus on clinical experience, as some teacher educators and accrediting agencies promoted the need to ground university-based programs in clinical practice and support that experience with academic coursework.[66] The turn to clinically based teacher education responded in part to the longstanding complaint that university-based programs consisted of theory separated from practice; it is interesting that this shift occurred in tandem with the growth of alternatives and new providers purportedly based in classroom practice.[67] The greater focus on practice led to a range of developments in the field, from teacher performance assessments, to residency models in which candidates essentially served as paid apprentices to mentor teachers while taking coursework, to an emphasis on "core" or high-leverage classroom practices—foundational, often research-based teaching "moves" or practices critical to helping students learn content—that candidates are taught to perform.[68] Tools such as the Danielson Framework, which emerged in the mid-1990s, attempted to organize and systemize such practices into the form of an observational rubric.

Articulating the professional knowledge base. In a bid to stabilize teaching's professional chops, teacher educators and researchers also worked to identify and articulate the specialized body of knowledge that distinguishes teachers from the generally well-informed or subject specialists. This work was already underway when TFA began, spurred by the 1986 Holmes and Carnegie reports. As early as 1989, for example, the American Association of Colleges for Teacher Education sponsored the publication of *The Knowledge Base for Beginning Teachers*, which one reviewer recognized as the field's attempt not only to "influence the content of teacher education programs . . . and assessments," but additionally, to "begin the difficult task of forming a consensus among teacher educators about what they should be doing."[69] Other such reviews were conducted by the Educational Testing Service, to develop teacher certification tests such as the Praxis exams.[70] In other cases, efforts over the past few decades to codify what teachers should know led to the articulation of specialized knowledge associated with teaching. Cognitive scientist Lee Shulman's notion of "pedagogical content knowledge"—the knowledge required to actually teach, not just know, a subject—became a defining core of this work.[71] More recent additions to the canon of specialized knowledge include recent findings in the science of learning and development, a literature around "core practices," deeper literacy around data and assessment, and a growing body of scholarship addressing culturally responsive pedagogy and "funds of knowledge."[72]

Evidence of effectiveness. Along with clarifying the specialized knowledge base associated with teaching, however, some teacher educators and critics alike presumed that true professionalism would require more in the way of proof: What evidence exists to show that university-based programs have made a difference to the quality of classroom teaching? Without stronger evidence to demonstrate the value of university-based programs to teachers' classroom performance, teacher educators have been hard pressed to advocate for their programs in what has become a data-focused environment. Catching hold of this issue in a 2008 journal article, teacher education researcher Pam Grossman invited the field to shore up both research and accountability associated with teacher preparation. In order to fulfill the conditions of a profession, Grossman argued, teacher educators needed to be able to show how university-based programs make a difference to student learning and, secondarily, the field needed to generate research that would enable teacher educators to make "strong claims about the effectiveness" of their programs.[73] Such an invocation was not without challenges, as teacher education scholars Aydarova and Berliner explain:

> [I]t is hard to define what experiences make for a quality teacher
> education program or what practices can ensure equitable outcomes
> for students. The fact that quality and equity can be achieved in
> so many different ways creates situations in which what looks to
> be disarray or poor choices by one scholar, is really thoughtfulness
> about the profession from another vantage point.[74]

Over its 30-year tenure, TFA has been a goad for so-called traditional programs to produce such evidence, in large part to combat the cultural trope of tired and terrible inner-city teachers, demonstrably ineffective despite their training. Against such stereotypes, TFA's promise of bright young people who require no specialized knowledge landed favorably, pressuring conventional teacher education to better account for its value, which wasn't readily apparent to the ordinary citizen. Writing about her TFA placement school in Washington Heights, one 1990 corps member described some of those traditional, experienced teachers in the system as "not ok": "I don't mean that they weren't creative. I mean they were awful—which is why complaints about TFAers' relative inexperience or weak commitment are so hard to take seriously."[75] TFA thus incited the production of scholarship aimed at assessing the effectiveness of TFA teachers in comparison to teachers trained in university-based programs and, in turn, the viability of TFA as a strategy for procuring teachers for underserved classrooms.[76] As Grossman, and Aydarova and Berliner, make clear, demonstrating teaching effectiveness and linking it to a training pathway is not easy, and studies have collectively offered a mixed picture. Some have taken the very lack of a consistent impact as conclusive, arguing it "should indicate to policymakers that TFA is likely not the panacea that will reduce disparities in educational outcomes."[77] Finally, even if evidence can be marshaled to identify weak and strong teachers and programs, many teacher educators question how it will be deployed, and advocate using such findings to support the improvement of weak teachers and programs rather than driving them out of the field.[78]

Social Justice Agenda for Change

In TFA's first round of recruitment materials, Wendy Kopp attempted to hitch the organization to a social justice agenda, as explored in Chapter 2. The initiative upped the ante over subsequent years, even claiming the mantle of a civil rights movement. Traditional teacher educators, however, have pushed back vehemently on that representation. Darling-Hammond, an early outspoken critic of TFA, asserted that inexperienced TFA teachers were likelier to harm than help those most vulnerable students: "It is especially disturbing to those who are concerned about the well-being of children in the poor rural and urban districts that TFA has targeted . . . [that] the debates over TFA and similar programs have scarcely considered the impact on the children in these schools."[79] In the early 1990s, as described in Chapter 4, university-based programs began to wrestle in earnest with multiculturalism, increasingly seeking to incorporate coursework and experiences that would help candidates become culturally responsive teachers. Many teacher educators associated with such programs have publicly proclaimed the social justice implications of preparing well-qualified urban educators through their scholarship and teaching. Yet here too there have been critics who have doubted the implementation of this agenda in university-based programs: Their concerns include a failure to engage candidates in reflecting on their field experiences, insufficient supervision and attention to social justice issues in practice teaching, and mixed results in changing teacher candidates' negative beliefs about urban communities.[80]

Accountability Context

Claims for the value of university-based teacher education have played out within a national and even global policy context defined more and more by accountability, feeding into what some teacher educators have dubbed "neoliberal management strategies"[81] and what others have described as long-awaited "clear, specific, real consequences for performance."[82] In policy terms, this translated into a national agenda of standards, accountability, and testing in education, a bipartisan approach nurtured by the first Bush and Clinton administrations, which matured into federal law with the passage of No Child Left Behind during the second Bush administration, and by the Obama administration's Race to the Top. Given the ramping up of testing and accountability in K–12 education, it was hardly surprising to see the same in teacher education. In the opinion of critics and some critical teacher educators, such as Martin Haberman, the fact that "schools of education are not required to make any follow up assessments of how well their graduates perform in the real world" demands that the "criterion of accountability . . . also be applied to the schools of education in universities and to alternative certification programs that prepare educators."[83] Unfortunately, broader opinion remained skeptical of teacher educators' ability to police themselves, resulting in the rise of external accountability measures. Widespread efforts to provide checks on the profession, such as assessing the quality of teacher preparation programs by the earlier mentioned VAM or ranking colleges of education and their preparation programs, represented crude but high-stakes ways of holding such programs to account and taking control out of the hands of teacher educators. Credentialing systems continued to exert regulatory control over university-based programs during this period, even as alternate routes attempted to ease the "roadblocks" of credentialing for their candidates.[84]

But this period also saw efforts, led by some of the nation's most distinguished educators, to grasp the levers of control on behalf of the profession, by tightening the link between standards for initial licensure, advanced certification, state program approval, and professional accreditation, and creating what education historian James Fraser described as a "strong, coherent, standardized *system*" for assessing the strength of the nation's teachers and teacher education.[85] The field's endeavors to raise standards in teacher education while maintaining authority over teacher preparation also led to peer-developed processes of evaluation, including the National Board for Professional Teaching Standards (NBPTS) and, by some accounts, the EdTPA, a performance assessment instrument created by Stanford University faculty.[86] The NBPTS, founded in 1987—"by teachers, for teachers," according to promotional language—works to advance the quality of teaching and learning through a voluntary advanced certification, while the EdTPA aims to improve preparation by redesigning teacher education "based on more clearly articulated constructions of teaching and learning."[87]

As Haberman asserted, neither university-based nor alternate routes to the classroom have been adequately held to account to date. And as Aydarova and Berliner have pointed out, this state of affairs exists in part because the field has struggled to define clear measures for what constitute high-quality teaching and high-quality teacher education programs. Publications describing and sharing strong exemplars have been balanced by another reality, summed up by Barmak Nassirian, director of federal relations and policy analysis for the American Association of State Colleges and Universities: "Conceptually, teacher prep has been in paralysis for some time now . . . this whole issue of quality assurance and accreditation is proving particularly vexing."[88]

Blurring the Lines

While this battle for control over the field and its professional status is real and ongoing, it is also more nuanced than a simple struggle between teacher educators and reformers. The wide variation within and across programs makes clean distinctions between alternate routes and more traditional pathways difficult, not to mention the lack of common and agreed upon definitions of what counts as "alternative" and "traditional." Grossman has gone so far as to say that the "terms such as *alternative* or *traditional* are all but meaningless in helping us to understand the characteristics of a program."[89] Perhaps more to the point, the focus on program designation distracts from thinking about how teachers in any pathway are learning to teach: The "either/or framework renders invisible the ideologies that shape and direct conceptions of teaching, learning, and the purpose of schools."[90]

As a result, some researchers suggest it is time to "abandon a zero-sum view of education reform agendas" and acknowledge a more contemporary blurring of the lines.[91] As one example of such blurring, the great majority of alternate routes to the classroom actually wind through traditional university-based teacher education territory: "Preparation coursework across pathways is more similar than different [and] many so-called alternative programs usually include coursework at a university."[92] In turn, some university-based programs have embraced a more clinical approach or teaching techniques popularized by alternate route programs.

Despite its marketing message to the contrary, TFA itself has largely paralleled the work of conventional university-based teacher preparation in its approach to training, from its initial Summer Institute (which relied on star teacher educators) through more recent years.[93] In fairly short order after the first Summer Institute, Kopp recognized the need to strengthen training for recruits and create supports for them once they began teaching, and looked again to university-based experts. And states' requirements for certification meant that TFA teachers had to somehow acquire key coursework components. Consequently, TFA has engineered fundamental changes to its training over the course of its existence. As education historian Jack Schneider points out, TFA has "consistently worked to improve its summer training, developing not only a coherent curriculum, but also a clear framework for lesson planning and classroom management, as well as robust systems of support, mentoring, and collaboration."[94] Ironically, even while maintaining its "alternative" rhetoric, TFA has often depended upon partnerships with existing schools of education to implement such improvements and satisfy credentialing requirements. If the short duration of TFA's training made it an outlier, the actual content of that training has been largely based on the curriculum of established university-based programs. Even TFA's development of "new" approaches has drawn heavily on existing ideas and practices in traditional teacher education, such as the provision of teacher training during the undergraduate senior year or induction support of TFA participants who elect to stay beyond their 2-year commitment.[95] Some in the field have cried foul at this double standard, in which upstart alternatives both decry and use the ideas and practices of university-based education. As teacher educator Lauren Anderson asserted, major philanthropic support has ignored university-based teacher education as an important source of knowledge and instead "incentivize[d] and subsidize[d] the transfer of knowledge from the university to the same entrepreneurial upstarts that are chiefly invested in narrative university-based teacher education as a problem."[96] Nonetheless, TFA's debt to traditional teacher preparation programs is real.

Other teacher educators, however, have found the encouragement of alternatives "not necessarily a bad thing," hoping that the introduction of these new models may "potentially stimulate innovation and help improve all types of teacher education."[97] Another faction, acknowledging that alternate pathways are unlikely to disappear, worries that the "dangerous dichotomy" of the debate between so-called traditional and alternate routes threatens social justice alliances that are necessary to improving the education of low-income students of color.[98] Indeed, many traditional teacher education providers have found it advantageous to embrace the development and operation of alternate route programs. Research critiques of TFA and other shortcut paths have helped such providers to raise questions about and even improve existing practices, while hosting alternate route programs has allowed university-based programs to retain that share of the teacher education market.[99]

In many cases, such partnerships have led to positive crosspollination of human resources and ideas. Instructors employed by university-based programs have taught alternate route candidates; the alternate pathways curriculum has borrowed from traditional programs, and university-based programs, in some cases, have deepened clinical practices and incorporated teaching techniques popularized by alternative programs. In an example of the latter, Lauren Gatti, a university-based teacher educator, described how the use of "champion techniques" and core practices across pathways have contributed to teacher educators' ability to name and systematize teaching skills. An urban teacher residency program, Leaders for Equity in Education, has included typical methods and foundations courses offered by the partnering university's faculty, but also provided for a "management techniques" course based on core concepts of Doug Lemov's *Teach Like a Champion*, an approach pioneered at the non-university Relay Graduate School of Education. University researchers Deborah Ball and Magdalene Lampert have worked with Lemov, whose approach is synonymous with alternate pathways, and have all influenced one another.[100]

CONCLUSION

In many ways, the challenges of TFA and its ilk to business as usual among teacher educators have forced the latter to articulate what university-based programs do well and take heed that their work is more closely connected to the immediate problems of practitioners. Given the increase nationally in alternate route programs, a growing group of teacher educators believes that teacher education should focus on "the essential ingredients in the preparation of all teachers" rather than clinging to traditional modes of preparation or anointing "one best" approach.[101] Ultimately, this chapter suggests that while teacher educators continue to struggle for legitimacy, there is increasing overlap across the variety of pathways to teaching. Alternate routes have pushed traditional providers to change their game, but at the same time, they have borrowed from those providers. This book's general thesis argues that neither the alternatives nor conventional university-based teacher education have satisfactorily solved the challenges of preparing high-quality teachers for all classrooms. With this chapter, we acknowledge the continuing stakes and uneven playing field set forth for traditional providers, but suggest that the respective efforts of traditional providers and alternatives have also intersected in ways that have served to push the field forward in confronting the persistent difficulties of preparing high-quality teachers.

CHAPTER 7

The Legacy of TFA

This book highlights a set of ideas about procuring and preparing teachers at what, in retrospect, was a pivotal moment for many of the trends that have come to define today's educational context.[1] Since 1990, TFA has radically expanded its presence, from its original six sites to its current involvement in 53 regions that, thanks to Teach For All (an international network of 28 organizations), now stretch across the globe.[2] Though only .2% of the nation's teachers are current or former TFA teachers, as a figurehead of the new reforms, especially alternate pathways, TFA has exerted an outsized impact. One in five new teachers now enters the classroom through paths other than 4-year undergraduate or university-based master's degree certification programs, and alternate route programs can be found throughout the country.[3] Additionally, TFA has spawned a powerful network, an "army of reform-minded alumni," many of whom have helped to shape policy and practice conducive to the new reforms.[4] TFA even found its way into American popular culture, appearing in Michelle Obama's bestselling book, adorning J. Crew T-shirts, and showing up in the provocative game Cards Against Humanity ("What's Teach For America using to inspire inner city children to success?").[5] Because TFA has had such a long life over a tumultuous period of change and a large geographic area, its legacy is vast and complicated. This chapter takes stock of significant aspects of this legacy, using our oral histories to illuminate areas of influence and larger questions provoked by TFA over the last 30 years as well as speak to the impact of TFA on participants' own lives and views.

TFA AND TEACHER TURNOVER

The lion's share of existing research has assessed TFA's impact in terms either of participants' teaching effectiveness compared to traditional-entry teachers, or of their persistence in teaching. We make no claims as to the former, other than to share the self-reports of our interviewees; as detailed in Chapter 5, they struggled mightily in their efforts to teach. Regarding the latter, critics have long rebuked TFA for treating teaching as a short-term steppingstone. Within our sample, four of 30 participants quit during their first year.[6] The overall 1990 cohort saw an attrition rate of close to 11 percent, "slightly higher than the national rate for first-year teachers," according to a *New York Times* article, but "far lower than the 25 to 50 percent turnover rates in the school districts where most of the newcomers were placed."[7] In fact, attrition among new teachers is highest in and most negatively affects schools serving low-income populations of color, exactly where TFA places corps members.[8] High turnover "leaves the very schools that most need stability and continuity continually searching for new teachers to replace those who leave," which is both costly and detrimental to students.[9] While 26 of our interviewees did fulfill at least their 2-year TFA commitment, only 10 made it past the 5-year mark, a roughly 60% attrition rate, compared to a national teacher attrition rate by year 5 of around 40%.[10] On the other hand, a study of three more recent TFA cohorts (2000–2002) found that over 60 percent of TFA teachers remained beyond their 2-year commitment and more than a third persisted more than 4 years. This is "markedly lower than the 50% [who persist beyond 4 years] estimated for new teachers across all types of schools" but, again, may be roughly comparable to general teacher turnover in similar high-poverty schools. The researchers who carried out this study concluded that TFA teachers "are far from being exclusively short-term in their intentions or actions."[11]

Even so, we agree that TFA has not solved the problem of teacher persistence. But we also suspect that, in the case of our participants, the static distinction of "stayed in teaching" versus "left teaching" misses the complexity of TFA's influence on participants' lives and professional journeys over time. If we consider how many 1990 alumni ended up working as college and university professors, school district personnel, and educational consultants or reformers in addition to K–12 teachers, approximately half of the total number (170) of 1990 alumni who reported careers on the website in 2009 were engaged in *education-related* work. Likewise, at the time of their interviews, just over half of our sample (16 participants) reported education-related positions (administrator, coach, curriculum developer, district-level work, higher education teaching) or fields (teacher education, education philanthropy, education reform); the remainder (14) being employed otherwise. Significantly, many acknowledged TFA as their gateway into education-related careers.[12]

Researchers who have studied the phenomenon of "role changing" associated with teachers trained by highly selective graduate programs assert that "as these well prepared teachers gain experience, they do leave teaching." Rather than leaving the field, however, such teachers often seek out other roles and opportunities in or related to education.[13] Role changers left classroom teaching because of poor working conditions in schools, the wish to have a bigger impact on urban education, and social pressure to achieve a higher status than teaching could afford.[14] These researchers suggest their results are generalizable to "well prepared teachers"; given our subjects' stories, it seems that these conclusions may also apply to teachers who enter teaching without strong preparation, but who possess a high level of cultural and social capital. Scholarship has long shown that teachers with more elite educational backgrounds, measured by attendance at elite undergraduate institutions, majors in subjects other than education, and high test scores, are those most likely to leave education.[15] The value of role changing aside—is it beneficial to keep these individuals within the larger field of education or does it hurt students when they leave the classroom, or both?—our work suggests that *both* well-prepared teachers *and* TFA participants with high levels of social capital are likely candidates for role changing. This, in turn, implies that social capital, when it collides with the constraints of urban teaching, may in fact exert significant influence on such teachers' decisions to leave teaching.

HOW TFA ALUMNI'S EXPERIENCES SHOW US TEACHER EDUCATION'S NEEDS

What else might the alumni testimonies and their experiences tell us about Teach For America and its legacy, teacher preparation, and working in schools that serve low income students or students of color? Perhaps the most significant common features the oral histories revealed across TFA participants' experiences are the lack of adequate preparation before and support for corps members during their teaching and, related to that, participants' recognition that being outstanding graduates from elite institutions did not compensate for their lack of preparation nor enable them to be successful in their TFA teaching. A third significant characteristic of their experiences was their naïveté about the context of the communities and conditions in the schools where they taught, a primary driver of teacher attrition.[16] These insights emerge directly from participants' interviews, but they also map onto critical policy concerns and, in what follows, we connect those findings from our interviews to larger policy takeaways that reflect TFA's legacy.

Need for More Effective Preparation

As the popular face of alternate routes, TFA represented the argument for doing things differently than the status quo of university-based programs. Supporters have argued that such alternatives provide highly motivated teachers in shortage areas and that TFA is a low-cost method for non–education majors and career-changers to enter the teaching field.[17] In rural areas such as the Mississippi Delta, for example, TFA has filled positions that might otherwise have gone begging.[18] Such contributions are predicated on the belief that what corps members need to know can be learned in a brief preparatory institute the summer before they assume their teaching position and on the job. The elision of existing preparation requirements suggests how little reformers valued that preparation and how much they expected that teachers could learn through experience. Wendy Kopp herself maintained that the "strongest schools develop their teachers tremendously so they become great in the classroom even in their first and second years."[19] And yet, according to our sources, neither their fast track into the classroom nor their placement school transformed them into highly qualified teachers. In fact, their stories attest to the need for more and better preparation than they received in order to be effective.

While the inaugural corps members' struggles—becoming an authority figure, managing a classroom, and teaching in an economically disadvantaged environment, as detailed in Chapter 5—mirrored those of many new teachers, the alumni's lack of preparation created particular difficulties for them. While teachers who matriculate through university-based programs also complain of feeling unprepared when they begin as teachers of record, they are likely to have been influenced by a range of experiences related to the profession before they head a classroom, all of which help to socialize them into the profession.[20] Our participants, on the other hand, were expected to meet all the challenges of learning to teach without such orienting experiences, leaving them to rely primarily on their common sense.

One of the alumni's chief complaints about the limited preparation they did get focused on what they perceived to be an excess of "theory" at the expense of "practical" knowledge. Traditionally trained teachers also typically complain of excessively "theoretical" preparation that failed to provide them with practical, relevant tools for teaching.[21] In general, teacher candidates have expressed impatience with learning about the theoretical dimensions of teaching and learning primarily because they haven't been helped to see how these ideas have a bearing on or can be translated into "real" teaching. This perennial issue stems in part from the historical institutional divide between schools and universities, where schools have commanded the so-called practical realm and universities represented theoretical concerns. Because of this persistent disconnect, teacher education critic Arthur Levine argues that university-based teacher education programs do not—really, cannot—adequately prepare their teacher candidates.[22] Yet the desire to detach theory from practice rests upon a false dichotomy, because theory in teaching "is embedded in and inseparable from practice." Effective teacher educators seek to expose teacher candidates to techniques and tools in conjunction with theoretical understandings, which are crucial to helping teachers develop their ability to adapt those tools and techniques to different contexts and learners.[23]

This widely perceived division between theory and practice dissolves, however, when new teachers learn and experience theory in the context of applied, high-leverage practices, so they see the ways in which theory manifests in practice. When real-life teaching becomes complicated, new teachers who lack this understanding of applied theory tend to revert to simplistic methods they may already have seen or experienced, which constitutes their "frame of reference."[24] Teachers then reproduce the methods they experienced as students, rather than reflect on the situation and, using higher-level theoretical understandings, innovatively adapt their teaching practice. Teacher preparation that enables teacher candidates to reflectively interpret situations that arise in classrooms and generate ideas for how to respond equips them to move past old assumptions toward more innovative practice.[25] A preparation program where critical concepts are modeled in practice and analyzed for further study and understanding is central to making teaching more than just generically pushing information at students. And having the opportunity to exercise these understandings in a carefully supervised and supported clinical experience would have helped participants to build a strong foundation for their teaching practice. But after just 8 somewhat chaotic weeks of the Summer Institute, where little if any exploration of critical concepts related to teaching in real classrooms occurred, the TFA alumni found themselves teachers of record, for the most part ill-prepared to do much more than reproduce what they had experienced as students. We argue that effective preparation, including rigorously supervised clinical experience and deep, theoretical grounding, could have helped them build a teaching practice that went beyond "common sense" and survival.

Participants' weak grasp of teaching concepts has echoed across the life of TFA. Decades after our interviewees faced down classrooms with little knowledge to sustain their teaching, participants continue to complain about truncated preparation that doesn't ready them for the challenges they will face. For example, Michael J. Steudeman, a TFA advisor who trained new TFA members between 2010 and 2012, described the Summer Institute as "trial-by-fire," noting that preparatory work in pedagogy, child development, and theory was limited to a short collection of "pre-Institute readings," meant for corps members to "study independently and without guidance or sustained discussions" before training began.[26] Olivia Blanchard, a 2011 corps member, recalled how her training focused on closing "the achievement gap," something that became a cornerstone of TFA's philosophy over time; but, Blanchard went on, "in my experience, many if not most corps members [were] confused about their purpose, uncertain of their skills, and struggling to learn the basics."[27] Single-minded attention toward closing the "achievement gap" by improving test scores may conflict with other important aspects of teaching in low-income schools, such as understanding systemic inequities in the schools, building on the knowledge base and assets of students' families, and simply making strong personal connections with the students to build curriculum based on their interests. Corps member Jessica Millen (2013) described her dissatisfaction with the Summer Institute's emphasis on "*talking* about how we were going to make a difference rather than learning how to be effective teachers who could ultimately 'make a difference.'"[28] And in her study of 2010–2011 new corps members, teacher educator Katherine Crawford-Garrett noted that, although selected for their "sharp intellects and leadership capabilities," few of the recruits felt they could draw on these resources to solve problems within schools and that "many doubted the integrity of their knowledge and deferred, instead, to curricular texts and outside experts when making instructional decisions."[29] Without preparation, TFA teachers were neither fully aware of the possibilities of what they could accomplish with their students, nor did they have the tools to identify or reach insightful educational goals.

Need for Ongoing Support—Induction and Mentoring

Another area in which participants might have gained some help would have been through the provision of in-service support. Many participants mentioned their gratitude for the support they got from TFA peers; some participants also described getting desperately needed mentoring informally, by way of their relationships with more experienced teachers at their schools. One other obvious place alumni looked to for support was the TFA organization. Many felt that closer contact with TFA during their first year of teaching would have made the experience less traumatic. Lori Lawson imagined that "instead of just plopping everybody in their cities," TFA could have "continued making everybody come together," something she believed would have helped her to fulfill her 2-year commitment. Sustained and substantive contact on the part of the TFA organization, she continued, would have sent the message, "You are all not alone . . . let's tackle real, practical stuff that you're dealing with now." Unfortunately, as Lawson and most of our interviewees recalled, "none of that happened."[30] Participants remembered little or no professional development or mentoring provided by the TFA organization during that first year.[31]

Some of those we interviewed felt it was not fair of TFA to persuade people to stay in the program when the organization possessed neither knowledge about the challenges corps members faced nor capacity to provide support. Sabin summoned up angry feelings at a letter TFA sent out that warned participants not to quit:

> [F]ew of the TFA people [i.e., organizational staff] had had teaching experience . . . and it just felt, this chastising letter, like, you guys don't even know what we are doing. That is the only involvement I

remember TFA having in my whole three years there and it wasn't a good one.[32]

Leo Flanagan agreed: "TFA was no help whatsoever. I think we had nothing to do with them the entire year."[33] In Jeffrey Simes's opinion, the organization's lack of support—which he characterized as a kind of abandonment—encouraged people to quit: "They quit us! They left! . . . We never saw anybody from TFA, never heard [from] anybody from TFA."[34] Because TFA was hard pressed to offer or encourage much induction support and because alumni lacked sufficient preparation, their vision of teaching tended to remain at a rather superficial level: that is, teaching as reactive, generally not guided by research, and not well connected to the contextual elements of the students themselves.

Contemporary teachers commonly cite the lack of professional support as a reason for leaving teaching; increasingly, research and policy over the last several decades have recognized the crucial need for ongoing support for all new teachers.[35] Some universities, schools, districts, and states have managed to create induction and mentoring experiences for beginning teachers, in order to better support and retain teachers during their early years in the profession.[36] Induction mentoring is generally understood to be a coherent and sustained professional development process, perhaps mandated by the state and provided to new teachers by a school district or university, that helps new teachers become acclimated to their school and more knowledgeable about their teaching following their pre-service preparation.[37] Teachers who receive mentoring are significantly more likely to stay in the classroom; mentoring also has a positive impact on classroom instructional practices and student achievement.[38] Yet despite positive press and some growth in numbers over the past 20 years, such programs are still a distinct minority—not because they are not helpful, but because they require additional funding and a high level of on-the-ground capacity.[39] Although induction and mentoring programs existed in 1990, they were not characteristic of most new teachers' experience; certainly, the majority of TFA participants we interviewed felt very much on their own when they began their teaching.

Even though many alumni expressed concern about their weak understanding of how to teach (a result of their sink-or-swim experience), a surprising majority concluded that teacher preparation does not matter, because one really only learns to teach by teaching. Jeffrey Simes discounted the utility of both the Summer Institute and the credentialing program in which he participated for a time.[40] Caroline Sabin denounced the education courses she took as an undergraduate at Harvard for their lack of rigor, declaring that the only way to be prepared to teach was to "know what is going to come at you," which for her meant being in the classroom.[41] Carlos Gomez, still teaching at the time of his interview, concurred with Sabin's view of teacher education courses. Having earned his credential while teaching in Compton, California, with TFA, Gomez found his Cal State courses "in general to be very underwhelming and just going through the motions just to get credit hours."[42] And Leo Flanagan, who spent his entire career in urban education, including many years as a principal, noted, "When I hire someone I have very specific outcomes of what I want them to be able to do, and I don't care how they got [them]."[43] While Andrew McKenzie did acknowledge the usefulness of his teacher education courses (because they occurred simultaneously with his teaching, so he could apply things immediately), he nonetheless felt he got most of his training "on the job, by simply going to [his] mentor's room and talking with him or talking with some of the other teachers."[44] Thus, participants' experiences tended to reaffirm for them not only the validity of entering teaching without pre-service training but the questionable value of such training. It seems counterintuitive: participants described vividly the difficult challenges they faced as unprepared novices but continued to disavow the potential value of pre-service preparation. Their stance makes sense, however, insofar as few were afforded the opportunity through preparation or in-service support to develop a more advanced, deeper understanding of teaching and what it involves. Instead, they assumed that what they learned by hard experience in their classrooms defined the limits of teacher practice. From our perspective as teacher educators, we respectfully disagree with their conclusion. There was an evolving body of knowledge that could have helped the TFA participants, had they had access to it, in their day-to-day work as well as in their growth as teaching professionals.

DO THE "RIGHT PEOPLE" MAKE THE BEST TEACHERS?

A second major influence of TFA has been its role in popularizing the notion that getting the "right" people in the classroom can solve what ails education and in focusing on pipeline at the expense of a larger picture of the educational enterprise. From the outset, Wendy Kopp's conception of TFA turned on recruiting an elite population: "This nation needs a Teacher Corps . . . [that] will appeal to the very 'best and brightest'—a group of individuals who will not respond to [other] current initiatives."[45] To be sure, TFA did not introduce the idea of attracting "better"—however defined—people into teaching, but it did revive the tendency of earlier eras, before the onset of credentialing requirements and the universal installation of teacher preparation within colleges and universities, to rely on desired personal characteristics and experiences, rather than training, as qualifications for teaching.[46] In perpetuating the "best and brightest" myth, TFA invoked a longstanding cultural faith in the ability of chosen

individuals, despite their lack of specialized knowledge or skills, to solve
the most intractable problems of the day.

At the heart of these assumptions lay the question of whether, simply
by virtue of their elite education and their identities, the TFA participants
could do better for children in underserved schools than could existing
teachers.[47] Researchers have not been able to agree on the effectiveness
of TFA teachers, as discussed in Chapter 6.[48] And though TFA has en-
deavored over time to improve the experiences and effectiveness of corps
members, the organization, along with similar programs, continues to
promote the idea that personal qualities outstrip thoughtful preparation
and experience, and so fosters the myth of "the best and the brightest" as
a solution to the most difficult challenges in education.

Recruiting "The Best"—Is It Enough?

Thanks to the high profile of TFA, the rhetoric of the "best and brightest" reverberates within contemporary media and policy conversations
about how to improve schooling for the most disenfranchised students.
Nearly 30 years after the first cohort of TFA corps members was selected
to "save" American's schools, recruitment of the "best and brightest"
has been called the key to success at top charter schools; and former U.S.
Secretary of Education Arne Duncan unleashed a publicity blitz to recruit
the "best and brightest" to the teaching profession.[49] Americans seem to
support the idea of the "best and brightest" becoming teachers, both because they believe teaching ability is "a natural talent" and because they
buy into the "best and brightest" narrative that promising, idealistic individuals can transcend the challenges of educating low-income students
by sheer dint of their hard work, dedication, and talent.[50] Perhaps not
coincidentally, this narrative allows society to ignore the larger systemic
and social challenges that have made education in underserved communities so difficult.

Unfortunately, the assumption that individuals with an elite college
background, idealism, and enthusiasm, along with some rudimentary training, will somehow solve the problems of the nation's hardest-
to-staff schools flies in the face of reality. Most obviously, the solution
to building better teachers cannot depend primarily on graduates from
elite colleges—the numbers are simply not in favor. Moreover, according
to the oral histories, the attributes that distinguished TFA recruits from
more traditionally trained teachers—their elite education, their idealism,
their achievements—did not automatically translate into teaching competence, as Kopp had predicted; the complexity of the work caught them
by surprise. Despite their attributes, our participants experienced many
of the same challenges as traditionally prepared teachers and, in some
cases, additional ones. And the presumption that anyone from a selective

college can pick up teaching without preparation and "save" underserved students ultimately set up and demoralized participants with whom we spoke when they could not live up to those unrealistic expectations. Such presumptions have additionally undermined the professional work of teaching by perpetuating troubling fictions about what it takes to teach and distracting attention from more constructive conversations.

Critics object to "shortcuts" such as TFA for undermining the professional nature of teaching by discounting the value of training and creating a two-tiered system.[51] They reason that if teacher candidates were to choose their vocation early and prepare well, they would become committed professional teachers who would stay in the classroom. While this seems sensible, it is not clearly borne out by research. A good number of those who choose a traditional entry to teaching from a very early point are making what is essentially an expedient choice—just as expedient as that of the corps members we interviewed. "Many teens . . . enter college to be teachers and complete the degree, even when they know it was the wrong choice; thus one reason why only about half of all college of education undergraduates ever teach."[52] Around the time our interviewees embarked upon their TFA teaching experience, over 50% of 1992–1993 bachelor's degree recipients who had prepared to teach did not apply for teaching jobs within the year following their graduation.[53] And many new teachers of the last several decades have approached teaching as "one of several in a series of careers they expected to have," suggesting a malleable commitment to the classroom.[54]

In this light, the focus on getting the "right people" into teaching seems to ignore what happens on the ground in the schools that most need qualified teachers. The problem is particularly pernicious for schools in large urban centers, such as those in which the alumni taught, where attrition rates far outpace those in suburban schools.[55] Ultimately, we argue, if the socializing influences of urban classrooms may well be more powerful than teacher characteristics and preparation pathway, then the relentless pursuit of the "best and the brightest" as a silver bullet solution for the challenges of educating low-income children of color seems misguided at best.

Community Context and the Conditions of Schooling

In putting its money on a particular kind of teacher candidate, TFA privileged a policy solution predicated on the problem of supply: Solving educational challenges meant attracting the right kind of teachers into classrooms. Some researchers have sought to shift the terms of this debate, arguing that the real problem has less to do with getting the right people into teaching than it does with keeping them there. As education researcher Richard Ingersoll claims, the reason that urban schools cannot adequately staff classrooms with qualified teachers is not because of recruitment problems, but rather, because too many teachers leave. This comes about not because of teachers' inherent characteristics (or lack thereof), but because of the organizational conditions of schools, chaotic and unsupportive, that drive many teachers away in the early stages of their careers.[56] Some of our interviewees who stayed in education for the long haul recalled educational settings during their TFA years where they believed they would still struggle, even with all the experience and knowledge they had gained in the intervening years, because conditions were so problematic.

Challenging working conditions, including dissatisfaction with administration, lack of influence on decisionmaking, decrepit school facilities, and lack of resources, constitute one of the primary reasons behind high teacher turnover (of both traditionally and alternatively trained teachers) in high-poverty schools.[57] A recent study of teacher turnover identified key drivers of attrition as dissatisfaction with testing and accountability pressures, lack of administrative support, lack of advancement opportunities, and unhappiness with working conditions.[58] Such findings seem to bear out researchers' argument that attrition from underserved schools is less about teachers' rejection of their students and more about teachers' desire to work in schools where they find more supportive teaching environments, including helpful administrators, collaborative faculties, and well-managed buildings.[59] Such elements are in short supply in dysfunctional, underserved schools.[60] For many young teachers, the wearing conditions of urban teaching lead to burnout and attrition. Particularly for those who may have entered the field motivated by ideals of service or social justice, teaching in such schools presents "an all-or-nothing proposition," requiring utter and complete dedication.[61]

Though some research has found preparation prior to entry (along with administrative support on the job) to be a prime determinant of turnover, other studies suggest that school conditions may outweigh the salience of preparation pathway.[62] For example, a study of over 2,000 TFA alumni (from the 2000, 2001, and 2002 cohorts) found that "Although the TFA school-based exit rates are high, there is some evidence that they are roughly similar to general teacher turnover rates in sites like those where TFA teachers are placed: low-performing schools serving high percentages of students of color and low-income students."[63] Our oral histories suggest that the conditions of urban schools served as a powerful equalizer among teachers. We found that many of the unique qualities alumni brought to teaching seemed to wash out once in their schools, providing them few advantages and suggesting that school conditions may have outweighed the differences in teacher characteristics between traditional-entry and TFA teachers.[64]

Rather than tackle these larger, more complex challenges, TFA belongs to a brand of education reform that has steadfastly disregarded the broader social context of communities and conditions of schools in the effort to improve education in economically disadvantaged areas. Such reforms have focused on treating a symptom, encouraging children to work harder, for example, wielding the "right people" and effective "management techniques" like a holy grail, as though effective teachers are somehow impervious to the larger structural factors that shape schools and communities. Ironically, as African Studies Professor Noliwe Rooks argued, TFA and its genre of initiatives have reaped success by promising to "narrow the achievement gap for students in areas that were highly racially segregated without addressing the poverty of segregation with which those students were surrounded."[65] Education reforms and theories that focus on individual students' need to work hard "sidestep" the "complex and often debilitating problems that structural poverty and racism create for students."[66] These reforms have failed to acknowledge the lived experiences of children in high-poverty areas, encouraged the segregation of children of color, and allowed schools to remain unequal.[67]

One way TFA could address these contextual conditions would be to help new teachers become knowledgeable about the historical, social, and economic conditions in which students negotiate their education, but that has not occurred. In addition to our interviewees' testimonies to this lapse in Chapters 4 and 5, TFA corps members from many cohorts over the program's history corroborate this ignorance. Anne Martin, from the 2008 corps, found "TFA's perspectives to be ill-informed about the community [metropolitan Atlanta] where I was working, and often superficial." Martin found that the lack of such knowledge influenced and diluted the curriculum: "From what I learned in my school and classes, TFA's suggested lesson cycle was inadequate and inappropriate to educate my students beyond rote memorization and procedural skills."[68]

In helping later cohorts to understand and conceptualize student achievement, TFA did not emphasize structural or systemic inequality. As Crawford-Garrett argued, "Without the opportunity to consider the ways in which U.S. society has systematically prevented poor and minority students from achieving educational and economic success," TFA teachers are left "with an overly simplistic narrative" that promotes "social mobility as an easily attainable, unequivocal good premised on the merits of the individual."[69] This tendency seems to have been less apparent for those we interviewed, who often credited their TFA experience for awakening them to intractable social and economic challenges that tripped up their students. But their experience was less defined by TFA's later laser focus on raising test scores than was that of subsequent TFA cohorts. Jessica Millen, a member of the 2013 corps, found both her school and TFA "focused on data and standardized testing to the detriment of what my young students needed." And the 3-day information session about New Orleans, where she taught, was not nearly enough to teach her about the culture of her school community in ways that could have supported her teaching.[70]

Another study, which investigated how 117 TFA alumni (from cohorts spanning 1991–2012) interpreted the causes of educational inequity, found that the overwhelming majority of respondents—more than 80%—tended to "frame the roots of educational inequity in terms of technical or managerial problems," revealing a "constrained and limited appreciation of inequity and the history of inequity in schools." Fewer than 15% of the study's respondents shared concerns about "reducing broader structures that systematically create racially and economically segregated schools."[71] Yet without deep understanding of such broader structures and their role in producing inequality, TFA teachers have tended to venerate shortsighted approaches to achievement, which ask children to demonstrate "grit" or pull themselves up by their bootstraps, without fully understanding the complicated history that created these children's educational situation. Indeed, some scholars have compared the presence and behavior of TFA teachers to America's earlier history of colonialist education, offering up the analogy of white teachers at the Native American Carlisle school or those who traveled south to teach freed people.[72]

Optimally, many university-based teacher educators favor educational practices that are "culturally responsive" and draw from the lived experiences of children who reside in high-poverty areas. Familiarity with students' lives, according to this line of thinking, enables teachers to create meaningful pedagogical experiences that connect the realities of children's lives with the acquisition of key content and skills.[73] Yet despite rhetorical support for this approach in university-based programs and efforts to distinguish such programs from alternate routes like TFA on this basis, research indicates that many traditional teacher education programs also struggle to engage candidates meaningfully in learning about and understanding the impact of structural factors on urban students' schooling and, especially, in operationalizing that knowledge instructionally. Teacher educators Mariana Souto-Manning and Christopher Emdin criticize university-based programs for commitments to equity that are "often strong in language and empty in lived experience" and further accuse many university-based programs of perpetuating an "'updated version of the 1960s and 1970s cultural deficit discourse.'"[74] Pointing to the overwhelming whiteness of the teaching population, the authors argue that, because university-based programs have failed to substantively shift practice toward diversity and inclusion, "white teachers graduate with a false perception of their commitments to diversity and social justice inherited from their teacher education programs and are . . . likely to frame racism as 'our students' problems.'"[75]

Another line of research highlights the limitations of university-based coursework in changing (white) candidates' perspectives on race. (While the conversation about social context includes many variables that shape children's opportunities, race is chief among them.) Because racism has so powerfully operated within American society since the country's inception, this argument goes, the work of helping candidates learn about racial identity in "ways that benefit individual teachers and support their work in schools and communities" may outstrip the time and capacity available in university-based programs and is, at the least, painstaking and uncertain.[76] As some teacher educators acknowledge, producing teachers who will "consistently support their minoritized students and persistently address racism" would require "doing teacher education differently."[77] The claims of both traditional and alternative preparation to a social justice agenda that aims to transform the education of low income students of color founder against the realities of the larger social context. Truly and meaningfully taking the social context into account begs for, as has been acknowledged, doing teacher education differently than it occurs now in either camp.

We are hardly the first nor unique in directing attention to the importance of the social context and conditions of schooling that shape the experiences of teachers and students in low-income communities of color. But we would argue that it is high time for reform approaches (including TFA) that have operated without addressing the significance of social context and school conditions to pay better attention. It should be clear that little if anything about schooling can be cut off from the larger social context and the conditions in which it occurs.

TFA ALUMNI'S INFLUENCE ON EDUCATION

Beyond these policy implications, there are now thousands of TFA alumni, many of whom occupy powerful positions in the public and private sectors, from "school administration to board of education seats to state senate offices, all the way to lobbying and staffer positions on Capitol Hill."[78] TFA encourages recruits to become educational leaders and policymakers; many alumni have also gone on to become influential entrepreneurs in education reform.[79] The TFA website boasts a "leadership force of 50,000+" alumni who have created advocacy organizations (such as RISE Colorado), organizations that train teachers (such as DC's Flamboyan Foundation), and charter school management organizations (such as IDEA Public Schools, which operates 30 pre-K to 12th-grade schools).[80] Not incidentally, many of these organizations build on the reform ideologies that define TFA, and are privately funded and operating outside of traditional public systems.

Many have used their TFA experience as a launchpad into education reform. After his time in TFA, interviewee Furman Brown devoted an extended period to learning about schooling before he created an innovative school model. While working for other start-up school reform organizations, Brown "spent 10 years designing a model before even sharing it with people," because he didn't want to raise expectations he couldn't fulfill.[81] Winning an Echo in Green prize [in 2004] "kind of changed everything," giving him the credibility to open his first New York City Generations High School in 2007, with union support; but the time to steep himself deeply in understanding education gave Brown the opportunity to think about how to do things differently at his school. [82]

Jennifer Denino, who taught for many years and held department head and other school leadership positions before becoming an education professor, similarly devoted time to learning about education after her 2 years with TFA. Dismayed about her inability to teach reading well, Denino enrolled in a master's program at Harvard's Graduate School of Education following her TFA teaching. While there, she learned she had good instincts about teaching but that she needed to learn more. For instance, where she had initially relied on a teaching guidebook, she later learned she could have spent more time helping her students to generate personal understandings of what they read. Denino's experience suggests how strong preparation has the potential to help new teachers see the possibilities in what they can accomplish with their students beyond what is routine or simply repetitive of how they were taught as students.

Not all TFA alums devoted time to learning more about the field, however, prior to taking leadership positions; some have acquired tremendous influence in education reform without necessarily gaining a deep and thorough knowledge of the field, inviting criticism from career teachers and education scholars. For instance, the TFA reformers who created the national charter school network, Knowledge is Power Program (KIPP), David Levin and Michael Feinberg, joined TFA in 1992 and began planning their new program in Houston, Texas, after just 1 year of teaching.[83] They borrowed heavily from Levin's first-year teaching mentor, classroom teacher Harriet Ball, to create their model; and though Ball's creative teaching strategies became central to the KIPP schools, the African American teacher was rarely mentioned in the broader media coverage of KIPP. Levin further "misinterpreted" Ball's methods, substituting a "no excuses" mantra for Ball's style in which care and love were central. Historian Emily Straus writes:

> The longstanding racial ideologies in Houston and in national school reform policy discourse elevated the aspirations of Feinberg and Levin, while silencing African American "Harriets," whose experience, thought, and leadership were neglected in . . . the nation's . . . ongoing search for better schooling for minority children.[84]

Feinberg and Levin's cultural capital as alumni of TFA and Ivy League schools advanced their education reform ideas despite their cursory understanding of the field. TFA had provided a hard-knocks, limited introduction to on-the-ground challenges of teaching and learning in an underserved school, but little preparation and deep knowledge development to serve broader thinking about the field before catapulting some alumni into decisionmaking positions. Without time and effort to become deeply informed about the field and its accretion of understandings about practice, as Brown and Denino did, those alumni holding leadership positions occupied an intellectually precarious, albeit powerful, position.

TFA'S INFLUENCE ON PARTICIPANTS' LIVES

Even when our interviewees and other TFA alumni did not hold decisionmaking positions in education or pursue careers in the classroom, Kopp seems to have predicted correctly that they would carry with them a changed perspective on education that would inform their subsequent work and lives. From the beginning, Kopp argued for the "idea power" associated with TFA. The young people involved would not only teach, but also "focus a new spirit on the educational system and the profession of teaching."[85] Ten years into the operation of Teach For America, Kopp had refined her notion of this "idea power," explaining that

> . . . a national teacher corps could produce a change in the very consciousness of our country. The corps members' teaching experiences were bound to strengthen their commitment to children in low-income communities and spur their outrage at the circumstances preventing these children from fulfilling their potential . . . those who would go into other sectors would remain advocates for social changes and education reform. They would become business leaders and newspaper editors, U.S. senators and Supreme Court justices, community leaders and school board members. And, because of their experience teaching in public schools, they would make decisions that would change the country for the better. [86]

In their oral history testimonies, our participants commonly remembered their commitment to TFA as a dual mission. They understood they would serve as teachers for 2 years, but also that they would draw on their experiences to advocate for the education of poor children, no matter what career they ultimately pursued.[87] As Brent Lyles commented, "The greatest achievement of Teach For America in my life was turning me into that education advocate that they talked about. You know, that's me."[88]

Participants believed that their TFA teaching experiences influenced their perspectives on and choices to advocate—in a broad variety of forms—for education. We do not claim that these experiences are generalizable to all the participants or that, following their experiences, TFA alumni were necessarily more likely to be involved in education or other civic activities than their non-TFA peers, for example. In fact, sociologists Doug McAdams and Cynthia Brandt called into question whether TFA "turned" participants like Brent Lyles to civic activity at all. In their large comparison study, McAdam and Brandt found that TFA participants accepted to TFA in 1993–1998 (including those who fulfilled their commitment, those who quit, and those who were accepted but never enrolled in TFA) together, relative to their age peers, participated at "very high levels" in all forms of civic/political participation.[89] But they also found that TFA completers consistently lagged behind the other two groups—those who quit and those who never matriculated—in their level of civic participation. We heard accounts from our interviewees, however, attesting to an abiding commitment to educational advocacy that came about as a result of their TFA experiences. In trying to reconcile these data, we suggest that perhaps the transformations described by our participants may say more about the type of person who applies to TFA in the first place than about the particular ways the program changes people; we also wondered if McAdam and Brandt, in their focus on broad indicators of civic participation, may have missed activities associated with the particular niche of educational advocacy that distinguished our interviewees' actions. In what follows, we describe how the TFA teaching experience influenced our participants' knowledge of systemic inequities that have shaped this country; we then examine how these new perspectives affected some of the participants and moved them to the small-scale, immediate, and local advocacy that they have practiced following their TFA experiences.

Our study participants came from a wide variety of backgrounds and brought a range of perspectives and expectations to their TFA experience, yet few would have predicted the way their experiences awakened them to the reality of larger social inequities in America. Because they studied at elite colleges and universities in the late 1980s, where the culture wars and identity politics shaped academic study, most participants had at least a theoretical awareness of the challenges posed by poverty and race in American society. But the reality of teaching in schools that served low-income students, many of color, drastically complicated that awareness. Furman Brown, who taught in Los Angeles with TFA, framed his awakening as radical, especially regarding his complicity (as a well-intentioned white man) in racism.

> I was totally clueless about South Central. I was as culturally
> clueless as I could have been. Probably, you know, sort of a liberal
> racism . . . it's a hard thing to accept of yourself, that . . . you're a
> big liberal racist . . . I actually, because of TFA, just had to confront

my own racism . . . You know, I was going to help people. How could I be racist? [90]

As he concluded, "I realized that our racial identity as a country and mine as an individual was [sic] much more complex [than I had thought]." Similarly, alumnus Mark Stephan recalled the confusing tangle of good intentions and cultural ignorance he experienced teaching in a rural North Carolina school. "[T]alk about a lesson in race, income, and also geography . . . I was basically a Northerner coming to a small Southern town and trying to be of help without realizing the complexity of race, class, Southern culture." Ultimately, that combination proved more than Stephan felt he could handle and he left the program early.[91]

Even for those who brought more developed political understandings of poverty and race to their experiences, TFA teaching was illuminating. Christina Brown, an African American woman who, after being a principal, went to work for a school reform organization, had come to TFA with a fairly sophisticated critique of racial inequality, power, and privilege in America by virtue of her lived experience. With lots of experience "being an 'other'" to shape her views, Brown found that "they [the white TFA participants and staff] just didn't get power and privilege and poverty and those issues that really were my main issues for being there." Nonetheless, as she explained, her TFA experience made the inequalities about which she cared deeply more concrete:

> It was my first real adult experience with poverty and just
> understanding what it meant to have power and privilege and what
> it meant not to, that I could leave, that I could go back, that I had
> choices and it didn't feel like these kids had choices.[92]

From the other end of the ideological spectrum, Heather Weller, who described herself as a nurse and mother in her interview, recalled the way in which her teaching experience challenged some of her fundamental, self-described conservative beliefs about opportunity in America.

> I was raised with the notion that in the United States there are
> opportunities and people who do not take advantage of those
> opportunities are lazy. And they're available to everybody and the
> lazy people don't take advantage of them. And what I ended up
> seeing was that growing up in such a stressful environment on so
> many levels, I mean the family unit was just nonexistent, money
> was nonexistent, living situations were nonexistent, nutrition was
> nonexistent, social—I don't know—values were nonexistent. So
> working in that environment and coming in contact with that
> and having it just slapped across my face and shoved down my

throat every day, I realized that what we speak of in our culture as opportunities are relative, in that they're only available to people who can take advantage of them.[93]

The violence of Weller's language—"slapped across my face" and "shoved down my throat"—speaks eloquently to her sense of being assaulted by evidence that failed to fit her understandings of society. We would also argue that her descriptions of the families and values as "nonexistent" suggest that, while she recognized the challenges of the community in which she taught, she may not have appreciated the larger historical forces that shaped that community and the assets therein.

Weller's reflection offers powerful evidence of a significant change in her beliefs, but does not necessarily reflect recognition of the constraining factors of poverty, family dissolution, and homelessness as the result of larger, structural factors. Other alumni, such as Furman Brown, found that "the structures themselves were . . . a huge part of the problem." For many, adopting a more structural critique meant revising their beliefs about the culpability of American society in existing inequities. As Brown realized, the "whole bootstraps metaphor is limited at best . . . [the TFA experience] definitely made it clear to me that the *structures* of our world, or our society, impact who's successful and who's not."[94] From watching her students' families, Lisa Robinson, who taught at an elementary school nestled in the Magnolia projects in New Orleans, witnessed the ways that economic disadvantage was institutionalized within the system. As she explained, the situation in the community where she taught was a "huge catch-22." Families trapped in the "system of poverty" found it nearly impossible to get out of the projects, because the "system is structured in such a way that someone who wants to get out of government assistance can't, you know, certainly can't easily."[95] In a variation on that theme, Felicia Clark noted the way her experiences revealed the systemic nature of educational disparities. Clark, who at the time of her interview served as the Los Angeles Unified School District math supervisor, began teaching in Lynwood, California, where she was aghast at the quality of education she saw offered to poor children of color. An African American woman herself, Clark recalled her own education in the public schools of Denver as quite good.

> I really thought that everyone who went to school got an education, and so I didn't have sympathy for dropouts initially. It's kind of like, "Well, you had the opportunity, and you didn't take it." And now I see, *systemically*, a lot of kids actually didn't really have a real, genuine opportunity.[96]

Like Weller, Clark found her original beliefs about equality of opportunity upended by her TFA teaching experience. But in her case, Clark linked what she understood as limited opportunity to "systemically" inequitable educational conditions.

To go from blaming students and their families for their situation to holding the larger system accountable marks a significant shift in perspective that took place for some TFA participants. Yet even this more complex accounting of the challenges faced by poor children of color often remains mired in what many progressive and multicultural theorists refer to as a deficit or "damage-centered" perspective. That is, even when communities' struggles are emphasized in order to hold those in power responsible for oppression, the focus on "brokenness . . . reinforces and reinscribes a one-dimensional notion of these people as depleted, ruined, and hopeless," with little room for agency.[97] According to a few participants, their TFA experiences helped them not only to see the challenges of their communities as a result of larger forces, but also to recognize the strengths and potential inherent in those communities. Both Furman Brown and Mark Stephan described how their initial ignorance about the culture of the communities where they taught contributed to their false assumptions about the nature and capacities of those communities, as well as their own roles. Brown's lack of cultural awareness, along with his eagerness to "help people," initially prevented him from appreciating the strengths of his students. He thought he was "going to go in and fix kids" but, in retrospect, Brown understood he could only have such a view because "I hadn't learned a whole lot about the resiliency and the brilliance of these kids."[98] Likewise, Stephan remembered thinking that he was "going to go in to help communities that can't help themselves . . . that have been hurt by the system." Yet such an approach, he realized, implied that he was "just . . . another person of privilege coming back to help out people who can't take care of themselves." Acknowledging the implicit "racial statements about power and about capacity" associated with his logic, Stephan ruefully wished he had approached his task differently. "'I'm going . . . to do what I can to help empower these communities . . . . That, upon reflection, is the mindset I would have liked to have had."[99]

EDUCATIONAL ADVOCACY (SMALL SCALE)

A well-known narrative associated with TFA showcases the influence of alumni as top directors and founders of "nationally prominent entrepreneurial education organizations" or in a host of more conventional administrative and district leadership positions across the country.[100] Yet many of our participants' stories indicated that, rather than acting from powerful, formal decisionmaking positions, they have acted in small-scale, localized ways to advocate for public education.[101] Their educational advocacy emerged across three main aspects of their personal lives: support for and commitment to public education for their children, education-related endeavors in their own communities, and conversations they had, private and public, about education. Even though they do not resemble the leadership roles in education and other influential fields that Kopp originally envisioned, the following examples illustrate some of the alumni's efforts in these areas and argue for their significance as sites of educational advocacy.

Commitment to public education for their children. For some alumni, their teaching in underserved schools persuaded them of the need for high-quality public schools for all children. Many believed that such high-quality public education would be widely available only if well-educated parents with high degrees of social and cultural capital became active members of their own local school systems. For those alumni, sending their children to public schools and becoming involved parents represented more than a simple choice—it was a pledge of support to the public system and a manifestation of political beliefs. For example, Carlos Gomez, a high school Spanish teacher and department chair at the time of his interview, who started his teaching career through TFA in Los Angeles, described his allegiance to public schooling for his children as having "started with Teach For America, and I think that's my commitment." As he elaborated: "we're [he and his wife, also a TFA alum and teacher] in a position of privilege as educators and we're committed . . . to the public education system." For him, decisions about his work and his family, especially where his children go to school, have been shaped by what he called "a piece of that Teach For America idealism," and the idea that "something is not as right as it should be and we've got to keep working at it."[102] His choices have come from an awareness not just of his children's experiences but also by how the school system benefits by having families with the privilege of strong educational backgrounds such as his engaged and involved in public education.

Jennifer Denino taught with TFA in New York City and, when interviewed, was beginning her career as a professor of education after many years of classroom teaching. She articulated the civic ideals that led her to believe strongly in public education not just for her own children, or a select segment of the population, but for all:

> I'm an advocate for people who believe that public education is for everyone. And I think that's still a message that people haven't fully embraced. I think that there are still people who believe that we are only preparing a certain segment of the population to go to college. [103]

Denino's idea that public schools should serve all citizens hearkens back to the roots of American common schools and Horace Mann's idea that the public school would be the "great equalizer."[104] Though her own experiences in TFA and subsequent classrooms often testified to the failure of Mann's ideals in contemporary schools, Denino's sentiments suggest that Mann's vision—that schools should be the meeting ground for all citizens and offer them the opportunity to transcend the circumstances into which they were born—has shaped her advocacy for public schools. Her political beliefs about public education and what it represents in a democratic society led to Denino's decision that "My kids will always go to public schools. I like public schools." [105]

Community-Based Advocacy. For those alumni who took part in community-based advocacy, some of their activity grew out of a personal interest in ensuring high-quality education for their own children. Advocacy on behalf of their own children's education has long been the preserve of white, middle-class parents and has often conflicted with the greater good. Scholars Amanda E. Lewis and John B. Diamond have described white suburban parents' fierce protection of resources in public school settings for their own children as "opportunity hoarding."[106] In this regard, the TFA participants' advocacy seemed different. For example, Caroline Sabin's concern for her children's opportunities was balanced by the work she did toward resource acquisition for all the families in her community, to the point of favoring proportionally more funding for low-income schools because they have less. Sabin taught with TFA in Los Angeles and, after years of teaching in private schools, settled into stay-at-home motherhood in a Boston suburb. As a volunteer, she has chaired a group called Citizens for Needham Schools, an organized grassroots effort that demanded local overrides to a state education funding proposition, Proposition 2½, to win more funding for Needham's schools budget. In this way, Sabin has committed herself to an overtly political form of advocacy work. She assumed a critical, unpaid, and on-the-ground role in the local politics of school funding, carrying out the small-scale, difficult work of canvassing, organizing, and advocating. As she explained, "rather than ask people every year for an increase, because it is a tremendous amount of work," the school committee "just shave[s], [the budget] for two or three years" until "the shaving is too much," and then they pursue an override.

> So then people like me will . . . run the campaign and we produce lots and lots of literature to try and explain what this particular chunk of money will pay for and what you [the voters] will lose if you don't approve it. . . . we try and find volunteers to work every single neighborhood in town and just talk to people. And the biggest challenge is . . . [that] people don't even show up for these votes . . . and that is why you get those neighborhood people,

because they know who is in that house and that he works killer hours and you really should get, have an absentee ballot, because, otherwise, he will never show up, that kind of stuff. . . . I do that kind of work.[107]

Sabin acknowledged that, like many middle-class families who can afford to do so, her family moved to Needham because they liked the schools, and she is motivated by her desire to have the schools "fully funded" for the benefit of her children. But at the same time, her work to increase school funding is deeply informed by a perspective on social inequality that she attributes to her years in TFA. Even though many of her neighbors balk at higher taxes, Sabin herself believes that it is their responsibility, as a more affluent community, to bear the burden of supporting their schools, so that precious state aid can go to those schools and communities with greater need.

[O]ne of the things you will hear people say, while we are saying we need to raise taxes, is, "What about the state? The state doesn't give Needham the kind of money it gives other places like Fall River and Lawrence [two less affluent communities in Massachusetts]." And the TFA side of me says, you know what? That is true: do you know how bad the schools are in Fall River and Lawrence? If more money should come into the state's hands, I still want all that extra money to go to Fall River and Lawrence. You . . . go to Disney, every year. You have the money to pay for . . . taxes. I don't want that state money, ever, to come to us. We don't need it and that is the TFA piece of me . . . that has informed my community work.

For some alumni who do not have children, their activities have come about primarily as a result of their interests in the well-being of others' children. Mark Stephan quit his TFA teaching position in North Carolina before the end of his first year and now works as a professor of environmental policy. He has volunteered in his community in a variety of ways, serving as a Big Brother and working on an advisory group for a local Superfund site (an environmental program run by the United States Environmental Protection Agency to address the most egregious toxic waste sites in the country). Stephan and his wife also focused their efforts on the elementary school near their home in Portland, Oregon, though they do not have children. Initially, they served in the school library, since the school could not afford a librarian (85% of the students receive free or reduced lunch). More recently, they were working to convince the superintendent of the need to secure more resources for the school. Stephan calls their activities, all of which revolve around deepening the quality of life in the community, "pragmatic and policy advocacy." Like Sabin, he credited his TFA experiences for his current involvement. "I have a hard time believing that I'd be an advocate for . . . K–12 education if I hadn't done Teach For America. I have also had a hard time believing that I would be as community-oriented as I am now [if not for TFA]."[108]

Neither Sabin nor Stephan holds a formal "office" or leadership position; rather, each has undertaken crucial, local voluntary work in service of their communities, work that recognizes the link between the health of their communities and the quality of education provided to its children. As Sabin's comments show, this work can be tedious and challenging. It occurs at the level of individual, personal relationships, as in, for example, Sabin's labors to persuade her neighbors to pay higher taxes for the benefit of their schools or Stephan's mentoring of a young boy in the community. In both Sabin's and Stephan's cases, these acts of advocacy spring from a view of what is just, equitable, and necessary to support a better society, a viewpoint they believe was nurtured by their experiences in TFA.

Advocacy through conversation. Though seemingly mundane, everyday conversation emerged as an important medium through which many of the alumni advocated for education. The alumni said they talk often and passionately about the inequities in the American educational system. We considered such conversations advocacy because of their impact on listeners, meaning their capacity to transform beliefs at an individual level, as well as their engagement of potentially influential individuals. Participants' words carry weight because of a combination of their own social capital and the credibility they hold because they taught in low-income communities. In some cases, alumni defended ideals that went against the grain of social sentiment about education.

Many of the alumni's conversations occurred within a close circle of family and friends, with the aim of "educating" them. For example, Priscilla Leon-Didion, who began teaching in Los Angeles with TFA and subsequently spent her career in education, much of it as a classroom teacher, explained that she often speaks about education at home: "In my household, you know, with my husband, [I'm] trying to explain to him intricacies of why this funding can be used for that . . . [and] not that funding." Yet Leon-Didion acknowledged that her private conversations with her husband about education are not simply for his edification: "Because he is also an advocate via me . . . I hear him say things to other people."[109] Her conversations thus reverberate beyond her relationship with her husband to reach a larger audience. Leon-Didion's case exemplifies how conversations served two important purposes, informing alumni's family and friends about educational issues and rippling outward to

include additional groups and networks of people. As well-educated individuals with high degrees of social and cultural capital, the TFA participants are likely to be sharing these in-depth discussions about inequities
in education with other individuals who possess high standing, influence,
and power in society. As a result, their collective views and actions could
conceivably affect broader sentiments and even decisions regarding educational policy, philanthropy, or elected leadership. In this regard, the
talk of the alumni may well be a formidable form of educational advocacy.

The significance of alumni's conversations lies not only in who they
talk to, but also what they talk about. According to interviewees, their talk
grows out of their desire to promote a particular set of beliefs about education, ultimately related to their vision of a just and equitable society. Having taught with TFA in North Carolina, Nichole Childs Wardlaw became
a certified nurse, midwife, and adjunct professor. She described how she
rallies her nursing students to fight against social inequities. "[O]ne of the
things that I drill into them is the whole piece about being active and having
a voice." Referring to debates about whether or not, during the Obama administration, the governor of her state would accept federal stimulus funds,
she recounted her efforts to galvanize her students:

> I'm like, "Look. Look at your politicians. Look at your governor
> who is on TV talking about, 'We don't need stimulus money!'"
> [Laughter]. You know? Think about what it is that is going on,
> and where the cuts are. And the biggest cuts are in education and
> healthcare, and I'm like, "Are you serious?" So yes, I'm definitely an
> advocate.[110]

Along with fiscal equity suits across the country, such views acknowledge that inadequate and unequal funding denies the educational
opportunity of students in high-poverty schools. While some cases have
secured favorable court rulings toward equalized funding, the obstacles
to carrying out the courts' orders has exposed the deep resistance to the
ideals of equity espoused by the TFA alumni here. Thus, the content of
alumni's conversations stakes out highly contested ground, but in making
the arguments, these alumni are working to keep these difficult issues and
a broad array of solutions, even unpopular ones, on the table.

Though we have argued for the significance of simple conversation,
some alumni with whom we spoke felt otherwise, and downplayed the
importance of their discussions about education. Kathy Feeley is a history
professor at a private liberal arts college in California who left her TFA
placement in New York City before completing her first year. She implied
that talk is cheap, compared to concrete actions. "I'm [not] talking about
going to political rallies, [I'm] just talking about it [education] informally

to people who may or may not agree, just in conversation."[111] Likewise, for all of her speaking out in a variety of venues about education, Caroline Sabin worried that simply talking might not be enough. "[P]eople . . . have heard that [i.e., about education] from me, but that is all word[s], right?"[112] In the end we believe our participants' words do have meaning. Their cultural capital and their experiences working in low-income schools give their words the resonance to inform a wider population about systemic inequities in nation's schools.

Participants identified their TFA experiences of teaching in poor schools and communities in the early 1990s as a critical influence on their post-TFA life choices, perspectives on American society, and commitments to and actions on behalf of educational opportunity over more than 2 decades. We recognize that the importance of TFA within their life narrative may be due to the fact that the experience occurred at a particularly pivotal "coming of age" moment in the interviewees' lives, as described in Chapter 2. Similarly, we acknowledge that participants' inclination to correlate their TFA experiences with subsequent beliefs and actions may be a result of the interview's focus on Teach For America, as opposed to other events that may have shaped their adult lives. Even taking into account such caveats, the interviews clearly demonstrate alumni's belief that their TFA experiences were one of the most significant influences to shape who they became and how they looked at the world.

CONCLUSION

Given the ink spilled on Teach For America, it seems obvious that the initiative has exerted an immense impact over the last 30 years. This chapter synthesizes familiar aspects of that impact, including the preponderance of TFA leadership in education reform organizations and the penetration of TFA's theory of action into mainstream assumptions about improving teaching and education in underserved schools. It also takes issue with that theory of action, identifying the problematic influence of TFA's devaluation of preparation, pipeline focus on elite college graduates, and willful ignorance of social context and school conditions. We additionally make a case for a less heralded sort of "impact," in the effects of the TFA experience on individual lives. Some of these effects shaped professional trajectories, drawing individuals such as Furman Brown, Andrew Mac-Kenzie, Christina Brown, and Jennifer Denino, for example, into the field of education across a variety of roles, when it isn't at all clear that they would have ended up there if not for TFA. Other aspects of the TFA experience reverberated more personally, informing individual beliefs and views about society and the role of education in mitigating inequality. These more personal takeaways, for many of our interviewees, led to various forms of advocacy, from support and volunteer work on behalf of public schools and districts to casual conversations within social networks, some of which included powerful opinion shapers and decision-makers.

Over the last 3 decades, TFA has been a figurehead for the merits of alternate routes in the polarized debate between alternate vs. traditional pathways to teaching. The complaints of our interviewees represent not just an indictment of TFA, but also a lamentably common experience among new teachers in urban schools then and now, whether "traditionally" or alternatively prepared for the classroom. Rather than use the alumni's experiences as yet more grist in the narrow argument about alternate vs. traditional pathways, we suggest two takeaways from our evidence. First, TFA missed a significant opportunity to rethink the pathway to the classroom, and second, this failure, along with the struggles of traditional teacher education programs, together illustrate how hard it is and has been to prepare and support effective teachers for schools serving disenfranchised communities.

More effective approaches to teacher preparation certainly exist, and many colleges and departments of teacher education are part of the larger field's discussions about how to make teacher education better.[113] States, districts, and even individual schools have also turned to mentoring and induction programs, to help new teachers exercise and develop their craft in substantive ways. It is worth noting, however, that university-based teacher preparation and associated efforts toward institutionalizing mentoring are constrained by lack of resources, capacity, and the kind of incentives that galvanize real change in bureaucratic systems. Likewise, seriously addressing school context will require a range of interventions, from "attention to the structures that develop, support, and facilitate the work of effective teachers" to broader initiatives that transcend the walls of the school to address larger structural inequalities.[114] Ultimately, the anguish suffered by the 1990 TFA participants when they took their place at the head of a classroom derives from a larger chain of concerns, many of which remain unaddressed today.

Table of Interviewees, Years in Classroom, and Career

TFA Interviewees	Years in the classroom	Career (as of 2009)
Participants who quit the first year		
Feeley, Kathy	months	History professor
Lawson, Lori	months	Teaches fundraising for non-profits
Schneider, Jane	months	Dermatologist
Stephan, Mark	months	Environmental policy professor
Participants who taught for 2 years		
Brewer, Diane	2 years	Theater professor
Brown, Furman	2 years	Director, school innovation organization
Downing, Spencer	2 years	History professor
Flanagan, Leo	2 years	Principal
Joftus, Scott	2 years	Educational consultant
Lyles, R. Brent	2 years	Director, education nonprofit
Norbert, Bill	2 years	Lawyer
Ramos, Marife	2 years	Human resources administrator
Simes, Jeffrey	2 years	Lawyer
Trasen, Jan	2 years	Lawyer
Participants who taught 3–8 years		
Bird, Eric	3 years	Golf course superintendent
Bond, Constance	3 years	VP, Woodrow Wilson National Fellowship Foundation
Clark, Felicia	3 years	Math curriculum leader at L.A. Unified
Rosenstock, Ellen	3 years	Producer, Leapfrog Enterprises

TFA Interviewees	Years in the classroom	Career (as of 2009)
Murray, Susanne*	4 years	Marketer for education technology
Turner-Weller, Heather	4 years	Nurse
Robinson, Lisa	5 years	Photographer
Sabin, Caroline	8 years	Homemaker
Schuhart, Arthur	8 years	English professor
Participants who taught 9–18 years		
Brown, Christina	10 years	Director of school reform organization
Leon-Didion, Priscilla	11 years	Science teacher
Childs Wardlaw, Nichole	12	Certified nurse midwife
Denino, Jennifer*	13	Education professor
McKenzie, Andrew	14	Instructional specialist & grad student
Terrell, Avis	17 years	Assistant principal
Gomez, Carlos	18 years	Spanish teacher

*Oral history narrators are conventionally not anonymized; however, two participants requested pseudonyms be used in association with their interviews and we complied.

Methodology

We recruited our subjects in the fall of 2008 by emailing all members of the 1990 cohort for whom the TFA website listed contact information (288 of about 480 original members) and inviting them to participate in an oral history interview. Fifty-six alumni responded and agreed to be interviewed. From this group, we selected 30 diverse individuals on the basis of four key variables: gender, undergraduate institution attended, region where they taught, and current career. We also considered program completion, and interviewed 24 individuals who finished their 2-year TFA commitment and six alumni (located via snowball sampling) who did not complete their 2-year commitment.[1]

Because of teaching's historically feminized nature, we wanted to understand the gender dynamics of an arguably elite pathway into teaching and so balanced our sample between men (12) and women (18). We also wanted to ensure a cross-section of the elite undergraduate institutions that participants attended, to illustrate the nature of their educational backgrounds. Gathering subjects who taught across the range of TFA sites enabled us to investigate both context-specific challenges as well as more general experiences associated with first year teaching in underserved schools. Finally, given our interest in understanding how participants' TFA experiences figured into their lives and professional choices over time, we also incorporated information about their current careers (which were listed on the 2008 TFA website) into our selection process.

Regarding the last of these variables, though our sample is not representative, we tried to select participants who roughly reflected both the range and frequency of careers that appeared on the website. We attended to whether participants' careers were related to education or outside of the field altogether and balanced our sample accordingly. More commonly, researchers have focused on whether TFA participants persist as classroom teachers or not, but we found that static distinction did not capture the complexity of individuals' professional journeys over time. We thus considered K–12 teachers, college and university professors, school district personnel, and educational consultants or reformers to be working in fields related to education. With this definition, approximately half of the total number (170) of alumni who reported careers on the website were working in a field related to education; in our sample, just over half (16 participants) reported working in careers related to education while the remainder (14) worked in other fields. Our sample also featured a range of classroom tenures (see Appendix A).

We conducted 30 in-depth, 2-hour oral history interviews, in which we addressed participants' backgrounds, TFA experiences, and subsequent career choices. Digital recordings of the interviews were transcribed and sent to participants for review. Data analysis was ongoing and involved reading transcripts and manual coding for emergent themes as well as themes developed *a priori*. We created several tables based on *a priori* themes, to systematically mine narrators' testimonies for specific information. To elicit new themes, both authors read the interview transcripts multiple times, independently noting initial codes. We then shared and reviewed our initial codes, to ensure that they accurately described the themes emerging in the data. Through this grounded theory approach, we then "focused" the codes as relevant themes were revealed. Once we had completed coding for each working theme, we separated data supporting each theme into separate theme files. Materials in each file helped us to develop our ideas about the significance, meaning, and place of these themes within our larger body of work.

We recognized the tension between appreciating the participants' stories as individual and idiosyncratic while also subjecting those stories to scholarly interpretation and analysis with the intention of drawing general insights to describe a particular historical moment.[2] We reconciled this potential conflict by referring to primary source materials, including studies, newspaper and journal articles, and reports, as well as secondary literature, to establish the larger context of urban teaching and Teach For America in the 1990s. Within this larger framework, we could then analyze and compare the subjective experiences of the TFA participants, and so understand what aspects of their stories might have been unique and what were largely shared experiences that reflected their situated (in terms of time and place) realities.

Notes

Foreword

1. *Forbes*. (2019). America's top charities. https://www.forbes.com/companies/teach-for-america/?list=top-charities/&sh=53ec1e111fb0
2. Marsh, D. (1979). The classroom effectiveness of Teacher Corps graduates: A national assessment. *The Journal of Classroom Interaction* 15(1), 25–33. http://www.jstor.org/stable/43997288
3. Department of Education, Washington, DC, *Teacher Corps: A Collection of Abstracts. A Program to Improve Educational Personnel Development and to Strengthen Educational Opportunities in Low-Income Schools.* (1965–1982), https://files.eric.ed.gov/fulltext/ED216003.pdf; C. Dziuban, (1967). The National Teacher Corps Program, 1966–67 Evaluation Report. Atlanta, GA: Atlanta Public Schools, https://www.academia.edu/27921619/The_National_Teacher_Corps_Program_1966_67_Evaluation_Report; Office of Education: Department of Health, Education, and Welfare. (1971). Report to the Congress, Assessment of the Teacher Corps Program at the University of Southern California and Participating Schools in Los Angeles and Riverside Counties. https://www.gao.gov/assets/210/202021.pdf.

Introduction

1. Alternate paths to the classroom sought to upend the status quo by circumventing the existing system of preparation, appealing to non-traditional candidates, provoking competitive change in traditional teacher education, and ratcheting up the quality of teachers. See Kenneth Zeichner and Elizabeth A. Hutchinson, "The Development of Alternative Certification Policies and Programs in the United States," in *Alternative Routes to Teaching: Mapping the New Landscape of Teacher Education*, ed. Pam Grossman and Susanna Loeb (Cambridge: Harvard University Press, 2008); Emily Feistritzer and Charlene K. Haar, *Alternate Routes to Teaching* (Upper Saddle River, NJ: Pearson Education, 2008). See also David Labaree, "Teach For America and Teacher Ed: Heads They Win, Tails We Lose," *Journal of Teacher Education* 61, nos. 1–2 (2010): 48–55, for an analysis of the marketing "marvel" that has propelled TFA to such popularity.
2. Education researchers Zeichner and Conklin suggest that the field of university-based teacher education has a "history of self critique," which has provoked calls over time for substantive change in the way teachers are prepared; likewise, they advocate for serious evaluation of nontraditional programs or alternate routes that critics have touted as solutions to or replacements for university-based teacher education. See Kenneth Zeichner and Hilary G. Conklin, "Beyond Knowledge Ventriloquism and Echo Chambers: Raising the Quality of the Debate in Teacher Education," *Teachers College Record* 118, no. 12 (2016): 3.

3. Karen Hammerness & Michele Reininger, "Who goes into early-entry programs?" in *Alternate Routes to Teaching: Mapping the New Landscape of Teacher Education,* eds. Pam Grossman and Susanna Loeb (Cambridge, MA: Harvard Education Press, 2008): 31–64.; Pierre Bourdieu, *The State Nobility* (Stanford, CA: Stanford University Press, 1996).

4. While much oral history practice has rightly focused on introducing the voices of disenfranchised and historically silenced individuals, Linda Shopes reminds us that interviews with the cultural elite can provide "the story underneath the story," which often goes missing from the public record. See Shopes (n.d.), "What Is Oral History?" http://history-matters.gmu.edu/mse/oral/oral.pdf.

5. Shopes, "What Is Oral History?"; Jack Dougherty, "From Anecdote to Analysis: Oral Interviews and New Scholarship in Educational History," *Journal of American History* 86, no. 2 (1999): 718.

6. Dougherty, "From Anecdote to Analysis," 718.

7. Mary Jo Maynes, Jennifer L. Pierce, and Barbara Laslett, *Telling Stories: The Use of Personal Narratives in the Social Sciences and History* (Ithaca: Cornell University Press, 2008); Dougherty, 718.

8. Maynes, Pierce, and Laslett, *Telling Stories*; Thomas Dublin and Walter Licht, *The Face of Decline: The Pennsylvania Anthracite Region in the Twentieth Century* (Ithaca, NY: Cornell University Press, 2000), 10.

9. Please see Appendix B for more about this book's methodology.

10. This is not to understate the significance of developments such as clinical residencies or the growing attention to induction support, but rather to acknowledge the uneven and inconsistent implementation of such developments across states and teacher education programs.

11. Carl Grant and Walter Secada, "Preparing Teachers for Diversity," in *Handbook of Research on Teacher Education,* ed. W. R. Houston (New York: Macmillan, 1990), 404.

12. Grant and Secada, "Preparing Teachers for Diversity," 404.

13. Michael Huberman (1989), "The professional life cycle of teachers," *Teachers College Record,* 91 (1) 31–57.

14. Zeichner and Conklin, "Beyond Knowledge Ventriloquism and Echo Chambers."

Chapter 1

1. Susan Chira, "In the Drive to Revive Schools, Better Teachers but Too Few," *New York Times,* August 27, 1990.

2. Ian Huschle, Director of Communications, Teach For America, quoted in Michel Marriott, "For Fledgling Teacher Corps, Hard Lessons," *New York Times,* December 5, 1990.

3. Wendy Kopp, "An Argument and Plan for the Creation of the Teacher Corps" (Undergraduate thesis, Princeton University, 1989), 4:1.

4. See, for example, Alexander W. Astin et al., *Cooperative Institutional Research Program, The American Freshman: National Norms for Fall 1987* (Los Angeles: Higher Education Research Institute, 1987), 4, regarding attitudes toward teaching among college freshman in 1987; see Valena White Plisko, *The Condition of Education,* 1983 edition, A Statistical Report (Washington, DC: National Center for Education Statistics, 1983), 184, as cited in Linda Darling-Hammond, *Beyond the Commission Reports. The Coming Crisis in Teaching* (Santa Monica, CA: The Rand Corporation, 1984), 15, for declining number and proportion of education degrees awarded. For impending teacher shortages, see Amy Stuart Wells, "Teacher Shortage Termed Most Critical in Inner-City Schools," *New York Times,* May 10, 1988.

5. Jack Schneider, *Excellence for All: How a New Breed of Reformers is Transforming America's Public Schools* (Nashville: Vanderbilt University Press, 2011), 83; see also Gerald A. Dorfman and Paul R. Hanna, "Can Education Be Reformed?," in *Thinking about*

America: The United States in the 1990s, eds. Annelise Anderson and Dennis L. Bark (Stanford: Hoover Institution Press, 1988), 387, quoted in Schneider.

6. "Help! Teacher Can't Teach," *Time*, June 16, 1980; "How to Teach Our Kids," Newsweek special edition, Education: A Consumer's Handbook, Volume Cxvi, no. 28, Fall/Winter 1990; Clinton B. Allison, "The American Teacher: Why Don't Teachers Get More Respect?" *Counterpoints* 6 (1995): 25–45.

7. Dan Lortie, *Schoolteacher: A Sociological Study* (Chicago: University of Chicago Press, 1975), eloquently establishes this dynamic; nearly 50 years later, Diana D'Amico Pawlewicz, *Blaming Teachers: Professionalization Policies and the Failure of Reform in American History* (New Brunswick, NJ: Rutgers University Press, 2020), revisits this dynamic in which teachers are simultaneously cast as essential to the success of schools and responsible for their failures.

8. For a review of scholarship on teachers' identity and its impact on public perceptions, see Judith Kafka, "In Search of a Grand Narrative: The Turbulent History of Teaching," in *Handbook of Research on Teaching*, 5th Edition, ed. Drew H. Gitomer and Courtney A. Bell (Washington, DC: American Educational Research Association, 2016), 69–126.

9. "Mickey Mouse" coursework derives from the assessment of James Bryant Conant, *The Education of American Teachers* (New York: McGraw-Hill, 1963). For critiques stretching back to the 1960s, in addition to Conant, see James Koerner, *The Miseducation of American Teachers* (Boston: Houghton Mifflin, 1963). More recent iterations of these criticisms can be found in a slew of 1980s reports, including The Holmes Group, *Tomorrow's Teachers* (East Lansing, MI: Author, 1986); Carnegie Task Force on Teaching as a Profession, *A Nation Prepared: Teachers for the 21st Century* (Washington, DC: Carnegie Forum on Education and the Economy, 1986); National Commission for Excellence in Teacher Education, *A Call for Change in Teacher Education* (Washington, DC: National Commission on Excellence in Teacher Education: American Association of Colleges for Teacher Education, 1985); and Southern Regional Education Board, Commission for Educational Quality, *Improving Teacher Education: An Agenda for Higher Education and the Schools. A Report to The Southern Regional Education Board by Its Commission for Educational Quality* (Atlanta, GA: Southern Regional Education Board, 1985). For broader syntheses of criticisms of teacher education, see James Fraser, *Preparing America's Teachers: A History* (New York: Teachers College Press, 2007), and Jack Schneider, "Marching Forward, Marching in Circles: A History of Problems and Dilemmas in Teacher Preparation," *Journal of Teacher Education* 69, no. 4 (September/October 2018), 330–340.

10. Doug Rossinow, *The Reagan Era: A History of the 1980s* (New York: Columbia University Press, 2015), 1.

11. Rossinow, *Reagan Era*, 29; William C. Berman, *America's Right Turn: From Nixon to Clinton*, 2nd ed. (Baltimore: Johns Hopkins University Press, 1998); Kevin M. Kruse and Julian E. Zelizer, *Fault Lines: A History of the United States since 1974* (New York: W.W. Norton & Company, 2019), 96.

12. Spencer Rich, "Clinton Vows to 'Honor Middle-Class Values,'" *Washington Post*, October 24, 1991, quoted in Rossinow, Reagan Era, 9.

13. Dorothy Shipps, "Echoes of Corporate Influence: Managing Away Urban School Troubles," in *Reconstructing the Common Good in Education: Coping with Intractable American Dilemmas*, ed. Larry Cuban and Dorothy Shipps (Palo Alto: Stanford University Press, 2000), 94.

14. William Reese, "Public Schools and the Elusive Search for the Common Good," in Cuban and Shipps, *Reconstructing the Common Good*, 14.

15. Rossinow, *Reagan Era*, 139.

16. Charles Payne, *So Much Reform, So Little Change* (Cambridge, MA: Harvard Education Press, 2008), 3.

17. James Patterson, *Restless Giant: The United States from Watergate to Bush v. Gore* (New York: Oxford University Press, 2007).

18. Elizabeth Hinton, *From the War on Poverty to the War on Crime: The Making of Mass Incarceration in America* (Cambridge, MA: Harvard University Press, 2016), 316.

19. Kruse and Zelizer, *Fault Lines,* 114.

20. On grassroots movements of the time, see Michael Stewart Foley, *Front Porch Politics: The Forgotten Heyday of American Activism in the 1970s and 1980s* (New York: Hill and Wang, 2013).

21. Rossinow, *Reagan Era,* 160.

22. Schneider, *Excellence for All,* 19.

23. Lisa McGirr, *Suburban Warriors: The Origins of the New American Right* (Princeton, NJ: Princeton University Press, 2001), 10.

24. Schneider, *Excellence for All,* 20.

25. Regarding legal challenges to school finance, see Michael A. Rebell, "Adequacy Litigations: A New Path to Equity?" in B*ringing Equity Back: Research for a New Era in American Educational Policy,* eds. Janice Petrovich, Amy Stuart Wells, and Alison Bernstein (New York: Teachers College Press, 2005); for the rise of homeschooling, see Milton Gaither, *Homeschool: An American History* (New York: Palgrave MacMillan, 2008). The expansion of and changes in special education are well documented in Robert Osgood, *The History of Special Education: A Struggle for Equality in American Public Schools* (Westport, CT: Praeger, 2007). Kathryn A. McDermott examines the complicated interactions of these factors within several states in "A National Movement Comes Home: State Politics and Educational Accountability in the 1990s," in *To Educate a Nation: Federal and National Strategies of School Reform,* eds. Carl F. Kaestle and Alyssa E. Lodewick (Lawrence, KS: University of Kansas Press, 2007), 117–43. For the end of court-ordered desegregation mandates, see Sean F. Reardon, Elena Tej Grewal, Demetra Kalogrides, and Erica Greenberg, "Brown Fades: The End of Court-Ordered School Desegregation and the Resegregation of American Public Schools," *Journal of Policy Analysis and Management* 31, no. 4 (Fall 2012): 876–904.

26. Susan Fuhrman, "Education Policy: A New Context for Governance," *Publius* 17, no. 3 (Summer 1987): 134.

27. Reese, "Public Schools," 13.

28. See, for example, *Business-Higher Education Forum, America's Competitive Challenge: The Need for a National Response* (Washington, DC: Business-Higher Education Forum, 1983); College Board Educational Equity Project, *Academic Preparation for College: What Students Need to Know and Be Able to Do* (New York: College Board, 1983); National Science Foundation, *Educating Americans for the 21st Century: A Plan of Action for Improving Mathematics, Science, and Technology Education for All American Elementary and Secondary Students So That Their Achievement Is the Best in the World by 1995* (Washington, D.C.: National Science Foundation, 1983); *Twentieth Century Fund, Making the Grade: Report of the Twentieth Century* Fund Task Force on Federal Elementary and Secondary Education Policy (New York: Twentieth Century Fund, 1983).

29. Kopp, "An Argument and Plan," 8.

30. Theodore Sizer, *Horace's Compromise: The Dilemma of the American High School* (Boston: Houghton Mifflin Company, 1984); John Goodlad, *A Place Called School: Prospects for the Future* (New York: McGraw-Hill Book Company, 1984); and Ernest Boyer, *High School: A Report on Secondary Education in America* (New York: Harper & Row, Publishers, 1983).

31. United States, National Commission on Excellence in Education, A Nation at Risk: The Imperative for Educational Reform (Washington D.C.: The National Commission on Excellence in Education, 1983).

32. Diane Ravitch, "Education in the 1980s: A Concern for 'Quality,'" *Education Week,* 10 January 1990.

33. A. Harry Passow, "Tackling the Reform Reports of the 1980s," *Phi Delta Kappan* 65, no. 10 (June 1984): 675; Ravitch, "Education in the 1980s."

34. United States, National Commission on Excellence in Education, *A Nation at Risk.*

35. Ernest Boyer, *High School: A Report on Secondary Education in America* (New York: Harper and Row, 1983), xii, cited in Schneider, p. 29.

36. Schneider, *Excellence for All,* 27.

37. Ravitch, "Education in the 1980s."

38. Laura S. Hamilton, Brian M. Stecher, and Kun Yuan, *Standards-Based Reform in the United States: History, Research, and Future Directions* (Santa Monica, CA: RAND Corporation, 2008).

39. Michael J. Petrilli, "A New Era of Accountability in Education Has Barely Just Begun," Flypaper (blog), September 25, 2009, https://fordhaminstitute.org/national/commentary/new-era-accountability-education-has-barely-just-begun.

40. Payne, *So Much Reform,* 2–3.

41. Thomas Timar and David Kirp, "Education Reform in the 1980s: Lessons from the States," *Phi Delta Kappan* 70, no. 7 (March 1989): 506.

42. David Labaree, "Teach for America and Teacher Ed: Heads They Win, Tails We Lose," *Journal of Teacher Education* 61, no. 1–2 (January 2010): 48–55.

43. Diane Massell, Michael W. Kirst, and Margaret Hoppe, *Persistence and Change: Standards-Based Reform in Nine States* (Philadelphia: Consortium for Policy Research in Education, 1997).

44. Schneider, *Excellence for All,* 32–33; Laura S. Hamilton, Brian M. Stecher, Julie A. Marsh, Jennifer Sloan McCombs, Abby Robyn, Jennifer Lin Russell, Scott Naftel and Heather Barney, *No Child Left Behind: Experiences of Teachers and Administrators in Three States* (Santa Monica, CA: Rand Corporation, 2007).

45. Fuhrman, "Education Policy," 137; David L. Clark and Terry Astuto, *The Significance and Permanence of Changes in Federal Educational Policy 1980–88* (Bloomington, IN: Policy Studies Center of the University Council for Educational Administration, 1986).

46. James W. Fraser and Lauren Lefty, *Teaching Teachers: Changing Paths and Enduring Debates* (Baltimore: Johns Hopkins University Press, 2018), 30.

47. Shipps, "Echoes of Corporate Influence," 82–105.

48. Denis P. Doyle, Bruce S. Cooper, and Roberta Trachtman, *Taking Charge: State Action in School Reform in the 1980s* (Indianapolis, IN: Hudson Institute, 1991), quoted in Shipps, "Echoes of Corporate Influence," 91.

49. Historians continue to add to a growing body of scholarship documenting this history; examples include Elizabeth Todd-Breland, *A Political Education: Black Politics and Education Reform in Chicago Since the 1960s* (Chapel Hill, NC: University of North Carolina Press, 2018); Clarence Taylor, *Knocking at Our Own Door: Milton A. Galamison and the Struggle for School Integration in New York City* (New York: Columbia University Press, 1997); Adina Back, "Exposing the 'Whole Segregation Myth': The Harlem Nine and New York City's School Desegregation Battles," in *North: Black Freedom Struggles Outside the South, 1940–1980,* eds. J. Theoharis and K. Woodard (New York: Palgrave Macmillan, 2003); Ruben Donato, *The Other Struggle for Equal Schools: Mexican Americans During the Civil Rights Era* (Albany, NY: State University of New York Press, 1997); Jack Dougherty, *More than One Struggle: The Evolution of Black School Reform in Milwaukee* (Chapel Hill, NC: University of North Carolina Press, 2004).

50. See Heather Lewis, *New York City Public Schools from Brownsville to Bloomberg: Community Control and Its Legacy* (New York: Teachers College Press, 2013); Russell Rickford, *We Are an African People: Independent Education, Black Power, and the Radical Imagination* (New York: Oxford University Press, 2016); and Jon N. Hale, *The Freedom Schools: Student Activists in the Mississippi Civil Rights Movement* (New York: Columbia University Press, 2016).

51. See, for example, Brittany Lewer, "Pursuing 'Real Power to Parents': Babette Edwards's Activism from Community Control to Charter Schools," in *Educating Harlem: A Century of Schooling and Resistance in a Black Community,* eds. Ansley T. Erickson and Ernest Morrell (New York: Columbia University Press, 2019), 276–297.

52. Seymour Fliegel, *Miracle in East Harlem: The Fight for Choice in Public Education* (New York: The Manhattan Institute, 1993), 7.

53. United States, National Commission on Excellence in Education, *A Nation at Risk*.

54. This history is explored more fully in Chapter 6, but 20 years earlier, both James Bryant Conant and James Koerner took aim at the preponderance of what Conant deemed "Mickey Mouse" pedagogical courses that squeezed out liberal arts coursework in their respective studies of teacher preparation, *The Education of American Teachers* (New York: McGraw-Hill, 1963) and *The Miseducation of American Teachers* (Boston: Houghton Mifflin, 1963).

55. This discussion tended to occur in the terms of supply and demand—see for example Lynn Olson and Blake Rodman, "Is There a Teacher Shortage? It's Anyone's Guess," *Education Week*, June 24, 1987—but perhaps the most compelling case for the decreasing appeal of teaching at the time can be found in Linda Darling-Hammond, *Beyond the Commission Reports. The Coming Crisis in Teaching* (Santa Monica, CA: The Rand Corporation, 1984).

56. Kopp, "An Argument and Plan," 25.

57. Timar and Kirp, "Education Reform in the 1980s," 506.

58. William R. Johnson, "Empowering Practitioners: Homes, Carnegie, and the Lessons of History," *History of Education Quarterly* 27, no. 2 (Summer 1987): 221–240.

59. Johnson, "Empowering Practitioners," 223.

60. Fraser and Lefty, *Teaching Teachers*. In the summary that follows, we are indebted to Fraser and Lefty for the synthesis found in their book's introduction and first chapter.

61. Fraser and Lefty, 26.

62. Fraser and Lefty, 28.

63. Reese, "Public Schools," 14.

64. Arthur Levine, *When Dreams and Heroes Died* (San Francisco: Jossey-Bass, 1980); see also the UCLA Higher Education Research Institute annual freshman surveys.

65. Arthur Levine and Deborah Hirsch, "Undergraduates in Transition: A New Wave of Activism on American College Campus [*sic*]," *Higher Education* 22, no. 2 (September 1991): 119–128.

66. Levine and Hirsch, "Undergraduates in Transition," 120, 126.

67. For example, see Thomas Moore, "Idealism's Rebirth," *U.S. News and World Report*, October 24, 1988, and Kathleen Teltsch, "New York City Attracts the Young as Volunteers," *New York Times*, August 23, 1987.

68. Robert C. Serow, "Students and Voluntarism: Looking Into the Motives of Community Service Participants," *American Educational Research Journal* 28, no. 3 (Fall 1991): 543–556.

69. Arthur Levine and Deborah Hirsch, "Undergraduates in Transition: A New Wave of Activism on American College Campus [*sic*]," *Higher Education* 22 (1991): 121.

70. George Bush, Republican Presidential Nomination Acceptance Speech (Republican National Convention, New Orleans, LA, August 18, 1988).

71. Robert A. Rhoads, "Student Protest and Multicultural Reform: Making Sense of Campus Unrest in the 1990s," *The Journal of Higher Education* 69, no. 6 (November-December 1998): 621–646.

72. Bethany L. Rogers, "'Better' People, Better Teaching: The Vision of the National Teacher Corps, 1965–1968," *History of Education Quarterly* 49, no. 3 (August 2009): 347–372; see especially note 5.

73. Wendy Kopp, *One Day, All Children: The Unlikely Triumph of Teach for America and What I Learned Along the Way* (New York, NY: Public Affairs, 2001), 24, 22.

74. Kopp, 34.

75. Teach For America Flyer, reprinted in Kopp, *One Day, All Children*, 36–37.

76. Kopp, "An Argument and Plan," 48.

77. Kopp, 52.

78. Kopp, 108.

79. Doug Rossinow, *The Politics of Authenticity: Liberalism, Christianity, and the New Left in America* (New York: Columbia University Press, 1998); Elizabeth Cobbs-Hoffman, *All You Need Is Love: The Peace Corps and the Spirit of the 1960s* (Cambridge, MA: Harvard University Press, 1998); Bethany L. Rogers, "Promises and Limitations of Youth Activism in the 1960s: The Case of the National Teacher Corps," *The Sixties* 1, no. 2 (2008): 187–207.

80. Kopp, *One Day, All Children.*

81. Christina Brown, interview with Megan Blumenreich, April 4, 2009.

82. David Labaree, "Teach For America and Teacher Ed," 49.

Chapter 2

1. Wendy Kopp, "An Argument and Plan for the Creation of the Teacher Corps" (Undergraduate thesis, Princeton University, 1989), 52.

2. Daniel Oscar, Recruitment letter, in Wendy Kopp, *One Day, All Children: The Unlikely Triumph of Teach For America and What I Learned Along the Way* (New York: Public Affairs, 2001), 30–31.

3. See Glen H. Elder, "Time, Human Agency, and Social Change: Perspectives on the Life Course," *Social Psychology Quarterly* 57, no. 1 (March 1994): 4–15; Richard G. Braungart and Margaret M. Braungart, "Life-Course and Generational Politics," *Annual Review of Sociology* 12 (1986): 205–231.

4. Elder, "Perspectives on the Life Course," 4.

5. Ivor F. Goodson and Pat Sikes, "Studying Teachers' Life Histories and Professional Practices," in *Life History Research in Educational Settings: Learning from Lives,* ed. Pat Sikes (Buckingham, U.K.: Open University Press, 2001), 57–74.

6. Margaret M. Braungart and Richard G. Braungart, "The Life-Course Development of Left- and Right-Wing Leaders from the 1960s," *Political Psychology* 11, no. 2 (June 1990): 252.

7. Daniel Oscar to Student Leaders, October 23, 1989, reprinted in Kopp, *One Day, All Children,* 30–32.

8. Kopp, *One Day, All Children,* xi

9. Caroline Sabin, interview with Megan Blumenreich, November 29, 2008.

10. Jeffrey Simes, interview with Bethany L. Rogers, February 9, 2009.

11. Andrew McKenzie, interview with Megan Blumenreich, February 8, 2009.

12. Donna Foote, "What Is Teach for America Really Like?" interview by Lucia Graves, *U.S. News & World Report,* March 5, 2008.

13. Lortie, *Schoolteacher: A Sociological Study* (Chicago: University of Chicago Press, 1975), 65.

14. Lortie, *Schoolteacher,* 65.

15. Sari K. Biklen, *School Work: Gender and the Cultural Construction of Teaching* (New York: Teachers College Press, 1995); Ellen Condliffe Lagemann, *An Elusive Science: The Troubling History of Education Research* (Chicago: University of Chicago Press, 2000); Amitai Etzioni, ed., *The Semi-Professions and Their Organization: Teachers, Nurses, Social Workers* (New York, NY: Free Press, 1969).

16. Sean P. Corcoran, William N. Evans, and Robert M. Schwab, "Women, the Labor Market, and the Declining Relative Quality of Teachers," *Journal of Policy Analysis and Management* 23, no. 3(2004): 449–470.

17. Edward Liu, Susan M Kardos, David Kauffman, Heather G. Peske, and Susan Moore Johnson, "'Barely Breaking Even': Incentives, Rewards, and the High Costs of Choosing to Teach" (working paper, Harvard University, 2000), 1, https://projectngt.gse.harvard.edu/files/gse-projectngt/files/barely_breaking_even_0700.pdf.

18. Sylvia A. Allegretto, Sean P. Corcoran, and Lawrence Mishel. *The Teaching Penalty: Teacher Pay Losing Ground* (Washington, DC: Economic Policy Institute, 2008); Eric A.

Hanushek and Steven G. Rivkin, "Pay, Working Conditions, and Teacher Quality," *Future of Children* 17, no. 1 (Spring 2007): 73.

19. In an interesting outlier, two of our 30 interviewees, both women of color, identified the teaching salary or getting paid as a benefit of doing TFA.

20. Eran Tamir, "Choosing to Teach in Urban Schools Among Graduates of Elite Colleges," *Urban Education* 44, no. 5 (2009): 527. See also Dan Lortie, *Schoolteacher*; Carmen A. Morales, "Education Majors: Why Teaching as a Career?" *Education* 114, no. 3 (Spring 1994): 340–343; Lagemann, *An Elusive Science*; Geraldine J. Clifford, "Man/Woman/Teacher: Gender, Family and Career in American Educational History," in *American Teachers: Histories of a Profession at Work*, ed. Donald Warren (New York: Macmillan, 1989), 293–343; Judith E. Lanier and Judith W. Little, "Research on Teacher Education," in *Handbook of Research on Teaching*, ed. Merlin C. Whitrock (New York: Macmillan, 1986), 527–569; Karen Zumwalt, and Elizabeth Craig, "Teachers' Characteristics: Research on the Demographic Profile," in *Studying Teacher Education: The Report of the AERA Panel on Research and Teacher Education*, eds. Marilyn Cochran-Smith & Ken Zeichner (Mahwah, NJ: Lawrence Erlbaum, 2005), 111–156.

21. Daniel C. Humphrey and Marjorie E. Weschler, "Insights into Alternative Certification: Initial Findings from a Nation," *Teachers College Record* 109, no. 3 (2007): 483–530.

22. Regarding elite undergraduate colleges, see Tamir, "Choosing to Teach in Urban Schools"; regarding Center X, see Brad Olson and Lauren Anderson, "Courses of Action: A Qualitative Investigation into Urban Teacher Retention and Career Development," *Urban Education* 42, no. 1 (2007): 5–29.

23. Tamir, "Choosing to Teach in Urban Schools." See also Pierre Bourdieu, "The Forms of Capital," in *Handbook of Theory and Research for the Sociology of Education*, ed. John Richardson (Westport, CT: Greenwood, 1986), 241–260; Pierre Bourdieu, The State Nobility (Stanford, CA: Stanford University Press, 1996);

24. Tamir, "Choosing to Teach in Urban Schools," 527. See also Helen Snodgrass, "Perspectives of High-Achieving Women on Teaching," *The New Educator* 6 (2010): 135–152.

25. Braungart and Braungart, "The Life-Course Development," 248–249. See also Bruno Bettelheim, "The Problem of Generations," in *Youth: Change and Challenge*, ed. Erik Erikson (New York, NY: Basic Books, 1963) and Erik Erikson, *Identity: Youth and Crisis* (New York, NY: Norton, 1968).

26. Braungart and Braungart, "The Life-Course Development," 249.

27. Simes, interview.

28. Robert V. Bullough and Kendra M. Hall-Kenyon, "The Call to Teach and Teacher Hopefulness," *Teacher Development* 15, no. 2 (2011): 128; Robert C. Serow, Deborah J. Eaker, and Krista D. Forrest, "'I Want to See Some Kind of Growth out of Them': What the Service Ethic Means to Teacher-Education Students," *American Educational Research Journal* 31, no. 1 (Spring 1994): 27–48.

29. Elaine Chin and John W. Young, "A Person-Oriented Approach to Characterizing Beginning Teachers in Alternative Certification Programs," *Educational Researcher* 36, no. 2 (2007): 77; see also Bethany L. Rogers, "Teaching and Social Reform in the 1960s: Lessons from National Teacher Corps Oral Histories," *Oral History Review* 35, no. 1 (2008): 39–67.

30. Spencer Downing, interview with Megan Blumenreich, April 1, 2009.

31. Sabin, interview.

32. Avis Terrell, interview with Megan Blumenreich, September 26, 2009.

33. Lori Lawson, interview with Megan Blumenreich, March 11, 2009.

34. Furman Brown, interview with Bethany L. Rogers, December 29, 2008, emphasis added.

35. Felicia Clark, interview with Bethany L. Rogers, December 12, 2008.

36. Christina Brown, interview with Megan Blumenreich, April 4, 2009.

37. Kathy Feeley, interview with Bethany L. Rogers, January 26, 2009.

38. Heather Weller, interview with Bethany L. Rogers, June 1, 2009.

39. Diane Brewer, interview with Megan Blumenreich, March 4, 2009.

40. Priscilla Leon-Didion, interview with Bethany L. Rogers, June 7, 2009.

41. Simes, interview.

42. R. Brent Lyles, interview with Bethany L. Rogers, April 1, 2009.

43. Scott Joftus, interview with Bethany L. Rogers, June 24, 2009.

44. Susanne Murray, interview with Bethany L. Rogers, February 10, 2013.

45. Brown, F., interview.

46. McKenzie, interview.

47. Constance Bond, interview with Megan Blumenreich, February 9, 2009.

48. Downing, interview.

49. Carlos Gomez, interview with Megan Blumenreich, May 6, 2009.

50. Leon-Didion, interview.

51. Marife Ramos, interview with Bethany L. Rogers, June 6, 2009.

52. Simes, interview.

53. Downing, interview.

54. Jan Trasen, interview with Megan Blumenreich, June 16, 2009.

55 Brewer, interview.

56. Lyles, interview.

57. Brown, F., interview.

58. Joftus, interview.

59. Leo Flanagan, interview with Megan Blumenreich, February 23, 2009.

60. Ellen Rosenstock, interview with Bethany L. Rogers, May 6, 2009.

61. Braungart and Braungart "The Life-Course Development," 266.

62. Murray, interview.

63. Downing, interview.

64. Jared Bernstein, "The Job Market for Young College Graduates," Economic Policy Institute, May 12, 2003, http://www.epi.org/publication/webfeatures_snapshots_archive_05132003/. See also Mark Alpert, "Tough Times for Most College Grads," *Fortune*, August 13, 1990, 12.

65. William Toombs and Kathie Thomas, "Jobs and Liberal Arts Graduates: Some Critical Relationships." *Research in Higher Education* 4, no. 2 (1976): 131–148.

66. Erikson, *Identity: Youth and Crisis*.

67. Braungart and Braungart "The Life-Course Development," 249–250; Robert Coles, *The Political Life of Children* (Boston: Atlantic Monthly Press, 1986); Richard Braungart, *Family Status Socialization and Student Politics* (Ann Arbor, MI: University Microfilms International, 1979).

68. One of our interviewees came to TFA a full decade after graduating college, having completed master's coursework; two others left graduate programs to participate in TFA, making them somewhat older than the rest of the pool.

69. Clark, interview; Terrell, interview; Brown, C., interview.

70. Mark Stephan, interview with Megan Blumenreich, April 9, 2009.

71. Jane Schneider, interview with Megan Blumenreich, February 24, 2009.

72. Joftus, interview.

73. Downing, interview.

74. Bill Norbert, interview with Megan Blumenreich, January 20, 2009; Bond, interview; Downing, interview; Weller, interview.

75. The religious backgrounds of our participants emerged as a particularly interesting area of the study: though we selected participants to represent many forms of diversity (see Appendix B for the methodology), religion was not a variable in our selection process.

76. The Official Catholic Directory via Center for Applied Research in the Apostolate, cited in Brian McGill, "Catholicism in the United States," *Wall Street Journal*, September 18, 2015, http://graphics.wsj.com/catholics-us/.

77. Janet Nolan, *Servants of the Poor: Teachers and Mobility in Ireland and Irish America* (Notre Dame, IN: University of Notre Dame Press, 2004); Bart Hellinckx, Marc Depaepe, and Frank Simon, "The Educational Work of Catholic Women Religious in the 19th and 20th Centuries: A Historiographical Survey," *Revue d'Histoire Ecclesiastique* 104, no. 2 (2009): 529–549; Hasia R. Diner, *Erin's Daughters in America: Irish Immigrant Women in the Nineteenth Century* (Baltimore, MD: Johns Hopkins University Press, 1983).

78. Sabin, interview.

79. Lawson, interview.

80. Carlos Gomez, interview with Megan Blumenreich, May 6, 2009.

81. Flanagan, interview.

82. Pew Research Center, *A Portrait of Jewish Americans: Findings from a Pew Research Center Survey of U.S. Jews* (Washington, DC: Pew Research Center, October 1, 2003).

83. See, for example, Ruth Markowitz, *My Daughter, the Teacher: Jewish Teachers in the New York City Schools* (New Brunswick, NJ: Rutgers University Press, 1993); Thomas R. Brooks, *Towards Dignity: A Brief History of the UFT* (New York, NY: United Federation of Teachers, 1967); and Jerald Podair, *The Strike That Changed New York: Blacks, Whites, and the Ocean Hill-Brownsville Crisis* (New Haven, CT: Yale University Press, 2004).

84. Joftus, interview.

85. Arthur Schuhart, interview with Megan Blumenreich, March 13, 2009.

86. To gauge the status of our participants' higher education background, we used the report, The American Freshman: National Norms for Fall, 1986, a large annual survey of first-time, full-time freshmen enrolled in a broad sample of institutions (https://files.eric.ed.gov/fulltext/ED278296.pdf). Of our 30 interviewees, 11 attended high selectivity private universities; eight went to very high selectivity, four-year non-sectarian private colleges; and three earned degrees from high selectivity public universities. Among the remaining eight participants, five attended institutions that did not appear in the HERI study; two of those institutions—the University of Chicago and College of the Holy Cross—would likely have been considered high selectivity institutions. The rest of the sample attended medium selectivity institutions, with the exception of one participant who graduated from a low selectivity institution and one woman who graduated from a selective, private, historically Black college. A large majority (about 80%) of the individuals we interviewed hailed from educational institutions and family educational status associated with the most elite levels of the stratified system illustrated in *The American Freshman, 1986* report. See Alexander W. Austin, Kenneth C. Green, William S. Korn, and Marilynn Schalit, *The American Freshman: National Norms for Fall 1986* (Los Angeles, CA: Higher Education Research Institute, UCLA, 1986).

87. Jerome Karabel, *The Chosen: The Hidden History of Admission and Exclusion at Harvard, Yale, and Princeton* (New York: Houghton Mifflin, 2005).

88. Gomez, interview.

89. Leon-Didion, interview.

90. Terrell, interview.

91. Flanagan, interview.

92. Schuhart, interview.

93. Braungart and Braungart "The Life-Course Development," 250; see also Rudolf Heberle, *Social Movements* (New York: Appleton-Century-Crofts, 1951) and Karl Mannheim, "The Problem of Generations," in *Essays on the Sociology of Knowledge* by Karl Mannheim, ed. Paul Kecskemeti (New York: Oxford University Press, 1952), 276–321.

94. Braungart and Braungart, "The Life-Course Development," 250.

95. Michael Elliot, "Shifting on its Pivot: The Year that Changed the World," *Time*, June 18, 2009.

96. McKenzie, interview.

97. Trasen, interview; Stephan, interview.

98. Lisa Robinson, interview with Megan Blumenreich, February 25, 2009.

99. Feeley, interview.

100. Brewer, interview.

101. Lawson, interview.

102. Robert A. Rhoades, "Student Activism as an Agent of Social Change: A Phenomeno-
logical Analysis of Contemporary Campus Unrest" (paper presented at the Annual Meeting of
the American Educational Research Association, Chicago, IL, March 24–28, 1997).

103. Philip G. Altbach and Robert Cohen, "American Student Activism: The Post-Six-
ties Transformation," *The Journal of Higher Education* 61, No. 1 (Jan–Feb, 1990), 48

104. Stephan, interview.

105. Brown, C., interview.

106. Simes, interview; Norbert, interview; Brown University Library Exhibitions,
"Anti–CIA Student Protests," Protest & Perspectives: Students at Brown 1960s-90s, https://
library.brown.edu/create/protest6090/anti-cia-student-protests/.

107. Lawson, interview.

108. Brown, C., interview.

109. Furman Brown majored in math and communications; Jennifer Denino majored
in finance because, as she laughingly explained, it did not require her to learn a second
language. The latter offers a good reminder that young people make many consequential
decisions on the basis of pragmatic, in-the-moment, or personal considerations rather than
as a result of carefully thought-out reasons.

110. Joftus, interview.

111. Brewer, interview.

112. Edward Said was a professor of literature at Columbia University, a public intellectual, political activist, and a founder of the academic field of postcolonial studies. A
literary critic who examined literature in light of social and cultural politics, Said was an
outspoken proponent of the political rights of Palestinians.

113. Robinson, interview.

114. Stephan, interview.

115. Brown, C., interview.

Chapter 3

1. Jeffrey Simes, interview by Bethany L. Rogers, February 9, 2009.

2. Wendy Kopp, "An Argument and Plan for the Creation of the Teacher Corps" (Undergraduate Thesis, Princeton University, 1989), 52.

3. Kopp, "An Argument and Plan," 73.

4. Kopp, "An Argument and Plan," 2.

5. Debates about what teachers should know and what characteristics equip them to
teach have a long past, aptly chronicled in James W. Fraser, *Preparing America's Teachers:
A History* (New York: Teachers College Press, 2007). Recent efforts to define the kinds of
knowledge, skills, and dispositions teachers must acquire include, for instance, Maynard
C. Reynolds (Ed.), *The Knowledge Base for the Beginning Teacher* (New York: Pergamon
Press, 1989); Frank B. Murray (Ed.), *The Teacher Educator's Handbook: Building a Knowl-
edge Base for the Preparation of Teachers* (San Francisco: Jossey-Bass, 1996); and Linda
Darling-Hammond and John Bransford (Eds.), *Preparing Teachers for a Changing World:
What Teachers Should Learn and Be Able to Do* (San Francisco: Jossey-Bass, 2005).

6. Mary Kennedy, "The Problem of Evidence in Teacher Education," in *The Role of the
University in the Preparation of Teachers,* ed. Robert A. Roth (London, U.K.: Falmer Press,
1999), 90.

7. Lisa Robinson, interview by Megan Blumenreich, February 25, 2009.

8. National Learning Corporation, Teacher License Examination Series, product description. https://passbooks.bookstore.ipgbook.com/common-branches--1-6---elementary-school-products-9780837380094.php?page_id=21

9. Spencer Downing, interview by Megan Blumenreich, April 1, 2009.

10. John Sikula, "National Commission Reports of the 1980s," in *Handbook of Research on Teacher Education: A Project of the Association of Teacher Educators,* ed. W. Robert Houston, Martin Haberman, and John Sikula (New York: Macmillan Publishing Company, 1990), 72–82.

11. William R. Johnson, "Empowering Practitioners: Holmes, Carnegie, and the Lessons of History," *History of Education Quarterly* 27 (Summer 1987): 221–240.

12. See, for example, C. Emily Feistritzer, "The Evolution of Alternative Teacher Certification," *The Educational Forum* 58, no. 2 (Winter 1994): 132–138.

13. James Bryant Conant, *The Education of American Teachers* (New York: McGraw-Hill, 1963); James Koerner, *The Miseducation of American Teachers* (Boston: Houghton Mifflin, 1963).

14. Lee Shulman, "Those Who Understand: Knowledge Growth in Teaching," *Educational Researcher* 15, no. 2 (Feb. 1986) 8.

15. Jack Schneider, *Excellence for All: How a New Breed of Reformers is Transforming America's Public Schools* (Nashville, TN: Vanderbilt University Press, 2011).

16. Today's TFA summer training is held in 17 different regions and generally involves 5 days of regional induction, a 5- to 7-week residential Institute, and a 1- or 2-week regional orientation.

17. See, for example, media accounts such as Laurel Shaper, "Teach For America Seeks Young Graduates," *Christian Science Monitor,* March 14, 1990; Deborah Appleman, "Teach For America: Is Idealism Enough?" *Christian Science Monitor,* August 8, 1990; and S. Tifft and D. Cray, "Crusaders in the Classroom: Teach For America Raises Recruits, Hopes and Questions," *Time,* July 23, 1990, 66. In a prelude to her specific criticisms of Teach For America, Linda Darling-Hammond censured the abbreviated pre-service training associated with alternate route programs and, especially, the assumptions that "subject matter preparation is the most crucial foundation for good teaching" and "teachers will learn pedagogical skills on the job." See Linda Darling-Hammond, "Teaching and Knowledge: Policy Issues Posed by Alternate Certification for Teachers," *Peabody Journal of Education* 67 (Spring 1990): 129.

18. Jack Schneider, "Rhetoric and Practice in Pre-Service Teacher Education: The Case of Teach For America," *Journal of Education Policy* 29, no. 4 (2014): 425–442.

19. Kopp, One Day All Children, 49.

20. Kopp, One Day All Children, 49; Laurel Shaper, "Teach For America Seeks Young Graduates," 13.

21. Kopp, *One Day All Children,* 49.

22. Appleman, "Teach For America: Is Idealism Enough?"

23. Ibid., 19.

24. Schneider, "Rhetoric and Practice," 428.

25. Kopp, *One Day All Children,* 51.

26. It is worth noting that this "transformation" was meant to occur as the alumni were also adjusting to the advent of post-college lives and adult responsibilities, which can be a challenging life stage for many young people.

27. Caroline Sabin, interview with Megan Blumenreich, November 29, 2008.

28. Christina Brown, interview with Megan Blumenreich, April 4, 2009.

29. Nichole Childs Wardlaw, interview with Bethany L. Rogers, February 23, 2009.

30. Lori Lawson, interview with Megan Blumenreich, March 11, 2009.

31. Kopp, *One Day All Children,* 50.

32. Brown, C., interview.

33. Avis Terrell, interview with Megan Blumenreich, September 26, 2009.

34. Heather Weller, interview with Bethany L. Rogers, June 1, 2009.

35. Furman Brown, interview with Bethany L. Rogers, December 29, 2008.

36. Jane Schneider, interview with Megan Blumenreich, February 4, 2009.

37. Historian Jack Schneider suggests that the training of TFA teachers has aligned closely with practices of traditional college- or university-based teacher education programs since its inception. See Schneider, "Rhetoric and Practice in Pre-Service Teacher Education." It's also worth noting that, in subsequent years, many teacher preparation institutions have created programs for TFA and other alternate route candidates that are based on existing state-approved coursework drawn from traditional teacher education programs. Some researchers have suggested that, given their different qualities and routes to the classroom, TFA and other alternate route candidates require a radically different approach to training, as opposed to a recycling or adaptation of existing teacher education coursework. See Heather Carter, Audrey Amrein-Beardsley, and Cory Cooper Hansen, "So NOT Amazing! Teach for America Corps Members' Education Program," *Teachers College Record* 113, no. 5 (2011): 861–894.

38. Brown, F., interview.

39. Simes, interview.

40. Scott Joftus, interview with Bethany L. Rogers, June 24, 2009.

41. Leo Flanagan, interview with Megan Blumenreich, February 23, 2009.

42. Terrell, interview.

43. Scott Joftus, interview with Bethany L. Rogers, June 24, 2009.

44. R. Brent Lyles, interview with Bethany L. Rogers, April 1, 2009.

45. Constance Bond, interview with Megan Blumenreich, February 9, 2009.

46. Lisa Robinson, interview with Megan Blumenreich, February 25, 2009.

47. See, for instance, Xiaofeng Steven Liu and Patrick Meyer, "Teachers' Perceptions of Their Jobs: A Multilevel Analysis of the Teachers Follow-Up Survey for 1994–95," *Teachers College Record* 107, no. 5 (May 2005): 985–1003.

48. Mark Stephan, interview with Megan Blumenreich, April 9, 2009.

49. Sylvia Chong, Low Ee Ling, and Goh Kim Chuan, "Developing Student Teachers' Professional Identities—An Exploratory Study," *International Education Studies* 4, no. 1 (2011): 30.

50. Jackie Walkington, "Becoming a Teacher: Encouraging Development of Teacher Identity through Reflective Practice," *Asia-Pacific Journal of Teacher Education* 33, no. 1 (2005): 53–64; D. Mayer, "Building Teaching Identities: Implications for Pre-Service Teacher Education," paper presented to the Australian Association for Research in Education, Melbourne, 1999.

51. Lisa Robinson, interview with Megan Blumenreich, February 25, 2009.

52. Joftus, interview.

53. Andrew McKenzie, interview with Megan Blumenreich, February 8, 2009.

54. Robinson, interview.

55. Spencer Downing, interview with Megan Blumenreich, April 1, 2009.

56. Arthur Schuhart, interview with Megan Blumenreich, March 13, 2009.

57. Downing, interview.

58. Edith Guyton and D. John McIntyre, "Student Teaching and School Experiences," in *Handbook of Research on Teacher Education*, ed. W. Robert Houston, Martin Haberman, and John Sikula (New York, NY: Macmillan Publishing Company, 1990), 514. See also M. Appleberry, "What Did You Learn from Student Teaching?" *Instructor* 85 (1976): 38–40; S. Nosow, "Students' Perceptions of Field Experience Education," *Journal of College Student Personnel* 16 (1975).

59. See Lauren M. Anderson and Jamy A. Stillman, "Student Teaching's Contribution to Preservice Teacher Development: A Review of Research Focused on the Preparation of Teachers for Urban and High-Needs Contexts," *Review of Educational Research* 83 (March 2013): 3–69.

60. Anderson and Stillman, "Student Teaching's Contribution," 4.

61. Catherine Cornbleth, "Institutional Habitus as the de facto Diversity Curriculum of Teacher Education," *Anthropology & Education Quarterly* 41 (September 2010): 280.

62. Guyton and McIntyre, "Student Teaching and School Experiences," 514.

63. Deborah Appleman, "Teach for America: Is Idealism Enough?" *Christian Science Monitor,* August 8, 1990, 19. https://www.csmonitor.com/1990/0808/eappl.html

64. Simes, interview.

65. Schuhart, interview.

66. Sharon Feiman-Nemser and M. Buchman, "Pitfalls of Experience in Teacher Education," Occasional Paper #65 (East Lansing, MI: Michigan State University, Institute for Research on Teaching), 1983.

67. W. Copeland, "The Nature of the Relationship between Cooperating Teacher Behavior and Student Teacher Classroom Performance," paper presented at the annual meeting of the American Educational Research Association, New York (1977).

68. Cornbleth, "Institutional Habitus," 287.

69. Guyton and McIntyre, "Student Teaching and School Experiences," 522.

70. Kopp, *One Day,* 94.

71. Priscilla Leon-Didion, interview with Bethany L. Rogers, June 7, 2009.

72. Robinson, interview.

73. Flanagan, interview.

74. Bill Norbet, interview with Megan Blumenreich, January 20, 2009.

75. Diane Brewer, interview with Megan Blumenreich, March 4, 2009.

76. McKenzie, interview.

77. Stephan, interview.

78. Jan Trasen, interview with Megan Blumenreich, June 16, 2009.

79. Spencer Downing, interview.

80. Caroline Sabin, interview with Megan Blumenreich, November 29, 2008.

81. Terrell, interview.

82. Guyton and McIntyre, "Student Teaching and School Experiences," 518. See also B. R. Tabachnick, T. Popkewitz, and K. Zeichner, "Teacher Education and the Professional Perspectives of Student Teachers," *Interchange* 10 (1979): 12–29.

83. Guyton and McIntyre, "Student Teaching and School Experiences."

84. Bond, interview.

85. Lyles, interview.

86. Kathy Feeley, interview with Bethany L. Rogers, January 26, 2009.

87. Trasen, interview.

88. Childs-Wardlaw, interview.

89. See Terry L. James, Carol P. Etheridge, and Dotsy A. Liles, "Student Teaching Delivery Via Clinical Training Sites: New Linkages, Structural Changes and Programmatic Improvements," *Action in Teacher Education* 13, no 2. (1991): 25, where authors problematize the fact that "too often student teaching content is based primarily on situation-specific phenomena of individual classrooms."

90. Lyles, interview.

91. Bond, interview.

92. Emily Straus, 1996 TFA alumna, personal communication, July 8, 2016.

93. Schneider, interview with Megan Blumenreich, February 4, 2009.

94. Brewer, interview.

95. Marife Ramos, interview with Bethany L. Rogers, June 6, 2009.

96. Robinson, interview.

97. Brown, F., interview.

98. Joftus, interview.

99. Eric Bird, interview with Megan Blumenreich, March 16, 2009.

100. Susanne Murray, interview with Bethany L. Rogers, February 10, 2013.

101. Brown, F., interview.

102. Simes, interview.

Chapter 4

1. Deborah Appleman, "Teach for America: Is Idealism Enough?", *Christian Science Monitor*, August 8, 1990: 19; Jack Schneider, "Rhetoric and Practice in Pre-Service Teacher Education: The Case for Teach For America," *Journal of Education Policy* 29, no. 4, 428; several of the oral histories referenced Carl Grant and his role.

2. Scott Joftus, interview with Bethany L. Rogers, June 24, 2009.

3. For an excellent review of this historical literature, see Judith Kafka, "In Search of a Grand Narrative: The Turbulent History of Teaching," in *Handbook of Research on Teaching*, 5th edition, ed. Drew H. Gitomer and Courtney A. Bell (Washington, DC: American Educational Research Association, 2016), 69–126.

4. Carlos Gomez, interview with Megan Blumenreich, May 6, 2009.

5. Andrew Hartman, "An Emerging Historiography of the Culture Wars," Society for U.S. Intellectual History, U.S. Intellectual History Blog, January 29, 2013, https://s-usih.org/2013/01/an-emerging-historiography-of-the-culture-wars/.

6. Gerald Graff, *Beyond the Culture Wars: How Teaching the Conflicts Can Revitalize American Education* (New York, NY: W.W. Norton & Company, 1992), 8.

7. Richard Bernstein, "The Rising Hegemony of the Politically Correct," *The New York Times*, October 28, 1990.

8. Joan Beck, "The Tyranny of Political Correctness," *Chicago Tribune*, December 20, 1990.

9. Spencer Downing, interview by Megan Blumenreich, April 1, 2009.

10. It should be noted that the movement of the 1990s represents the latest in a long history of efforts on the part of teacher educators to prepare teachers to work with children from different backgrounds than their own, as seen, for example, in the interwar years' "cultural gifts" movement—see Diana Selig, *Americans All: The Cultural Gifts Movement* (Cambridge, MA: Harvard University Press, 2008)—or the efforts in the 1960s to tailor teacher education experiences toward fitting teachers to work with "disadvantaged" populations; for example, Vernon Haubrich, "Teachers for Big City Schools," in *Education in Depressed Areas*, ed. Harry Passow (New York: Teachers College Press, 1970), 243–261 and Harry Passow, "Diminishing Teacher Prejudice," in *The Inner-City Classroom: Teacher Behaviors*, ed. Robert Strom (Columbus, OH: Charles E. Merrill Publishing Company, 1966), 93–110.

11. James A. Banks, "Teaching Multicultural Literacy to Teachers," *Teaching Education* 4, no. 1 (1991): 133–142.

12. Ana Maria Villegas and Tamara Lucas, *Educating Culturally Responsive Teachers: A Coherent Approach* (Albany, NY: State University of New York, 2002), p. xii. Emphasis added.

13. Carl Grant and Walter Secada, "Preparing Teachers for Diversity," in *Handbook of Research on Teacher Education*, ed. W. R. Houston (New York: Macmillan, 1990), 404; James S. Coleman et al., "Equality of Educational Opportunity," (1966), https://eric.ed.gov/?id=ED012275.

14. National Center for Education Statistics, 1992, cited in Mary Louise Gomez, "Prospective Teachers' Perspectives on Teaching 'Other People's Children,'" in *Currents of Reform in Preservice Teacher Education*, eds. Kenneth Zeichner, Susan Melnick, and Mary Louise Gomez (New York: Teachers College Press, 1996), 111.

15. Motoko Rich, "Where Are the Teachers of Color?" *New York Times*, April 11, 2015.

16. Gomez, "Prospective Teachers' Perspectives," 111. See also Children's Defense

Fund, The State of America's Children, 1991 (Washington, DC: Children's Defense Fund, 1991), 24; 2.

17. Gomez, "Prospective Teachers' Perspectives," 111.

18. John Goodlad, *Teachers for Our Nation's Schools* (San Francisco: Jossey-Bass, 1990), 264.

19. Gomez, "Prospective Teachers' Perspectives," 111. See also American Association of Colleges for Teacher Education, AACTE/Metropolitan Life Survey of Teacher Education Students (Washington, DC: AACTE, 1990).

20. Gomez, "Prospective Teachers' Perspectives," 113.

21. William Wayson, "Multicultural Education in the College of Education: Are Future Teachers Prepared?" in *Multicultural Education: Knowledge and Perceptions,* ed. Camilla A. Heid (Bloomington, IN: Indiana University, Center for Urban and Multicultural Education, 1988), 17.

22. A. R. Contreras, "Multicultural Attitudes and Knowledge of Education Students at Indiana University" (presentation, Annual Meeting of the American Educational Research Association, New Orleans, LA, April 1988), 14.

23. Gomez, "Prospective Teachers' Perspectives," 117, 138.

24. Kenneth Zeichner, "Educating Teachers for Cultural Diversity," in *Currents of Reform in Preservice Teacher Education,* ed. Kenneth Zeichner, Susan Melnick, and Mary Louise Gomez (New York: Teachers College Press, 1996), 143. See also Courtney Cazden and Hugh Mehan, "Principles from Sociology and Anthropology: Context, Code, Classroom, and Culture," in *Knowledge Base for the Beginning Teacher,* ed. Maynard Reynolds (Washington, DC: American Association of Colleges for Teacher Education, 1990), 47–57; James Comer, "Educating Poor Minority Children," *Scientific American* 259 (1988): 42–48; and James Banks, "Teaching Multicultural Literacy to Teachers."

25. Zeichner, "Educating Teachers for Cultural Diversity," 143. See also Hugh Mehan and T. Trujillo, *Teacher Education Issues* (Research & Policy series no. 4) (Santa Barbara: University of California Linguistic Minority Research Project, 1989).

26. Gomez, "Prospective Teachers' Perspectives," 125.

27. Grant and Secada, "Preparing Teachers for Diversity," 413.

28. Ibid., 420.

29. Leo Flanagan, interview with Megan Blumenreich, February 23, 2009.

30. Joftus, interview.

31. Jeffrey Simes, interview with Bethany L. Rogers, February 9, 2009.

32. Flanagan, interview.

33. Joftus, interview.

34. Christina Brown, interview with Megan Blumenreich, April 4, 2009.

35. Wendy Kopp, *One Day All Children: The Unlikely Triumph of Teach For America and What I Learned Along the Way* (New York: Public Affairs, 2001), 50–51.

36. Jane Schneider, interview with Megan Blumenreich, February 24, 2009; Diane Brewer, interview with Megan Blumenreich, March 4, 2009. Here she refers to the popular 1980s talk show hosted by Phil Donohue, who used to circulate through the audience with his microphone, looking to capture emotional reactions for entertainment.

37. Caroline Sabin, interview with Megan Blumenreich, November 29, 2008.

38. Eric Bird, interview with Megan Blumenreich, March 16, 2009.

39. Ellen Rosenstock, interview with Bethany L. Rogers, May 6, 2009.

40. Nichole Childs Wardlaw, interview with Bethany L. Rogers, February 23, 2009.

41. Marife Ramos, interview with Bethany L. Rogers, June 6, 2009.

42. Flanagan, interview.

43. Brown, C., interview.

44. Avis Terrell, interview with Megan Blumenreich, September 26, 2009.

45. Downing, interview.

46. Lori Lawson, interview with Megan Blumenreich, March 11, 2009.

47. Terrell, interview.

48. Jan Trasen, interview with Megan Blumenreich, June 6, 2009.

49. Lisa Robinson, interview with Megan Blumenreich, February 25, 2009.

50. For example, see Emily E. Straus, *Death of a Suburban Dream* (Philadelphia, PA: University of Pennsylvania Press, 2014) for an incisive analysis of Black–Latinx struggles over schooling in Compton, California, over the last half-century.

51. Sabin, interview.

52. Sabin, interview.

53. Brown, C., interview.

54. Brown, C., interview.

55. Brown, C., interview.

56. Brown, C., interview.

57. Brown, C., interview.

58. Enough of the interviewees mentioned this individual for us to identify her; however, for our purposes, it was far more important to understand our participants' ideas about and responses to her than to substantiate her identity.

59. Gomez, interview.

60. Gomez, interview.

61. Marife Ramos, interview with Bethany L. Rogers, June 6, 2009.

62. Priscilla Leon-Dideon, interview with Bethany Rogers, June 7, 2009.

63. Ibid.

64. Schneider, interview.

65. Schneider, interview.

66. Andrew McKenzie, interview with Megan Blumenreich, February 8, 2009.

67. Heather Weller, interview with Bethany L. Rogers, June 1, 2009.

68. Weller, interview.

69. Scott Joftus, interview with Bethany L. Rogers, June 24, 2009.

70. Joftus, interview.

71. Kathy Feeley, interview with Bethany L. Rogers, January 26, 2009.

72. Downing, interview.

73. Flanagan, interview.

74. McKenzie, interview.

75. James A. Banks, Marilyn Cochran-Smith, Luis Moll, Anna Richert, Kenneth Zeichner, Pamela LePage, Linda Darling-Hammond, Helen Duffy, and Morva McDonald, "Teaching Diverse Learners," in *Preparing Teachers for a Changing World: What Teachers Should Learn and Be Able to Do*, eds. Linda Darling-Hammond and John Bransford (San Francisco: Jossey-Bass, 2005), 232–274.

76. Gloria Ladson-Billings, "Toward a Theory of Culturally Relevant Pedagogy," *American Education Research Journal* 32, no. 3 (1995): 465–491; Ana Maria Villegas, Culturally Responsive Pedagogy for the 1990s and Beyond: Trends and Issues paper No. 6 (Washington, DC: ERIC Clearinghouse on Teacher Education, 1990).

77. Martin Haberman, "The Rationale for Training Adults as Teachers," in *Empowerment Through Multicultural Education*, ed. Christine E. Sleeter (Albany, NY: SUNY Press, 1991), 285.

78. See, for example, C. Bennett, A. Okinaka, and W. Xiao-yang, "The Effect of a Multicultural Education Course on Preservice Teachers' Attitudes, Knowledge, and Behavior" (presentation, Annual Meeting of the American Educational Research Association, New Orleans, LA, April 1988); Zeichner, "Educating Teachers for Cultural Diversity," 162; and Ana Maria Villegas, "Restructuring Teacher Education for Diversity" (presentation, Annual Meeting of the American Educational Research Association, Atlanta, GA, April 1993).

79. Martin Haberman, "Can Cultural Awareness Be Taught in Teacher Education Programs?" *Teaching Education* 4 (1991): 25–32.

80. James A. Banks, Marilyn Cochran-Smith, Luis Moll, Anna Richert, Kenneth

Zeichner, Pamela LePage, Linda Darling-Hammond, Helen Duffy, with Morva McDonald, "Teaching Diverse Learners," in *Preparing Teachers for a Changing World: What Teachers Should Learn and Be Able To Do*, Linda Darling-Hammond and John Bransford (eds.) (San Francisco: Jossey-Bass, 2005), 247.

81. Mark Stephan, interview with Megan Blumenreich, April 9, 2009.

Chapter 5

1. Ellen Rosenstock, interview by Megan Blumenreich, May 6, 2009.

2. Lisa Delpit, "Multiplication Is for White People": *Raising Expectations for Other People's Children* (New York, NY: The New Press, 2012), 73.

3. As to whether the TFA teachers were better than whoever else would have ended up in those classrooms, we are not equipped to say; the larger point is that the learning curve our interviewees experienced came at the expense of their students.

4. Regarding work with diverse communities, see Cynthia Onore and Bonny Gildin, "Preparing Urban Teachers as Public Professionals Through a University–Community Partnership," *Teacher Education Quarterly* 37, no. 3 (2010): 27–44. For support needed by new teachers, see Sharon Feiman-Nemser, "Beyond Solo Teaching," *Educational Leadership* 69, no. 8 (2012): 10.

5. See, for example, Karen Hammerness, Linda Darling-Hammond, John Bransford (with David Berliner, Marilyn Cochran-Smith, Morva McDonald, and Kenneth Zeichner), "How Teachers Learn and Develop," in *Preparing Teachers for a Changing World: What Teachers Should Learn and Be Able to Do*, eds. Linda Darling-Hammond and John Bransford (San Francisco, CA: Jossey-Bass, 2005), 358–389; Michael Huberman, "The Professional Life Cycle of Teachers," *Teachers College Record* 91, no. 1 (1989) 31–57; Margaret Berci, "The Autobiographical Metaphor: An Invaluable Approach to Teacher Development," *Journal of Educational Thought* 41, no. 1 (Spring, 2007) 63–90; and Karen Hammerness, *Seeing Through Teachers' Eyes* (New York, NY: Teachers College Press, 2006).

6. Kathy Carter, "Teachers' Knowledge and Learning to Teach," in *Handbook of Research on Teacher Education: A Project of the Association of Teacher Educators*, eds. W. Robert Houston, Martin Haberman, and John P. Sikula (New York: Macmillan, 1990).

7. Kathleen Topolka Jorissen, "Successful Career Transitions: Lessons from Urban Alternate Route Teachers Who Stayed," *High School Journal* 86, no. 3 (2003) 41–51.

8. Huberman, "The Professional Life Cycle of Teachers," 33.

9. Sharon Feiman-Nemser, "Beyond Solo Teaching," 10.

10. Marieke Pillen, Douwe Beijaard & Perry den Brok (2013) Tensions in beginning teachers' professional identity development, accompanying feelings and coping strategies, *European Journal of Teacher Education*, 36:3, 240–260, DOI: 10.1080/02619768.2012.696192; Sharon Feiman-Nemser, "Beyond Solo Teaching," 10.

11. Hammerness et al., "How Teachers Learn and Develop," 379; see also David Berliner, "Expertise: The Wonder of Exemplary Performances," in *Creating Powerful Thinking in Teachers and Students: Diverse Perspectives*, eds. J. Mangieri and C. C. Block (Fort Worth, TX: Harcourt Brace College Publishers, 1994), 161–186; Sharon Feiman-Nemser, "Learning to Teach," in *Handbook of Teaching and Policy*, eds. Lee Shulman and Gary Sykes (New York, NY: Longman, 1983), 150–171; V. Richardson and P. Placier, "Teacher Change," in *Handbook of Research on Teaching*, 4th edition, ed. V. Richardson (Washington, DC: American Educational Research Association, 2001), 905–947.

12. Hammerness et al., "How Teachers Learn and Develop," 379.

13. Pillen, Beijaard, and de Brok, "Tensions in Beginning Teachers' Professional Identity Development," 242.

14. Deborah P. Britzman, *Practice Makes Practice: A Critical Study of Learning to*

Teach (Albany, NY: State University of New York Press, 2003).

15. Spencer Downing, interview by Megan Blumenreich, April 1, 2009.

16. Megan Trexler, "(Re)reading Identity Narratives: Developing Strategies for Negotiating Authority in the Composition Classrooms" *Young Scholars in Writing: Undergraduate Research in Writing and Rhetoric* 4 (2006): 3–14.

17. Rosenstock, interview.

18. Mark Stephan, interview with Megan Blumenreich, April 9, 2009.

19. Pamela LePage, Linda Darling-Hammond, and Hanife Akar (with Cris Guiterrez, Evelyn Jenkins-Gunn, and Kathy Rosebrock), "Classroom Management," in *Preparing Teachers for a Changing World: What Teachers Should Learn and Be Able to Do*, eds. Linda Darling-Hammond and John Bransford (San Francisco: Jossey-Bass, 2005), 327–357.

20. Karen Hammerness, "Classroom Management in the United States: The View from New York City," *Teaching Education* 22, no. 2 (2011): 155.

21. H. Richard Milner IV & F. Blacke Tenore, "Classroom Management in Diverse Classrooms," *Urban Education* 45, no. 5 (2010): 598.

22. R. Brent Lyles, interview with Bethany L. Rogers, April 1, 2009.

23. Lisa Robinson, interview with Megan Blumenreich, February 25, 2009.

24. Bill Norbet, interview with Megan Blumenreich, January 20, 2009.

25. Robinson, interview.

26. LePage et al., "Classroom Management," 340.

27. Ibid.

28. LePage et al., "Classroom Management," 327.

29. Lee Canter and Marlene Canter, *Assertive Discipline: Positive Behavior Management for Today's Classroom* (Santa Monica, CA: Canter & Associates, 1987).

30. Linda Darling-Hammond, "Who Will Speak for the Children? How 'Teach For America' Hurts Urban Schools and Children," *Phi Delta Kappan* 76, no. 1 (1994): 21–34.

31. Memories of the Canter book among interviewees were scant; thus, much of what we note here derives from the memories of one of the authors, Megan Blumenreich, who was a 1990 TFA participant.

32. Hammerness, "Classroom Management in the United States," 151–167. See also Frank Merret and Kevin Wheldall, "How Do Teachers Learn to Manage Classroom Behavior? A Study of Teachers' Opinions about Their Initial Training with Special Reference to Classroom Behavior Management," *Educational Studies* 19, no. 1 (1993): 91–106; LePage et al., "Classroom Management," 350. On the adoption of research-based approaches to classroom management, see Madeline Will, "Are Classroom Teachers Learning Classroom Management? It Varies," *Education Week*, October 20, 2020, retrieved from https://www.edweek.org/teaching-learning/are-aspiring-teachers-learning-classroom-management-it-varies/2020/10 and Laura Pomerance and Kate Walsh, 2020 *Teacher Prep Review: Clinical Practice and Classroom Management* (Washington, DC: National Council on Teacher Quality, 2020). Retrieved from: www.nctq.org/publications/2020-Teacher-Prep-Review:-Clinical-Practice-and-Classroom-Management

33. Kathy Feeley, interview with Bethany L. Rogers, January 26, 2009.

34. Eric Bird, interview with Megan Blumenreich, March 16, 2009.

35. Robinson, interview.

36. Leo Flanagan, interview with Megan Blumenreich, February 23, 2009.

37. Christina Brown, interview with Megan Blumenreich, April 4, 2009.

38. Robinson, interview. Several TFA alumni who went on to start charter schools and charter school networks, such as the KIPP schools, built those schools around a culture of strict behavioral discipline. While it is beyond the scope of our data, it is tempting to speculate that the TFA teachers' raw experiences, without deeper understanding of the complex and nuanced aspects of classroom management, may have led them to believe in such "assertive" discipline as the most effective way of achieving order.

39. William Ayers, "Introduction," in *City Kids, City Schools,* eds. William Ayers, Gloria Ladson-Billings, Greg Michie, and Pedro A. Noguera (New York, NY: The New Press, 2008), xxvi.

40. Hammerness et al., "How Teachers Learn and Develop," 378.

41. For texts on creating well-organized structures, see Ruth Charney, *Teaching Children to Care: Classroom Management for Ethical and Academic Growth, K–8* (Glenfield, MA: Northeast Foundation for Children, 2002); and Paula Denton and Roxann Kriete, *The First Six Weeks of School* (Turners Falls, MA: Northeast Foundation for Children, Inc., 2000). For a chapter available at the time on procedures for classroom management, see Walter Doyle, "Classroom Management Techniques," in *Student Discipline Strategies: Research and Practice,* ed. Oliver C. Moles (New York: State University of New York Press, 1990), 113–127.

42. Scott Joftus, interview with Bethany L. Rogers, June 24, 2009.

43. Furman Brown, interview with Bethany L. Rogers, December 29, 2008.

44. Richard L. Curwin and Allen N. Mendler, Discipline with Dignity (Alexandria, VA: Association for Supervision & Curriculum Development, 1999).

45. Downing, interview.

46. Bird, interview.

47. Constance Bond, interview by Megan Blumenreich, February 9, 2009.

48. Hammerness, "Classroom Management in the United States," 155.

49. Christina Brown, interview with Megan Blumenreich, April 4, 2009.

50. Jennifer Denino, interview with Megan Blumenreich, January 20, 2009).

51. Avis Terrell, interview with Megan Blumenreich, September 26, 2009.

52. Felicia Clark, interview with Bethany L. Rogers, December 12, 2008.

53. Lori Lawson, interview with Megan Blumenreich, March 11, 2009.

54. See, for example, Jeannie Oaks, *Keeping Track: How Schools Structure Inequality* (New Haven, CT: Yale University Press, 1985).

55. For instance, Howard Gardner, *Multiple Intelligences* (New York, NY: Basic Books, 1993).

56. Susan Chira, "For Freshman Teacher Corps, a Sobering Year," *New York Times,* June 26, 1991.

57. Ayers, "Introduction," xxvi.

58. Lyles, interview.

59. Lawson, interview.

60. Caroline Sabin, interview with Megan Blumenreich, November 29, 2008.

61. Lyles, interview.

62. See James Bryant Conant, *Slums and Suburbs: A Commentary on Schools in Metropolitan Areas* (NY: McGraw-Hill, 1961), for an example of the documentation of "slum" school conditions; for more recent examples of arguments on behalf of specialized teacher preparation for urban teachers, see Tyrone C. Howard and H. Richard Milner IV, "Teacher Preparation for Urban Schools," in H. Richard Milner IV and Kofi Lomotey (eds), *Handbook of Urban Education* (New York: Routledge, 2014), 199–216; Martin Haberman, Star Teachers (Houston: Haberman Educational Foundation, 2005) and Jack Helfelt, Robert M. Capraro, Mary Margaret Capraro, Elizabeth Foster, and Norvella Carter, "An Urban Schools–University Partnership that Prepares and Retains Quality Teachers for 'High Need' Schools," *The Teacher Educator* 44, no. 1 (2009): 1–20.

63. Onore and Gildin. "Preparing Urban Teachers as Public Professionals"; K. Matsko and Karen Hammerness, "Unpacking the 'Urban' in Urban Teacher Preparation: Making a Case for Content-Specific Teacher Preparation," *Journal of Teacher Education* 65, no. 2 (2014): 128–44.

64. Onore and Gildin. "Preparing Urban Teachers as Public Professionals," 28.

65. Jonathan Kozol, *Savage Inequalities* (New York, NY: Crown Publishers, Inc., 1991).

66. Kozol, *Savage Inequalities*. For culturally relevant approaches to teaching, see Ayers, "Introduction" and Milner IV and Tenore, "Classroom Management in Diverse Classrooms."

67. Jeffrey Simes, interview with Bethany L. Rogers, February 9, 2009.

68. Arthur Schuhart, interview with Megan Blumenreich, March 13, 2009.

69. See, for example, Thomas Toch, "Drafting the Best and the Brightest," *U.S. News and World Report*, January 29, 1990, 52 and Deborah Appleman, "Teach for America: Is Idealism Enough?", *Christian Science Monitor*, August 8, 1990, 19, for "best and brightest" coverage; Wendy Kopp, *One Day All Children: The Unlikely Triumph of Teach For America and What I Learned Along the Way* (New York, NY: Public Affairs, 2001), 30–31.

70. Kopp, 30–31.

71. Jane Schneider, interview with Megan Blumenreich, February 24, 2009.

72. Lawson, interview.

73. Ellen Rosenstock, interview with Megan Blumenreich, May 6, 2009.

74. Brown, C., interview.

75. Simes, interview.

76. Feeley, interview.

77. Norbet, interview.

78. Joftus, interview.

79. Stephan, interview.

80. Huberman, "The Professional Life Cycle of Teachers," 42.

81. Lawson, interview.

82. Joftus, interview.

83. Stephan, interview.

84. Ibid.

85. Feeley, interview.

86. Rosenstock, interview.

87. Lawson, interview.

88. Marife Ramos, interview with Bethany L. Rogers, June 6, 2009.

89. Norbet, interview.

90. Bird, interview.

91. Daniel Oscar, "Recruitment Letter," quoted in Wendy Kopp, *One Day All Children*, 30–31.

Chapter 6

1. James Fraser, *Preparing America's Teachers: A History* (New York, NY: Teachers College Press, 2007).

2. Judith Kafka, "In Search of a Grand Narrative: The Turbulent History of Teaching," in Drew H. Gitomer and Courtney A. Bell, *Handbook of Research on Teaching*, 5th Ed. (Washington, D.C.: American Educational Research Association, 2016), 69–126; Christine Ogren, *The American State Normal School: An Instrument of Great Good* (New York, NY: Palgrave Macmillan, 2005).

3. Nancy Hoffman, Woman's *"True" Profession: Voices from the History of Teaching* (Cambridge, MA: Harvard Education Press, 2003), 43–44, cited in Fraser, *Preparing America's Teachers*, 42.

4. Susan B. Carter, "Incentives and Rewards to Teaching," in *American Teachers: Histories of a Profession at Work,* ed. Donald Warren (New York: Macmillan Publishing Company, 1989), 49–62; John L. Rury, "Who Became Teachers? The Social Characteristics of Teachers in American History," in Warren, *American Teachers*, 9–49; Christine Ogren, "The History and Historiography of Teacher Preparation in the United States: A Synthesis, Analysis, and Potential Contributions to Higher Education History," in *Higher Education:*

Handbook of Theory and Research 28, ed. Michael B. Paulsen (New York: Springer, 2013): 405–458.

5. Fraser, *Preparing America's Teachers*; Michael W. Sedlak, "'Let Us Go and Buy a School Master': Historical Perspectives on the Hiring of Teachers in the United States, 1750–1980," in Warren, *American Teachers*, 257–290.

6. Fraser, *Preparing America's Teachers*, 207.

7. Ogren, "The History and Historiography of Teacher Preparation," 431.

8. William R. Johnson, "Teachers and Teacher Training in the Twentieth-Century," in Warren, *American Teachers*, 243; Ellen C. Lagemann, *An Elusive Science: The Troubling History of Education Research* (Chicago: University of Chicago Press, 2000).

9. Johnson, "Teachers and Teacher Training," 243.

10. James D. Koerner, quoted in Fraser, *Preparing America's Teachers*, 263.

11. Seymour B. Sarason, Kenneth S. Davidson, and Burton Blatt, *The Preparation of Teacher: An Unstudied Problem in Education* (Cambridge, MA: Brookline Books, 1986), ii.

12. James W. Fraser and Lauren Lefty, *Teaching Teachers: Changing Paths and Enduring Debates* (Baltimore: Johns Hopkins University Press, 2018), 27.

13. James Bryant Conant, *The Education of American Teachers* (New York: McGraw-Hill, 1963); James D. Koerner, *The Miseducation of American Teachers* (Boston: Houghton Mifflin, 1963).

14. See James C. Stone, *Breakthrough in Teacher Education* (San Francisco, CA: Jossey-Bass, 1968).

15. Panel on Education Research and Development of the President's Science Advisory Committee, Innovation and Experiment in Education (Washington, DC: U.S. Government Printing Office, 1964), 30; Harry N. Rivlin, "Teachers for the Schools in Our Big Cities" (paper prepared for the University of Pennsylvania Schoolmen's Week Program, Philadelphia, PA, October 12, 1962), 5, quoted in Education in *Depressed Areas*, ed. A. Harry Passow (New York: Teachers College Press, 1963), 237. Urban teachers at the time were often disparaged as "second rate," deficient in teaching skills, and unconcerned with their students. This characterization, however, fails to take into account how poverty and deprivation afflicted the working conditions of urban schools; it also elides the gulf between the well-educated white, male scholars, researchers, reformers and writers making these judgments and the urban school staff who were largely Black, female, or otherwise disempowered. For criticisms of urban teachers, see Larry Cuban, *To Make a Difference: Teaching in the Inner City* (New York: Free Press, 1970), 237; Richard Wisniewski, *New Teachers in Urban Schools: An Inside View* (New York: Random House, 1968), 214; and Seymour Levey, "Are We Driving Teachers Out of Ghetto Schools?" *American Education* 3, no. 5 (May 1967): 2–4. For more nuanced consideration of urban teachers' motives and identities, see Michèle Foster, *Black Teachers on Teaching* (New York: The New Press, 1997).

16. James Bryant Conant, *Slums and Suburbs: A Commentary on Schools in Metropolitan Areas* (New York: McGraw-Hill Book Company, Inc., 1961), 2–3.

17. Amy Kovner, "A Plea from the Ghetto," reprinted in Ron Van Doren, "Missionaries in the Classroom" (Washington, DC: U.S. Government Publishing Office, 1967), 4.

18. Richard Graham, "The Teacher Corps: One Place to Begin," *NASSP Bulletin* 52, no. 330 (October 1968): 49–61; Milton Gold, "Programs for the Disadvantaged at Hunter College," *Phi Delta Kappan* 48, no. 7 (March 1967): 365; *Promising Practices from the Projects for the Culturally Deprived* (Chicago, IL: Research Council of the Great Cities Program, 1964); *The Teachers College Journal* 37 (October 1965).

19. John O'Brian, "A Master's Degree Program for the Preparation of Teacher of Disadvantaged Youth," in *Preparing to Teach the Disadvantaged*, eds. Bruce W. Tuckman and John O'Brian (New York: Free Press, 1969); Leonard Kornberg, "Meaningful Teachers for Alienated Children," in Passow, *Education in Depressed Areas*, 262–277.; Vernon F. Haubrich, "Teachers for Big-City Schools," in Passow, *Education in Depressed Areas*, 243–261; see also *Action for the Improvement of Teacher Education* (Washington, DC: American Association of Colleges of Teacher Education, 1965), 111–125, and Nick Juravich, "'Harlem Sophistication':

Community-Based Paraprofessional Educators in Harlem and East Harlem," in *Educating Harlem: A Century of Schooling and Resistance in a Black Community,* eds. Ansley T. Erickson and Ernest Morrell (New York: Columbia University Press, 2019), 234–256.

20. Bethany L. Rogers, "'Better' People, Better Teaching: The Vision of the National Teacher Corps, 1965–1968," *History of Education Quarterly* 49, no. 3 (August 2009): 347–372. Part of the 1965 Higher Education Act, the NTC operated in nearly 700 sites across the nation before being dismantled by Ronald Reagan's Education Consolidation and Improvement Act in 1981.

21. Fraser, *Preparing America's Teachers,* 213.

22. Graham, "The Teacher Corps"; Liston and Zeichner, *Teacher Education,* 14.

23. This is not to say that alternative paths such as emergency certification did not already exist, but the 1980s essentially introduced an officially recognized path to classroom teaching that did not involve the traditional education school experience.

24. The following derives from Alan H. Jones, "Teacher Education and the 1980s: A Decade to Forget—Or to Remember," *California Journal of Teacher Education* 10, no. 2 (1983): 1–16.

25. Kenneth M. Zeichner, "The Struggle for the Soul of Teaching and Teacher Education in the USA," *Journal of Education for Teaching* 40, no. 5 (2014): 559.

26. See Lauren Gatti, *Toward a Framework of Resources for Learning to Teach* (New York: Palgrave Macmillan, 2016), 11; 13.

27. Gatti, *Toward a Framework of Resources,* 21.

28. Gatti, *Toward a Framework of Resources,* 21.

29. Zeichner, "The Struggle for the Soul of Teaching," 551–552; Linda Darling-Hammond and John Bransford, *Preparing Teachers for a Changing World* (San Francisco, CA: Jossey Bass, 2005).

30. Gary Natriello, "The Policy Context for the Evolution of Teacher Education Reform in New Jersey," *Teachers College Record* 119, no. 14 (2017): 2.

31. Natriello, "The Policy Context"; the TNTP website describes its program origins, https://tntp.org/about-tntp.

32. Wendy Kopp, "An Argument and Plan for the Creation of the Teacher Corps," (Undergraduate thesis, Princeton University, 1989). Early cohorts of TFA corps members were placed in hard-to-staff schools and districts that desperately needed teachers; later, however, critics accused TFA of sweetheart deals with districts that threatened the positions of existing, credentialed teachers. See Dana Goldstein, *The Teacher Wars: A History of America's Most Embattled Profession* (New York: Doubleday, 2014), 201, and Valerie Strauss, "Teach For America Recruits Get Preference for Teaching Jobs," *Washington Post,* August 29, 2013, https://www.washingtonpost.com/news/answer-sheet/wp/2013/08/29/how-teach-for-america-recruits-get-preference-for-teaching-jobs/?arc404=true.

33. Ken Zeichner and Elizabeth A. Hutchinson, "The Development of Alternative Certification Policies and Programs in the United States," in *Alternative Routes to Teaching,* eds. Pam Grossman and Susanna Loeb (Cambridge, MA: Harvard Education Press, 2008), 22.

34. Marilyn Cochran-Smith, "Relocating Teacher Preparation to New Graduate Schools of Education," *The New Educator* 17, 1(2021): 1–20.

35. Daniel Friedrich, "'We Brought It Upon Ourselves': University-Based Teacher Education and the Emergence of Boot-Camp-Style Routes to Teacher Certification," *Education Policy Analysis Archives* 22, no. 2 (2014): 1–21.

36. See Grossman and Loeb, *Alternative Routes to Teaching;* Gatti, *Toward a Framework of Resources,* 17.

37. Zeichner and Hutchinson, "The Development of Alternative Certification Policies," 24; Joel McFarland et al., "Characteristics of Public School Teachers Who Completed Alternative Route to Certification Programs," *The Condition of Education 2018* (Washington, DC: National Center for Education Statistics, 2018), 14.

38. Elena Aydarova and David C. Berliner, "Navigating the Contested Terrain of Teacher Education Policy and Practice: Introduction to the Special Issue," *Education Policy*

Analysis Archives 26, no. 25 (2018): 2. On the nature of teacher education over the last 20 years, see Robert J. Bullough, "Recalling 40 Years of Teacher Education in the USA: A Personal Essay," *Journal of Education for Teaching* 40, no. 5 (2014): 474–491; Christine Sleeter, "Equity, Democracy, and Neoliberal Assaults on Teacher Education," *Teaching and Teacher Education* 24, no. 8 (2008): 1947–1957; Lois Weiner, "A Lethal Threat to US Teacher Education," *Journal of Teacher Education* 58, no. 4 (2007): 274–286; and Ken Zeichner, "Competition, Economic Rationalization, Increased Surveillance, and Attacks on Diversity: Neo-Liberalism and the Transformation of Teacher Education in the U.S," *Teaching and Teacher Education* 26, no. 8 (2010): 1544–1552.

39. Zeichner, "The Struggle for the Soul of Teaching," 556; Fraser and Lefty, *Teaching Teachers*.

40. See Testimony before the U.S. House of Representatives Committee on Education and the Workforce, Subcommittee on 21st Century Competitiveness, 108th Congress (2003) (statement of Kati Haycock, President, The Education Trust); see also William L. Sanders and June C. Rivers, Research Report: Cumulative and Residual Effects of Teachers on Future Student Academic Achievement (Knoxville, TN: University of Tennessee Value-Added Research and Assessment Center, 1996), https://www.heartland.org/_template-assets/documents/publications/3048.pdf. For an excellent synthesis of this trend in education policymaking and its effects, see Goldstein, *The Teacher Wars,* chapter 9.

41. Linda Darling-Hammond, "Teacher Education and the American Future," *Journal of Teacher Education* 61, no. 1–2 (2010): 38.

42. Darling-Hammond, "Teacher Education and the American Future," 38.

43. American Statistical Association, ASA Statement on Using Value-Added Models for Educational Assessment, Executive Summary (Alexandria, VA: ASA, 2014).

44. Zeichner, "The Struggle for the Soul of Teaching," 556.

45. Aydarova and Berliner, "Navigating the Contested Terrain"; Zeichner, "The Struggle for the Soul of Teaching," 556. See also Michael Mitchell, Michael Leachman, and Kathleen Masterson, *A Lost Decade in Higher Education* (Washington, DC: Center on Budget and Policy Priorities, 2017); "25 Years of Declining State Support for Public Colleges," *The Chronicle of Higher Education,* March 2, 2014; and Christopher Newfield, *Unmaking the Public University* (Cambridge, MA: Harvard University Press, 2008).

46. Zeichner, "The Struggle for the Soul of Teaching," 555.

47. The ability of alternate route teachers to earn a credential while also teaching as a teacher of record became an issue when the NCLB law required a "highly qualified" teacher for every student, and "highly qualified" was essentially equated to certification. As a concession to the alternate route programs, state laws often allowed candidates in pursuit of their certification to count as "highly qualified."

48. Fraser and Lefty, *Teaching Teachers,* 15–16.

49. Zeichner, "The Struggle for the Soul of Teaching," 552; Darling-Hammond, "Teacher Education and the American Future," 35–47. Regarding jurisdictional challenges, see Pam Grossman, "Responding to Our Critics: From Crisis to Opportunity in Research on Teacher Education," *Journal of Teacher Education* 59, no. 1 (2008): 10–23; and Andrew Abbott, *The System of the Professions: An Essay on the Division of Expert Labor* (Chicago: University of Chicago Press, 1988).

50. Viv Ellis and Jane McNicholl, *Transforming Teacher Education: Reconfiguring the Academic Work* (New York and London: Bloomsbury Academic, 2014); Ken Zeichner and César Peña-Sandoval, "Venture Philanthropy and Teacher Education Policy in the U.S.: The Role of the New Schools Venture Fund," *Teachers College Record* 117, no. 5 (2015): 1–44.

51. Arthur Levine, "Teacher Education Must Respond to Changes in America," *Phi Delta Kappan* 92, no. 2 (2010): 19–24.

52. See Cochran-Smith, "Relocating Teacher Education." For examples of such arguments, see Sleeter, "Equity, Democracy"; Lauren Anderson, "Private Interests in a Public

Profession: Teacher Education and Racial Capitalism," *Teachers College Record* 121, no. 4 (2019): 1–38; Mariana Souto-Manning, "Transforming University-Based Teacher Education: Preparing Asset-, Equity-, and Justice-Oriented Teachers Within the Contemporary Political Context," *Teachers College Record* 121, no. 6 (2019): 1–26; and Zeichner and Peña-Sandoval, "Venture Philosophy and Teacher Education Policy."

53. Anderson, "Private Interest in a Public Profession," 3.

54. David C. Berliner, "Effects of Inequality and Poverty vs. Teachers and Schooling on America's Youth," *Teachers College Record* 115, no. 12 (2013).

55. Zeichner, 2016; Ken Zeichner and Hilary Conklin, "Beyond Knowledge Ventriloquism and Echo Chambers: Raising the Quality of the Debate on Teacher Education," *Teachers College Record* 118, no. 12 (2016): 1–38.

56. Fraser and Lefty, *Teaching Teachers*, 11.

57. Harry Judge, "Foreword: A Beginning or an End?" in Michael Fullan et al., *The Rise and Stall of Teacher Education Reform* (Washington, D.C.: American Association of Colleges for Teacher Education, 1998), vi, cited in Fraser, Preparing America's Teachers, 232.

58. Zeichner and Conklin, "Beyond Knowledge Ventriloquism," 3; Linda Darling-Hammond, "Teacher Education and the American Future," 35–36.

59. Aydarova and Berliner, "Navigating the Contested Terrain," 6. For examples of self-critique on the part of teacher educators, see also B. Othanel Smith, *A Design for a School of Pedagogy* (Washington, DC: U.S. Department of Education, 1980); The Holmes Group, *Tomorrow's Teachers* (East Lansing, MI: Author, 1986); Carnegie Task Force on Teaching as a Profession, *A Nation Prepared: Teachers for the 21st Century* (Washington, DC: Carnegie Forum on Education and the Economy, 1986); Carnegie National Commission on Teaching & America's Future, *What Matters Most: Teaching for America's Future* (New York: Author, 1996); John I. Goodlad, *Educational Renewal: Better Teachers, Better Schools* (Hoboken, NJ: Wiley, 1998); National Council for Accreditation of Teacher Education (NCATE), Transforming Teacher Education through Clinical Practice: A National Strategy to Prepare Effective Teachers (Washington, DC: NCATE, 2010);.

60. Darling-Hammond, "Teacher Education and the American Future," 39.

61. Cochran-Smith, "Relocating Teacher Education." See also Linda Darling-Hammond, *Doing What Matters Most: Investing in Quality Teaching* (New York: National Commission on Teaching & America's Future, 1997); Morva McDonald and Ken Zeichner, "Social Justice Teacher Education," in *Handbook of Social Justice in Education*, eds. William Ayers, Therese Quinn, and David Stovall (Philadelphia, PA: Taylor & Francis, 2009), 595–610; and Ana María Villegas, "Diversity and Teacher Education," in *Handbook of Research on Teacher Education: Enduring Questions in Changing Contexts*, 3rd edition., eds. Marilyn Cochran-Smith, Sharon Feiman-Nemser, D. John McIntyre, and Kelly E. Demers (New York: Routledge/Association of Teacher Educators, 2008), 551–558.

62. Linda Darling-Hammond, "Who Will Speak for the Children? How 'Teach For America' Hurts Urban Schools and Students," *Phi Delta Kappan* 76, no. 1 (1994): 22.

63. Darling-Hammond, "Teacher Education and the American Future," 39.

64. Barbara L. Bales, "Teacher Education Policies in the United States: The Accountability Shift Since 1980," *Teaching and Teacher Education* 22, no. 4 (2006): 395–407; see also W. D. Hawley, "Systematic Analysis, Public Policy-Making, and Teacher Education," in *Handbook of Research on Teacher Education*, ed. R. W. Houston (New York: Macmillan, 1990), cited in Bales.

65. David Hurst et al., *Overview and Inventory of State Education Reforms: 1990 to 2000* (Washington, DC: National Center for Education Statistics, 2003).

66. Zeichner and Bier, "Opportunities and Pitfalls," 27; NCATE, *Transforming Teacher Education*.

67. Zeichner and Bier, "Opportunities and Pitfalls"; Deborah Ball and Francesca

Forzani, "The Work of Teaching and the Challenge for Teacher Education," *Journal of Teacher Education* 60, no. 5 (2009): 497–511; Cochran-Smith, "Relocating Teacher Preparation."

68. Cochran-Smith, "Relocating Teacher Preparation"; Pam Grossman, Karen Hammerness, and Morva McDonald, "Redefining Teacher: Re-Imagining Teacher Education," *Teachers and Teaching, Theory and Practice* 15, no. 2 (2009): 273–290; Magdalene Lampert, "Learning Teaching in, from and for Practice: What Do We Mean?" *Journal of Teacher Education* 61, no. 1–2 (2010): 21–34.

69. Mary M. Kennedy, "Knowledge Base for the Beginning Teacher: Two Views," *Journal of Teacher Education* 40, no. 6 (1989): 53. See also Maynard C. Reynolds (ed.), *The Knowledge Base for Beginning Teachers* (New York: Pergamon Press, 1989).

70. See, for instance, Anne Reynolds, Richard J. Tannen, and Michael Rosenfeld, *Beginning Teacher Knowledge of General Principles of Teaching and Learning: A National Survey* (Princeton, NJ: Educational Testing Service, 1992).

71. Lee S. Shulman, "Those Who Understand: Knowledge Growth in Teaching," *Educational Researcher* 15, no. 2 (1986): 4–14; Lee S. Shulman, "Knowledge and Teaching: Foundations of the New Reform," *Harvard Educational Review* 57, no. 1 (1987): 1–22.

72. See, for example, Linda Darling Hammond, Channa Cook-Harvey, Brigid Barron, and David Osher, "Implications for Educational Practice of the Science of Learning and Development," *Applied Developmental Science* 24, no. 2 (2020): 97–140; Pam Grossman (ed.), *Teaching Core Practices in Teacher Education* (Cambridge, MA: Harvard Education Press, 2018); Tonya Bartell, Robert Floden, and Gail Richmond, "What Data and Measures Should Inform Teacher Preparation? Reclaiming Accountability," *Journal of Teacher Education* 69, no. 5 (2018): 426–428; Luis C. Moll, Cathy Amanti, Deborah Neff, and Norma Gonzalez, "Funds of Knowledge for Teaching: Using a Qualitative Approach to Connect Homes and Classrooms," *Theory into Practice* 31 (1992): 132–141; and Gloria Ladson-Billings, "Toward a Theory of Culturally Relevant Pedagogy," *American Educational Research Journal* 32, no. 3 (1995): 465–491.

73. Pam Grossman, "Responding to Our Critics." See also Andrew Abbott, *The System of the Professions: An Essay on the Division of Expert Labor* (Chicago: University of Chicago Press, 1988).

74. Aydarova and Berliner, "Navigating the Contested Terrain," 6–7.

75. Sara Mosle, "Scenes from the Class Struggle: My Year at New York's P.S. 98," *The New Republic*, December 16, 1991, 30.

76. Donald Boyd, Pamela Grossman, Hamilton Lankford, Susanna Loeb, and James Wyckoff, "How Changes in Entry Requirements Alter the Teacher Workforce and Affect Student Achievement," *Education Finance and Policy* 1, no. 2 (2006): 176–216; Linda Darling-Hammond, Debora J. Holtzman, Su Jin Gatlin, and Julian Vasquez Heilig, "Does Teacher Preparation Matter? Evidence about Teacher Certification, Teach for America, and Teacher Effectiveness," *Education Policy Analysis Archives* 13, no. 42 (2005): 1–51; Steven Glazerman, Daniel Mayer, and Paul Decker, "Alternative Routes to Teaching: The Impacts of Teach for America on Student Achievement and Other Outcomes," *Journal of Policy Analysis and Management* 25, no. 1 (2006): 75–96; Thomas J. Kane, Jonah E. Rockoff, and Douglas O. Staiger, "What Does Certification Tell Us about Teacher Effectiveness? Evidence from New York City," *Economics of Education Review* 27, no. 6 (December 2008): 615–631; Ildiko Laczko-Kerr and David C. Berliner, "The Effectiveness of 'Teach for America' and Other Under-Certified Teachers on Student Academic Achievement: A Case of Harmful Public Policy," *Education Policy Analysis Archives* 10, no. 37 (2002); Margaret Raymond, Stephen Fletcher, and Javier Luque, "Teach for America: An Evaluation of Teacher Differences and Student Outcomes in Houston, Texas" (Stanford, CA: The Hoover Institution, Center for Research and Education Outcomes, 2001).

77. Julian Vasquez Heilig and Su Jin Jez, *Teach For America: A Review of the Evidence* (Boulder and Tempe: Education and the Public Interest Center & Education Policy Research Unit, 2010), 4.

78. Ken Zeichner, "The Struggle for the Soul of Teaching," 557.

79. Darling-Hammond, "Who Will Speak for the Children?" 22.

80. Cynthia Onore and Bonny Gildin, "Preparing Urban Teachers as Public Professionals," *Teacher Education Quarterly* 37, no. 3 (2010): 27–44.

81. Ethan L. Hutt, Jessica Gottlieb, and Julia Cohen, "Diffusion in a Vacuum: EdTPA, Legitimacy, and the Rhetoric of Teacher Professionalization," *Teaching and Teacher Education* 69 (2018): 53.

82. Martin Haberman, "A Modest Proposal for Making Teacher Education Accountable: How to Make University-Controlled Teacher Education and Alternative Certification Programs Accountable for the Quality of Teachers in Schools Serving Children and Youth in Poverty," in *Transforming Teacher Education: What Went Wrong with Teacher Training, and How We Can Fix It*, eds. Valerie Hill-Jackson and Chance W. Lewis (Sterling, VA: Stylus Publishing, 2010), 129.

83. Haberman, "A Modest Proposal," 130.

84. Fraser and Lefty, *Teaching Teachers*, 27.

85. Fraser, *Preparing America's Teachers*, 235, emphasis added.

86. Despite its roots as a peer-developed tool, implementation of the EdTPA has been highly contested by teacher educators across the country. See, for example, Christine Clayton, "Voices from Student Teachers in New York: The Persistence of a Subtractive Experience of the EdTPA as a Licensure Exam for Initial Certification," *Education Policy Analysis Archives* 26 (2018).

87. "Elevating Teaching, Empowering Teachers," National Board for Professional Teaching Standards, May 20, 2020, https://www.nbpts.org/vision-and-impact/vision/; Aydarova and Berliner, "Navigating the Contested Terrain," 3.

88. Linda Darling-Hammond and Jeannie Oakes, *Preparing Teachers for Deeper Learning* (Cambridge, MA: Harvard Education Press, 2019); Nassirian, cited in Liana Loewus and Stephen Sawchuk, "Yet Another Group Sets Out to Accredit Teacher Prep Programs," *Education Week*, October 12, 2017, https://www.edweek.org/teaching-learning/yet-another-group-sets-out-to-accredit-teacher-prep-programs/2017/10.

89. Grossman, "Responding to Our Critics," 20.

90. Lauren Gatti, *Transformative Teacher Preparation: A Framework of Resources for Learning to Teach. In: Toward a Framework of Resources for Learning to Teach* (New York: Palgrave Macmillan, 2016), 12.

91. Ethan Hutt, Jessica Gottlieb, and Julia Cohen, "Diffusion in a Vacuum: EdTPA, Legitimacy, and the Rhetoric of Teacher Professionalization," *Teaching and Teacher Education* 69 (2018): 59.

92. Zeichner and Conklin, "Beyond Knowledge Ventriloquism," 3. Authors point out that the difference between traditional and alternate route preparation lies less in the content of the coursework and more in the timing: Traditional paths require teachers to complete the majority of their coursework prior to becoming teachers of record while many alternate route candidates work as teachers of record while pursuing their coursework.

93. Jack Schneider, "Rhetoric and Practice in Pre-Service Teacher Education: The Case of Teach For America," *Journal of Education Policy* 29, no. 4 (2014): 425–442.

94. Jack Schneider, "Rhetoric and Practice," 426.

95. Mary Jo Madda, "Teach for America Responds to Criticism, Seeks to Reform," *EdSurge*, September 8, 2014.

96. Lauren Anderson, "Private Interest in a Public Profession: Teacher Education and a Racial Capitalism," *Teachers College Record* 121, no. 6 (2019): 5.

97. Zeichner, "The Struggle for the Soul of Teaching," 559.

98. Conra D. Gist, "Teacher Development for Community, Justice and Visionaries," in *Portraits of Anti-racist Alternative Routes to Teaching in the U.S.: Framing Teacher Development for Community, Justice, and Visionaries*, ed. Conra D. Gist (New York: Peter Lang, 2017), 1.

99. Mari Koerner, Doug Lynch, and Shane Martin, "Why We Partner with Teach for America: Changing the Conversation," *Phi Delta Kappan* 89, no. 10 (June 2008): 726–729.

100. These examples come from Gatti, *Transformative Teacher Preparation*, 33.

101. For documentation of the increase in alternate route programs, see C. Emily Feistritzer, *Profile of Alternative Route Teachers* (Washington, DC: Center for Education Information, 2005). For citation, see Marilyn Cochran-Smith, "Taking Stock in 2005: Getting Beyond the Horse Race," *Journal of Teacher Education* 56, no. 1 (2005): 3–7.

Chapter 7

1. Portions of Chapter 7 were previously published in Bethany L. Rogers and Megan Blumenreich, "Reframing the Conversation: Insights from the Oral Histories of Three 1990 TFA Participants," *Teachers College Record* 115, no. 6 (June 2013): 1–46, and Megan Blumenreich and Bethany L. Rogers, "TFA and the Magical Thinking of the 'Best and the Brightest,'" *Education Policy Analysis Archives* 24, no. 13 (February 2016): 1–35. The authors are grateful to the journal editor and publisher for their permission to reprint them here.

2. Matthew A.M. Thomas, Emilee Rauschenberger, and Katherine Crawford-Garrett (eds.), *Examining Teach For All: International Perspectives on a Growing Global Network* (New York: Routledge, 2021); Kathrine Crawford-Garrett and Matthew A.M. Thomas, "Teacher Education and the Global Impact of Teach For All," *Oxford Research Encyclopedia of Education* (Oxford: Oxford University Press, 2018), 1–26; Stephen Exley, "The Unstoppable Rise of Teach For All," *Times Educational Supplement,* January 3, 2014, https://www.tes.com/news/unstoppable-rise-teach-all-0.

3. Anya Kamenetz, "For Teachers, Many Paths into the Classroom. . . Some Say Too Many," National Public Radio, September 12, 2014, https://www.npr.org/sections/ed/2014/09/12/347375798/for-teachers-many-paths-into-the-classroom-some-say-too-many.

4. James W. Fraser and Lauren Lefty, *Teaching Teachers: Changing Paths and Enduring Debates* (Baltimore: Johns Hopkins University Press, 2018), 28.

5. Liana Loewus, "Teach for America Gets a J. Crew Tee," *Education Week,* December 5, 2012, https://www.edweek.org/teaching-learning/teach-for-america-gets-a-j-crew-tee/2012/12; Theresa Mooney, "As Seen on TV! Teach for America in Pop Culture," Teach For America, July 1, 2019, https://www.teachforamerica.org/stories/as-seen-on-tv-teach-for-america-in-pop-culture.

6. Our sample is not random; we chose a diverse sample using variables of gender, undergraduate institution attended, region where taught, and current career; we also considered program completion. For details, see Appendix B.

7. Susan Chira, "For Freshman Corps, A Sobering Year," *New York Times,* June 26, 1991.

8. Richard Ingersoll, "The Teacher Shortage: A Case of Wrong Diagnosis and Wrong Prescription," *NASSP Bulletin* 86, no. 631 (2002): 16–31.

9. Morgaen L. Donaldson and Susan Moore Johnson, "TFA Teachers: How Long Do They Teach? Why Do They Leave?" *Phi Delta Kappan* 93, no. 2 (October 2011): 47–51; Richard M. Ingersoll, *Why Do High-Poverty Schools Have Difficulty Staffing their Classrooms with Qualified Teachers?* (Washington, D.C.: Center for American Progress, 2004).

10. Richard Ingersoll, Lisa Merrill, and Daniel Stuckey, *Seven Trends: The Transformation of the Teaching Force,* Updated April 2014 (Philadelphia, PA: Consortium for Policy Research in Education, University of Pennsylvania, 2014), 24, 23. The data cited refer to cumulative percent attrition of beginning teachers by years of experience between 1993 and 2003.

11. Donaldson and Johnson, "TFA Teachers: How Long Do They Teach?"; see also Richard M. Ingersoll and Thomas M. Smith, "The Wrong Solution to the Teacher Shortage," *Educational Leadership* 60, no. 8 (2003): 30–33.

12. Such role-changing over time, particularly within the larger field of education, has been noted among other groups of teachers who have been considered "elite" in terms of their education. See Karen Hunter Quartz et al., "Careers in Motion: A Longitudinal Retention Study of Role Changing Patterns Among Urban Educators," *Teachers College Record* 110, no. 1 (2008): 218–50; Eran Tamir, "Choosing to Teach in Urban Schools Among Graduates of Elite Colleges," *Urban Education* 44, no. 5 (2009): 522–544.

13. Quartz et al., "Careers in Motion," 239; Brad Olson and Lauren Anderson, "Courses of Action: A Qualitative Investigation into Urban Teacher Retention and Career Development," *Urban Education* 42, no. 1 (2007): 23.

14. Olson and Anderson, "Courses of Action."

15. Linda Darling-Hammond and E. M. Sclan, "Who Teaches and Why: Dilemmas of Building a Profession for Twenty-First Century Schools," in *The Handbook of Research on Teacher Education*, 2nd ed., ed. John P. Sikula (New York, NY: Macmillan, 1996): 67–101; Cassandra M. Guarino, Lucrecia Santibañez, and Glenn A. Daley, "Teacher Recruitment and Retention: A Review of the Recent Empirical Literature," *Review of Educational Research* 76, no. 2 (2006): 173–208; Richard Murnane et al., *Who Will Teach? Policies That Matter* (Cambridge, MA: Harvard University Press, 1991); Todd R. Stinebrickner, "Estimation of a Duration Model in the Presence of Missing Data," *Review of Economics and Statistics* 81, no. 3 (1999): 529–542. See also Andrew Thomas, "Social Networks and Career Paths of Urban Teachers: Effects of Career Decision-Related Communication Networks on Teacher Retention" (unpublished doctoral dissertation, University of California, Los Angeles, 2005).

16. Eric A. Hanushek, John F. Kain, & Steven G. Rivkin, "Why Public Schools Lose Teachers," *Journal of Human Resources* 39, no. 2 (2004): 326–354.

17. Guili Zhang and Nancy Zeller, "A Longitudinal Investigation of the Relationship Between Teacher Preparation and Teacher Retention," *Teacher Education Quarterly* 43, no. 2 (Spring 2016): 73–92.

18. Chris Curren, "Teach for America Placement and Teacher Vacancies: Evidence from the Mississippi Delta," *Teachers College Record* 119, no. 2 (2017): 1–24.

19. Wendy Kopp, quoted in Motoko Rich, "At Charter Schools, Short Careers by Choice," *The New York Times,* August 26, 2013, https://www.nytimes.com/2013/08/27/education/at-charter-schools-short-careers-by-choice.html.

20. Trexler, "(Re)reading Identity Narratives," 3–14.

21. Arthur Levine, *Educating School Teachers* (Washington, DC: Education Schools Project, 2006).

22. Arthur Levine, "The School-College Divide and Teacher Preparation," Education Week, January 4, 2007. The issue of the theory-practice divide appears across the literature on teacher education; many such recent sources have focused on better integrating theory and practice within university-based teacher education. See, for instance, Linda la Velle, "The Theory-Practice Nexus in Teacher Education: New Evidence for Effective Approaches," *Journal of Education for Teaching* 45, no. 4 (2019): 369–372; Oliver McGarr, Emmanuel O'Grady and Liam Guilfoyle, "Exploring the Theory-Practice Gap in Initial Teacher Education: Moving Beyond Questions of Relevance to Issues of Power and Authority," *Journal of Education for Teaching* 43, no. 1 (2017): 48-60; Tony Yeigh and David Lynch, "Reforming Initial Teacher Education: A Call for Innovation," *Australian Journal of Teacher Education* 42, no. 12 (2017): 112-127.

23. Linda Darling-Hammond, *Powerful Teacher Education: Lessons From Exemplary Programs* (San Francisco, CA: Jossey-Bass, 2006), 37.

24. Mary Kennedy, "The Problem of Evidence in Teacher Education," in *The Role of the University in the Preparation of Teachers,* ed. Robert A. Roth (London: Falmer Press, 1999), 56. See also Dan C. Lortie, *Schoolteacher: A Sociological Study* (Chicago: University of Chicago Press, 1975).

25. Kennedy, "The Problem of Evidence in Teacher Education," 56.

26. Michael J. Steudeman, "Ignoring the Ghost of Horace Mann: A Reflective Critique of Teach For America's Solipsistic Pedagogy," in *Teach For America Counter-Narratives: Alumni Speak Up and Speak Out,* eds. T. Jameson Brewer and Kathleen DeMarrais (New York: Peter Lang, 2015), 48.

27. Olivia Blanchard, "I Quit Teach for America," *The Atlantic,* September 23, 2013, https://www.theatlantic.com/education/archive/2013/09/i-quit-teach-for-america/279724/.

28. Jessica Millen, "The TFA Bait and Switch: From 'You'll Be Making a Difference' to 'You're Making Excuses,'" in Brewer & DeMarrais, eds., *Teach For America Counter-Narratives,* 19.

29. Katherine Crawford-Garrett, *Teach For America and the Struggle for Urban School Reform: Searching for Agency in an Era of Standardization* (New York: Lang, 2013), 89.

30. Lori Lawson, interview with Megan Blumenreich, March 11, 2009.

31. Today, TFA offers professional development to corps members during the school year but, according to Barbara Miner, who studied this aspect of TFA, such increased support did not occur until individual states tightened their requirements for provisional licensing. See Barbara Miner, "Looking Past the Spin: Teach For America," *Rethinking Schools* 24, no. 3 (2010), https://rethinkingschools.org/articles/looking-past-the-spin-teach-for-america/.

32. Caroline Sabin, interview with Megan Blumenreich, November 29, 2008.

33. Leo Flanagan, interview with Megan Blumenreich, February 23, 2009

34. Jeffrey Simes, interview with Bethany L. Rogers, February 9, 2009.

35. Jack Helfelt, Robert M. Capraro, Mary Margaret Capraro, Elizabeth Foster, and Norvella Carter, "An Urban School-University Partnership that Prepares and Retains Quality Teachers for 'High Need' Schools," *The Teacher Educator* 44, no. 1 (2009): 1–20.

36. Robert Bullough, Jr., "Mentoring and New Teacher Induction in the United States: A Review and Analysis of Current Practices," *Mentoring and Tutoring: Partnership in Learning* 20, no. 1 (2012): 57–74.

37. Michael Strong, New Educator, 1 no. 3, 181–198 (July 2005), https://eric.ed.gov /?id=EJ819914.

38. Darling-Hammond, *Powerful Teacher Education,* 339–340;

39. R. Ingersoll, R. and M. Strong, (2011). "The Impact of Induction and Mentoring Programs for Beginning Teachers: A Critical Review of the Research." *Review of Education Research* 81(2), 201–233. doi:10.3102/0034654311403323; Strong, "Teacher Induction, Mentoring, and Retention" 181–198.

40. Simes, interview. Interestingly, however, Simes did find the student teaching portion of the Summer Institute to be of value, situated as it was in the real world of classroom practice.

41. Sabin, interview.

42. Carlos Gomez, interview with Megan Blumenreich, May 6, 2009.

43. Flanagan, interview.

44. Andrew McKenzie, interview with Megan Blumenreich, February 8, 2009.

45. Wendy Kopp, "An Argument and Plan for Creation of the Teacher Corps" (Senior Thesis, Princeton University, 1989), 45; Kopp, *One Day All Children: The Unlikely Triumph of Teach For America and What I Learned Along the Way* (New York: Public Affairs, 2001).

46. For an overview of this history, see Megan Blumenreich and Bethany L. Rogers, "TFA and the Magical Thinking of the 'Best and the Brightest,'" *Education Policy Analysis Archives* 24, no. 13 (February 2016): 1–35

47. This line of argument derives from Blumenreich and Rogers, "TFA and the Magical Thinking of the 'Best and the Brightest,'" 13.

48. See Linda Darling-Hammond, Debora J. Holtzman, Su Jin Gatlin, and Julian Vasquez Heilig, "Does Teacher Preparation Matter? Evidence about Teacher Certification, Teach for America, and Teacher Effectiveness," Education Policy Analysis Archives 13, no.

42 (2005): 1–51; Teach For America Editorial Team, "Are Teach for America Teachers Effective?" Teach For America, March 6, 2018, https://www.teachforamerica.org/stories/are-teach-for-america-teachers-effective

49. Richard Whitmire, "For the Union, Inconvenient Truths about Charter Schools and Teacher Quality," New York Daily News, April 9, 2018, https://www.nydailynews.com/opinion/richard-whitmire-top-teachers-work-great-charters-article-1.2137246; Stephanie Simon and Nirvi Shah, "Duncan Launches Campaign to Recruit 'Best and Brightest' Teachers- Librarians Cheer Court Win for Google's Online Book Database," Politico, November 15, 2013, https://www.politico.com/tipsheets/morning-education/2013/11/duncan-launches-campaign-to-recruit-best-and-brightest-teachers-librarians-cheer-court-win-for-googles-online-book-database-212543.

50. Shane J. Lopez, "Americans Want the Best and the Brightest to Be Teachers," Gallup, May 18, 2019, http://www.gallup.com/poll/149222/Americans-Best-Brightest-Teachers.aspx.; T. Jameson Brewer and Sarah Matsui, "Living in Dialogue: Teach For America Counter-Narratives: Two Alumni Books Reframe the Discourse," National Education Policy Center, August 3, 2015, https://nepc.colorado.edu/blog/teach-america.

51. Linda Darling-Hammond, "Who Will Speak for the Children? How 'Teach For America' Hurts Urban Schools and Students," Phi Delta Kappan 76, no. 1 (1994): 21–34; Linda Darling-Hammond, Ruth Chung, and Fred Frelow, "Variation in Teacher Preparation: How Well Do Different Pathways Prepare Teachers To Teach," Journal of Teacher Education 53, no. 4 (2002): 286–302; James Jelmberg, "College-Based Teacher Education Versus State-Sponsored Alternative Programs," Journal of Teacher Education 47, no. 1 (1996): 60–66; Ildiko Laczko-Kerr and David C. Berliner, "The Effectiveness of 'Teach for America' and Other Under-certified Teachers on Student Academic Achievement: A Case of Harmful Public Policy," Education Policy Analysis Archives 10, no. 37 (2002); Betty E. Steffy and Michael P. Wolfe, "A Life-Cycle Model for Career Teachers," Kappa Delta Pi Record 38, no. 1 (2001): 16–19.

52. Kenneth C. Gray, Getting Real: Helping Teens Find Their Future (Thousand Oaks, CA: Corwin Press, 2009), 115.

53. Robin R. Henke et al., America's Teachers: Profile of a Profession, 1993–1994 (Washington, D.C.: U.S. Department of Education, Office of Research and Improvement, 1997).

54. Susanne Moore Johnson and The Project on the Next Generation of Teachers, Finders and Keepers: Helping New Teachers Survive and Thrive in Our Schools (San Francisco: Jossey-Bass, 2004), 28.

55. Hamilton Lankford, Susanna Loeb, and James Wyckoff, "Teacher Sorting and the Plight of Urban Schools: A Descriptive Analysis," Educational Evaluation and Policy Analysis 24, no. 1 (2002): 37–62.

56. Richard M. Ingersoll, Teacher Turnover, Teacher Shortages, and the Organization of Schools (Seattle, WA: University of Washington: Center for the Study of Teaching and Policy, 2001); Richard M. Ingersoll, "The Teacher Shortage: A Case of Wrong Diagnosis and Wrong Prescription," NASSP Bulletin 86, no 631 (2002): 16–31.

57. Desiree Carver-Thomas and Linda Darling-Hammond, Teacher Turnover: Why It Matters and What We Can Do About It (Palo Alto, CA: Learning Policy Institute, 2017), 6. See also Charles Payne, So Much Reform, So Little Change (Cambridge, MA: Harvard Education Press, 2008).

58. Carver-Thomas and Darling-Hammond, Teacher Turnover.

59. Johnson and Project on the Next Generation of Teachers, Finders and Keepers.

60. Charles Payne, So Much Reform, So Little Change (Cambridge, MA: Harvard Education Press, 2008).

61. Olson and Anderson, "Courses of Action," 14.

62. See Carver-Thomas and Darling-Hammond, Teacher Turnover, vi, who argue that preparation pathway has a meaningful effect on attrition.

63. Donaldson, "The Promise of Older Novices," 20.

64. Bethany L. Rogers and Megan Blumenreich, "Reframing the Conversation: Insights From Oral Histories of Three 1990 TFA Participants," *Teachers College Record* 115 (2013), 1–46.

65. Noliwe Rooks, *Cutting School: Privatization, Segregation, and the End of Public Education* (New York: The New Press, 2017), 43.

66. Steven Goodman and Michelle Fine, *It's Not about Grit: Trauma, Inequity, and the Power of Transformative Teaching* (New York: Teachers College Press, 2018), 2.

67. Rooks, *Cutting School*, 43.

68. Anne Martin, "Elite by Association, but at What Expense? Teach for America, Colonizing Perspectives and a Personal Evolution," in Brewer and DeMarrais, eds., *Teach for America Counter-Narratives*, 115.

69. Crawford-Garrett, *Teach for America and the Struggle for Urban School Reform*, 125

70. Millen, "The TFA Bait and Switch," 19.

71. Tina Trujillo, Janelle Scott, and Marialena Rivera, "Follow the Yellow Brick Road: Teach For America and the Making of Educational Leaders," *American Journal of Education* 123, no. 3 (2017): 365.

72. Christopher Emdin, *For White Folks Who Teach in the Hood . . . and the Rest of Y'all Too: Reality Pedagogy and Urban Education* (Boston: Beacon Press, 2016), 7.

73. See, for example, Goodman and Fine, *It's Not about Grit*.

74. Mariana Souto-Manning and Christopher Emdin, "On the Harm Inflicted by Urban Teacher Education Programs: Learning from the Historical Trauma Experienced by Teachers of Color," Urban Education (2020): 2. See also Gloria J. Ladson-Billings, "Is the Team All Right? Diversity and Teacher Education," *Journal of Teacher Education* 56, no. 3 (2005): 231.

75. Souto-Manning and Emdin, "On the Harm," 2; Audrey Thompson, "Tiffany, Friend of People of Color: White Investments in Anti-Racism," *International Journal of Qualitative Studies in Education* 16, no. 1 (2003): 10.

76. Ann Mogush Mason, "Taking Time, Breaking Codes: Moments in White Teacher Candidates' Exploration of Racism and Teacher Identity," *International Journal of Qualitative Studies in Education* 29, no. 8 (2016): 1046.

77. Christine Sleeter, "Wrestling with Problematics of Whiteness in Teacher Education," *International Journal of Qualitative Studies in Education* 29, no. 8 (2016): 1065; see also Christine Sleeter, L. I. Neal, and Kevin K. Kumashiro, eds., *Diversifying the Teacher Workforce* (New York: Routledge, 2014).

78. Fraser and Lefty, *Teaching Teachers*, 49.

79. Trujillo, Scott, and Rivera, "Follow the Yellow Brick Road"; Kerry Kretchmar, Beth Sondel, and Joseph Ferrare, "The Power of the Network: Teach For America's Impact on the Deregulation of Teacher Education," *Educational Policy* 32, no. 3 (May 2018): 423–453.

80. "Teach For America: 25 Years of Impact," *Teach For America*, accessed February 15, 2018.

81. Furman Brown, interview with Bethany L. Rogers, December 29, 2008.

82. Brown, F., interview.

83. The following discussion of KIPP draws from Emily Straus, "The Black and White Business of School Reform in Houston: The Careers of Harriet Ball," in Race, Place, and Power in Houston, Texas: The Past and Present of Megapolitan Texas, eds. Brian D. Behnken, Alexander X. Byrd, and Emily E. Straus (Baton Rouge, LA: Louisiana State University Press, forthcoming). In 2018, Feinberg was dismissed after accusations of sexual misconduct.

84. Straus, "The Black and White Business of School Reform," n.p.

85. Wendy Kopp, "An Argument and Plan for the Creation of the Teacher Corps" (Undergraduate Thesis, Princeton University, 1989), 52.

86. Wendy Kopp, *One Day All Children*, 7.

87. At the end of our interview protocol, we explicitly asked whether the interviewee considered him- or herself an education advocate. In nearly all of the interviews, we found that participants' continuing commitment to the improvement of education for poor students and their notion of themselves as "education advocates" came up long before the question itself did.

88. R. Brent Lyles, interview with Bethany L. Rogers, April 1, 2009.

89. Doug McAdam and Cynthia Brandt, "Assessing the Effects of Voluntary Youth Service: The Case of Teach for America," *Social Forces* 88, no. 2 (December 2009): 953.

90. Brown, F., interview.

91. Mark Stephan, interview with Megan Blumenreich, April 9, 2009.

92. Christina Brown, interview with Megan Blumenreich, April 4, 2009.

93. Heather Weller, interview with Bethany L. Rogers, June 1, 2009.

94. Brown, F., interview.

95. Lisa Robinson, interview with Megan Blumenreich, February 25, 2009.

96. Felicia Clark, interview with Bethany L. Rogers, December 12, 2008, emphasis added.

97. Eve Tuck, "Suspending Damage: A Letter to Communities," *Harvard Education Review* 79, no. 3 (Fall 2009): 409–27.

98. Brown, F., interview.

99. Stephan, interview.

100. See "Research," Teach For America, https://www.teachforamerica.org/what-we-do/impact/research; see also Monica Higgins, Wendy Robison, Jennie Weiner, and Frederick Hess, "Creating a Corps of Change Agents: What Explains the Success of Teach For America?" *Education Next* 11, no. 3 (2011).

101. Again, though participants attributed their interest in public education to their TFA experiences, it is possible they would have been inclined toward civic-mindedness or have had similar growth experiences had they not participated in TFA. See McAdam and Brandt, "Assessing the Effects."

102. Gomez, interview.

103. Jennifer Denino, interview with Megan Blumenreich, January 20, 2009.

104. It is important to note, however, that Mann's vision did not include a place for African Americans within the "common" fabric of the nation.

105. Denino, interview.

106. Amanda E. Lewis and John B. Diamond, *Despite the Best Intentions: How Racial Inequity Thrives in Good Schools* (New York: Oxford University Press, 2015).

107. Sabin, interview.

108. Mark Stephan, interview.

109. Priscilla Leon-Didion, interview with Bethany L. Rogers, June 7, 2009.

110. Nichole Childs Wardlaw, interview with Bethany L. Rogers, February 23, 2009.

111. Kathy Feeley, interview with Bethany L. Rogers, January 26, 2009.

112. Sabin, interview.

113. Linda Darling-Hammond and Jeannie Oakes, *Preparing Teachers for Deeper Learning* (Cambridge, MA: Harvard Education Press, 2019); Darling-Hammond, *Powerful Teacher Education*; Elizabeth Green, *Building a Better Teacher: How Teaching Works* (and How To Teach It to Everyone) (New York: W.W. Norton & Company, 2014); Pasi Sahlberg, "Lessons from Finland," *American Educator* 35, no. 2 (2011): 32–36.

114. Barnett Berry, Alesha Daughtrey, and Alan Weider, *Teaching Effectiveness and the Conditions that Matter Most in High-Needs Schools: A Policy Brief* (Carrboro, NC: The Center for Teaching Quality, 2009); see also Nicole Mirra and John Rogers, "The Overwhelming Need: How the Unequal Political Economy Shapes Urban Teachers' Work Conditions," *Urban Education* 55, no. 7 (2016): 1045–1075

Appendix B

1. We had no formal way of determining participants' race, though we did try to control informally for a racially diverse sampling. On snowball sampling: "By asking a number of people who else to talk with, the snowball gets bigger and bigger as you accumulate new information rich cases." See Michael Patton, *Qualitative Evaluation and Research Methods*, 2nd Ed. (Thousand Oaks, CA: Sage Publications, 1990).

2. Susan Smulyan, "Choosing to Teach: Reflections on Gender and Social Change," *Teachers College Record* 106, no. 3 (2004): 513–543; Diane L. Wolf, Feminist Dilemmas in Fieldwork (Boulder, CO: Westview Press, 1996).

Index

About the Authors

Megan Blumenreich is professor of Childhood Education at The City College of New York, City University of New York. Megan began her career in education teaching in Compton, CA as a 1990 TFA corps member; she later worked as the director of The Learning Center, an educational program for children affected with HIV at The Special Needs Clinic, an interdisciplinary clinic located at New York-Presbyterian Hospital. Since 2002, she has taught at City College. Her research focuses on qualitative research and urban education. She is the editor in chief of *The New Educator,* a quarterly journal with a focus on preparing and supporting new teachers.

Bethany L. Rogers is associate professor in the Educational Studies department at the College of Staten Island, City University of New York (CUNY), and in the Urban Education doctoral program at the CUNY Graduate Center. A historian of education, she uses the lens of the past to understand educational inequities today, focusing her research primarily on the postwar history of teachers, urban communities and schooling, and education reform, as well as the connection of those histories to contemporary policy. A public school parent and teacher educator, she has worked to strengthen university-based teacher preparation on the ground from her faculty position and, between 2016–2020, as a state director for teaching fellowships at the Woodrow Wilson National Fellowship Foundation.